ZACK HAMPLE

THE BASEBALL

Zack Hample is a baseball fan best known for having snagged 4,662 baseballs (and counting) from 48 different major league stadiums. Hample has been featured in hundreds of newspapers and magazines, including *Sports Illustrated, People, Men's Health, Maxim, Playboy, The New York Times, The Wall Street Journal,* and *USA Today.* He has also appeared on NPR, ESPN, FOX Sports, CNN International, *The Rosie O'Donnell Show,* the CBS Evening News with Katie Couric, and *The Tonight Show* with both Jay Leno and Conan O'Brien. Hample's first book, *How to Snag Major League Baseballs,* was published in 1999 when he was 21 years old. His last book, *Watching Baseball Smarter,* was published in 2007 and is currently in its 16th printing. Hample, a New York City native, runs a business called "Watch With Zack" through which he takes people to games and guarantees them at least one ball. He also snags baseballs to raise money for the charity Pitch In For Baseball and writes a popular blog called *The Baseball Collector.*

www.zackhample.com

D0030205

ALSO BY ZACK HAMPLE

Watching Baseball Smarter
How to Snag Major League Baseballs

THE

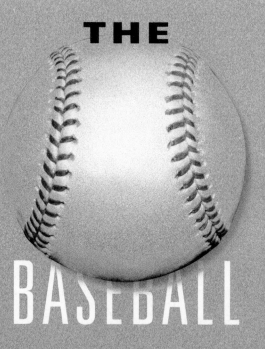

BASEBALL

Stunts, Scandals, and Secrets Beneath the Stitches

ZACK HAMPLE

ANCHOR SPORTS
Anchor Books
A Division of Random House, Inc.
New York

AN ANCHOR SPORTS ORIGINAL, MARCH 2011

Copyright © 2011 by Zack Hample

Library of Congress Cataloging-in-Publication Data
Hample, Zack, 1977–
The baseball : stunts, scandals, and secrets beneath the stitches /
by Zack Hample.
p.   cm.
ISBN 978-0-307-47545-9
1. Baseball—United States—History.   2. Baseball—Social aspects—
United States.   I. Title.
GV863.A1H36 2011
796.3570973—dc22
2010043551

Book design by R. Bull

www.anchorbooks.com

Printed in the United States of America
10 9 8 7 6 5 4 3 2 1

This one's for my dad.

CONTENTS

CHAPTER 10 BATTING PRACTICE 212

The First 60 Seconds • General Advice on Positioning • Left
Field versus Right Field • Home Run Balls • Ground Balls •
The Glove Trick (and Other Devices)

CHAPTER 11 HOW TO GET A PLAYER TO THROW
YOU A BALL 228

Dress for Success • A Mishmash of Strategies • Don't Be
Annoying • Tailor Your Request to the Situation • Where to
Go and When to Be There • If It Rains

CHAPTER 12 THE GAME ITSELF 244

What Are the Odds? • Foul Ball Theory • Game Home Runs
• Nice Catch! Now What? • Third-Out Balls and Other
Tosses • After the Final Out

CHAPTER 13 TOP 10 LISTS AND OTHER THINGS
OF INTEREST 270

Top 10 Ballhawks of All Time • Top 10 Memorable
Ballhawking Moments • Top 10 Stadiums for Ballhawking •
Spring Training, Home Run Derby, and the Postseason •
Ballhawking Etiquette • Documenting Your Collection

INTRODUCTION

I know this might be asking a lot, but can we forget about steroids for a moment? And while we're at it, can we stop griping about instant replay and ticket prices and everything else? Baseball is still the national pastime, and whether you're just a regular fan or a multimillionaire A-list celebrity, catching a foul ball—or better yet, a home run—might be the ultimate American experience. Ask Charlie Sheen. Back in April 1996, he bought 2,615 outfield seats at an Angels game to increase his odds of snagging a home run ball.

It didn't work.

As hard as it might seem (particularly for Sheen) to leave the stadium with a souvenir, it used to be much harder. At the turn of the 20th century, fans weren't even allowed to keep balls. Teams typically used just a few balls per game, so whenever one landed in the seats, a stadium employee retrieved it and put it back into play. Naturally, by the end of each game the balls were so dirty and discolored that they were tough to see, especially at dusk. No one thought much about this until 1920—more than two decades before teams started wearing helmets—when a batter named Ray Chapman was fatally hit in the head by a pitch that he barely saw. Soon after, umpires were instructed to keep new, clean balls in play.

The tradition of keeping foul balls, while impossible to trace back to one particular moment, got a major boost the following season when a 31-year-old New York Giants fan named Reuben Berman refused to return a ball, got kicked out of the Polo Grounds, sued the team for mental anguish, and won. Now, nearly a century later, catching and keeping balls is such a big part of the game that some fans enjoy this pursuit as much as the game itself.

I know because I'm one of them.

Since 1990 I've snagged 4,662 baseballs at 48 different major league stadiums. Of course, when I first started going to games, I didn't know what I was getting myself into. There weren't any blogs about snagging baseballs. I didn't know what a so-called ballhawk was. The whole thing was a mystery, and I just wanted to catch *one* ball. But now that I've reeled in thousands of them and had some time to reflect, I've discovered that the ball is more than just a five-ounce sphere of cork, rubber, yarn, and cowhide. It's a major source of history and controversy and hilarity. Did you know that Babe Ruth once tried to catch a ball that was dropped from an airplane? Or that several NASA astronauts have thrown ceremonial first pitches from outer space? (See "Stunts" on page 54.) Remember when Kramer got hit in the head by a foul ball on *Seinfeld*? Or when Carrie snagged a ball on *Sex and the City*? (See "Foul Balls in Pop Culture" on page 67.) Do you know how many fans have been killed by balls at major league games? Or the story about Dave Winfield nearly getting thrown in jail after killing a bird with a ball in Toronto? (See "Death by Baseball" on page 42.) Are you aware that Rawlings uses nearly one thousand feet of yarn and thread inside every ball? Or that the balls get stamped with invisible ink that only shows up under a black light? (See "The Rawlings Method" on page 151.) Did you know that the juiced-ball controversy dates back to the 1860s? Or that the cover of the ball used to be made of horsehide that was purchased from dog food companies? (See "The Evolution of the Ball" on page 89.)

Gathering these facts was lots of fun—it helped to have Rawlings, Major League Baseball, and the Hall of Fame on my side—but when I first started doing the research, explaining the book to people was oddly difficult.

"It's about baseballs," I'd say.

"You're writing a baseball book?"

"No . . . I mean . . . yes. I mean, it's about base-*balls* . . . you know? The ball—the actual baseball itself."

(Cue the awkward silence.)

"Oh, like, how the ball is made?"

Yeah, how the ball is made—but this book covers so much more. I'm still not quite sure how to describe it, but if there's one thing I've learned from going to hundreds of games and snagging thousands of balls and meeting tens of thousands of fans, it's that there's something about base-balls that makes people crazy. This book is a celebration of the ball—and of those people.

PART ONE

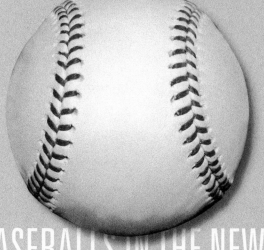

BASEBALLS IN THE NEWS

Base ball fans—the radicals—are so anxious to get a base ball that has history attached to it, that they willingly risk arrest for petty theft. They are willing to fight amongst themselves for such a ball, if necessary. A blackened optic or a busted breezer, in their opinion, is a mere incident—if they only can get that pellet.
—*Sporting Life* magazine, July 22, 1916

CHAPTER 1

THE SOUVENIR CRAZE

"BALL GRABBERS, READ THIS"

Way back in 1915, a first-class stamp cost two cents, a gallon of gas went for a quarter, and a game-used baseball fetched three bucks. At least, that was the going rate at the Polo Grounds when a Yankee fan named Guy Clarke snagged one in the left-field bleachers, got arrested for refusing to return it, and had to pay a $3 fine. That was a lot of money back then, but we're not talking about any old ball. It was a ninth-inning home run hit by Yankees shortstop Roger Peckinpaugh against the Boston Red Sox. Considering what that ball would sell for today, it was totally worth it. The editors at the *New York Times,* however, didn't see it that way, and on May 8, 1915—one day after the incident—the paper ran a short article called "Ball Grabbers, Read This." It was a warning, and the message was clear: if you steal a baseball, you're gonna get busted.

This was old news.

And it wasn't entirely true.

Clarke was just one of the unlucky few who got prose-cuted; fans had been snapping up baseballs for years, and by 1915 more than two dozen balls were disappearing at the Polo Grounds each week. Yeah, these balls were expensive—owners were paying $15 per dozen—but beyond the financial burden, it didn't really matter. If a few balls were lost here and there, the home plate umpire simply replaced them.

That's not how things worked when the National League formed in 1876. High-quality balls were so scarce that each one was expected to last an entire game, and if the ball went missing, the players went looking for it. As a result, fans policed themselves whenever a ball landed in the crowd and made sure that it was returned. It had to be. There was no room for debate. But when foul balls flew completely over the grandstand and landed outside the ballpark, they were much harder to recover. These balls were often grabbed by little kids who didn't have enough money to buy tickets, so teams came up with a solution: anyone who returned a ball got to watch the game for free.

This reward system was effective at first, but kids even-tually began to value the ball more than the opportunity to watch grown men play with it. (Can you blame them?) On June 1, 1887, *Toronto World* reported that "fifteen balls were knocked over the left field fence at Buffalo Monday and were stolen by bad boys."[1] In other words, teams weren't just losing balls during games; kids were taking them during batting practice as well. What began as a

---

[1] The Buffalo Bisons were a National League team from 1879 to 1885. They moved to the International League in 1886 and have been a minor league franchise ever since.

nuisance—a missing ball every once in a while—was turning into an epidemic.

On May 1, 1897, *The Sporting News* declared that "the souvenir craze" was affecting games in the South. In 1899 the Washington Senators hired a group of boys to retrieve baseballs. By 1901 teams were spending so much money on balls that the National League Rules Committee suggested penalizing batters who fouled off good pitches. On May 2, 1902, the *Detroit Free Press* said, "Baseballs that go into the stands at St. Louis are hopelessly lost, the man who first gets his hands on the flying sphere clinging to it." Sometime around 1903, it was rumored that on one occasion when a fan at the Polo Grounds refused to return a ball, John McGraw, the Hall of Fame manager of the New York Giants, retaliated by stealing the guy's hat.

Major League Baseball took action the following season by officially giving teams the right to retrieve balls that were hit into the stands. This new measure worked in some cases, but for the most part all it did was piss off the fans and make them more determined than ever not to cooperate.

In 1905 a Cubs fan named Samuel Scott was arrested in Chicago after catching a foul ball and refusing to hand it over to an usher. Cubs president James Hart personally confronted him and signed a larceny complaint, but the charges were dropped the next day when Scott, a member of the Board of Trade, threatened to sue for assault and false arrest.

Things got progressively worse from there.

"Brooklynites seem to prize highly balls which go into the bleachers," reported the *New York Tribune* in 1908.

"Women are as bad as men about stealing baseballs;

Charles Weeghman, an unsung hero among modern-day ballhawks, was the first owner to let fans keep foul balls.

they aren't so skillful in hiding them," said baseball manufacturer Tom Shibe in 1911.

"The practice of concealing balls fouled into the grandstand or bleachers has reached disgusting proportions in New York," claimed *Sporting Life* magazine in 1915.

Cubs owner Charles Weeghman felt otherwise. He recognized the foul ball frenzy as a business opportunity—a chance to bring more folks to the ballpark—and on April 29, 1916, he began letting fans keep the balls they caught. Two and a half months later, the Phillies' business manager billed Weeghman for eight baseballs that were hit into the stands during BP, but that was the price of good PR. The October 1916 issue of *Baseball* magazine praised Weeghman in a lengthy staff editorial. "The charm of novelty, of possible gain might lure far more spectators than enough to pay for the lost balls," it said. "At any rate, Mr. Weeghman evidently thinks so. For he has recently inaugurated this common-sense policy in his park at Chicago."

Other owners just didn't get it.

"Why should a man carry away an object worth $2.50 just because he gets his hands on it?" asked Colonel "Cap" Huston, part-owner of the Yankees. "When people go to a restaurant, do they take the dishes or silverware home for souvenirs?"

Most teams generously donated used balls to servicemen during World War I, but continued bullying the regular fans.

Enter Reuben Berman.

On May 16, 1921, Berman, a 31-year-old stockbroker from Connecticut, caught a foul ball during a Reds-Giants game at the Polo Grounds, and when the ushers demanded that he return it, he responded by tossing it deeper into the crowd. Berman was whisked away by security personnel, taken to the team offices, threatened with arrest, and ejected from the stadium. Giants management figured that was the end of it, but nearly three months later Berman's attorney served the team with legal papers, claiming that his client had been unlawfully detained and had suffered mental anguish and a loss of reputation. The case was tried in New York's Supreme Court, and Berman was awarded $100—far less than the $20,000 sum originally sought by his attorney, but the message was delivered.

"Reuben's Rule" (as it came to be known) was the real turning point, although change didn't happen all at once. Several owners still refused to give in, and as a result, there were a few more high-profile clashes between fans and security personnel. The most outrageous incident took place in 1923, when an 11-year-old boy named Robert Cotter was arrested and thrown in jail for pocketing a ball at the Baker Bowl in Philadelphia. The following day he was released by a sympathetic judge who said, "Such an act on the part of a boy is merely proof that he is following his most natural impulses. It is a thing I would do myself."

Seven years later in Chicago, with Weeghman long gone as Cubs owner, there was another ugly incident involving a young fan. Arthur Porto, age 17, caught a Hack Wilson foul ball and brawled with stadium security when they tried to take it from him. He and his two friends, who had joined the scuffle, were booked for disorderly conduct. The next day in court the judge dismissed the charges and ruled that a ball hit into the crowd belongs "to the boy who grabs it."

There were still a few more altercations in the 1930s, and during World War II teams once again donated balls to the armed forces. During that time fans were asked to return whatever they snagged, but that was the end of it.

Ballhawking bliss, along with a whole new set of controversies, was about to begin.

STEVE BARTMAN

Steve Bartman is responsible for the biggest ball-related controversy in history. Most sports fans know his name, but few are aware of the entire wacky aftermath. The original incident occurred on October 13, 2003—Game 6 of the National League Championship Series at Wrigley Field. It was the top of the eighth inning. One out. Runner on second base. The Cubs were beating the Marlins, 3–0, and needed just five more outs to advance to the World Series. They hadn't been there since 1945. They hadn't won it since 1908. Momentum was finally on their side— until Luis Castillo lofted a seemingly harmless fly ball down the left-field line. Cubs left fielder Moises Alou ran into foul territory and probably would've made the catch had a certain fan not reached out of the stands and deflected it.

That fan was Steve Bartman.

Alou flung his glove in disgust, and the crowd directed its wrath at Bartman, who had to be escorted out by stadium security for his own safety. When play resumed, the Marlins rallied for eight runs and put the game away.

Poor Bartman. Not only did half a dozen police cars have to gather outside his home that night to protect him and his family, but things got worse the next day after the Cubs blew their lead in Game 7 and failed to reach the World Series. Bartman became an instant scapegoat for generations of disgruntled Cubs fans, received death threats, had to change his phone number, and was forced into hiding. Illinois governor Rod Blagojevich suggested that he enter the witness protection program, while Florida governor Jeb Bush offered him asylum. Bartman proceeded to turn down interview requests and endorsement deals, and he eventually rejected a $25,000 offer to autograph a photo of himself at a sports memorabilia convention.

Here's where it gets weird.

Several months later, a successful restaurateur named Grant DePorter bought the infamous foul ball at an auction for $113,824. DePorter, hoping to rid the Cubs of their curse, recruited Michael Lantieri, an Academy Award–winning special effects expert, to blow up the ball at Harry Caray's restaurant. The stunt was covered live on CNN, ESPN, and MSNBC and was written up by more than 4,000 newspapers. Then, a year later, at a much less publicized event, DePorter used the remnants of the ball to make a dish he named "Foul Ball Spaghetti." What remained of the ball was boiled; the steam was captured and distilled and added to the recipe.

JEFFREY MAIER

Jeffrey Maier was the most infamous baseball fan before Bartman, and he attained his notoriety by doing the same thing: reaching out of the stands and interfering with a ball that was still in play. Luckily for Maier, who was just 12 years old at the time, he was treated as a hero because his interference happened to help the home team. And not just any team—the New York Yankees.

It was October 9, 1996—Game 1 of the American League Championship Series. The Yankees were trailing the Baltimore Orioles, 4–3, with one out in the bottom of the eighth, when Derek Jeter spanked a deep drive toward the short porch in right field. Orioles right fielder Tony Tarasco reached the blue padded wall as the ball was descending and leaped to make the catch—but he never got the chance because Maier stuck out his glove and deflected the ball back into the stands.[2] Right-field umpire Rich Garcia ruled it a home run, prompting Tarasco and Orioles manager Davey Johnson to argue like mad. And they were right—slow-motion replays indicated that the ball would not have cleared the wall if not for Maier—but the bad call stood, and the Yankees won the game (and eventually the World Series) in extra innings. The Orioles filed an official protest, and even though Garcia admitted that there was fan interference, the protest was denied by American League president Gene Budig. Maier appeared on national talk shows and was given the key to New York City by Mayor Rudy Giuliani.

RED SOX WORLD SERIES BALLS

When Red Sox first baseman Doug Mientkiewicz caught the final out of the 2004 World Series, he found an extra way to get his name in the papers: by deciding to keep the ball for himself. Mientkiewicz, a former Gold Glove winner who had entered the game as a defensive replacement for David Ortiz in the bottom of the seventh, felt that he

---

[2] Let the record show, once and for all, that Maier did not "catch" the ball. Not only was he glorified for breaking a rule, but the media mistakenly credited him with having athleticism.

deserved to keep it since he caught it. Red Sox fans and management disagreed. Their team had finally overcome "the Curse of the Bambino"[3] and won its first championship in 86 years. In their minds, this was one of the most important balls in the history of the sport, and it belonged in the team's museum. Mientkiewicz held out, and as the negative media attention intensified, he joked to a *Boston Globe* reporter that the ball was his "retirement fund." Or *was* he joking? On the same day he caught it, Barry Bonds's 700th career home run ball sold for $804,129 through an online auction.

How did the Mientkiewicz saga end? It was easy. First the Red Sox traded him to the Mets for a minor leaguer. Then they filed a lawsuit against him. Then they dropped the charges when he agreed to let an independent mediator settle the dispute. Finally he lent the ball to the Sox for a year and then donated it to the Hall of Fame.

When Boston won the World Series again in 2007, a whole new controversy erupted over the final-out ball. This time it ended up in the hands of catcher Jason Varitek, who initially said he planned to return it to the team, but later admitted that he gave it to reliever Jonathan Papelbon. When the team asked Papelbon for the ball, he claimed that his dog ate it.

"He plays with baseballs like they are his toys," said the pitcher of his bulldog, Boss. "He jumped up one day on the counter and snatched it. He likes rawhide. He tore that thing to pieces."

Papelbon vowed to keep what was left of the ball, but later told the New England Sports Network that he'd

---

[3] If you don't know what this is, pick up a copy of *Watching Baseball Smarter* and turn to page 203.

thrown it out. "It's in the garbage in Florida somewhere," he said.

Team officials took his word and did not file charges.

BARRY BONDS HOME RUN BALLS

It wasn't just the steroids that caused controversy for Barry Bonds. On four separate occasions, it was the product of his alleged steroid use—the home run balls themselves—that created a buzz.

73RD HOME RUN OF 2001 When Mark McGwire hit 70 home runs in 1998 to break the single-season record, his final home run ball sold for more than $3 million. Three years later, when Bonds surpassed him by hitting 73 homers, the final ball ended up in court. Video replays showed a fan making the catch in the tip of his glove, but after the ensuing melee in the right-field stands of what was then called Pacific Bell Park, a different fan held up the ball and was quickly escorted to safety by security personnel. The first fan, Alex Popov, sued the other fan, Patrick Hayashi, for ownership of the ball, claiming that Hayashi had stolen the prized souvenir from him. Fourteen months after number 73 had been hit, the judge ordered the men to sell the ball and split the money. Comic book mogul Todd McFarlane (who had bought the McGwire ball) paid $517,500 for it—far less than Popov needed to cover his legal costs. Hayashi's lawyers went pro bono, and a full-length documentary called *Up for Grabs* was made about the whole ordeal.

700TH CAREER HOME RUN Six months before Bonds hit his 700th career homer, a fan in Los Angeles purchased every ticket in the right-field pavilion for two of the sea-

Up for Grabs *is the best documentary ever made about a baseball.*

son's last three Giants games at Dodger Stadium—6,458 tickets in all. The fan, a 28-year-old investment banker named Michael Mahan, hoped that Bonds would hit the historic blast during one of those contests, but unfortunately for him, the Giants slugger connected two weeks too soon. Unfortunately for the Dodgers, who had offered a reduced group rate on the seats, Mahan resold thousands of the tickets for a profit.

On September 17, 2004, when Bonds connected on number 700, the milestone ball landed in the left-center-field bleachers in San Francisco. Steve Williams, the man who snagged it, had two separate lawsuits filed against him by fans who claimed that he'd stolen it from them during the scrum. One of those fans, an accomplished Bay Area ballhawk named Alex Patino, insisted that he had possession of the ball after sitting on it. Because of the lack of evidence (and perhaps the absurdity of the claim), the judge dismissed the charges and allowed Williams to sell the ball.

756TH CAREER HOME RUN On August 7, 2007, Bonds launched his record-breaking 756th home run toward the right-center-field bleachers at San Francisco's AT&T Park, sparking such a wild melee for the ball that a fan in a wheelchair was knocked over and an usher nearly died from an asthma attack. Fashion designer Marc Ecko ended up buying the ball for $752,467 and creating a website where fans could vote for its fate. Eight days and 10 million votes later, the public decided to "brand" the historic ball with an asterisk and send it to the Hall of Fame. (The other two options included sending the ball sans brand to the Hall or putting it on a rocket and launching it into

Barry Bonds's 756th home run ball was "branded" with an asterisk carved into the cowhide.

space.) Bonds responded by threatening to boycott his own induction if the Hall accepted the branded ball. Gilbert Arenas, an All-Star point guard on the NBA's Washington Wizards, offered to buy the ball from Ecko for $800,000. Ultimately Ecko branded the ball and donated it to Cooperstown after a lengthy negotiating process.

762ND CAREER HOME RUN Ever since an FBI sting in the mid-1990s nabbed dozens of high-profile memorabilia counterfeiters, specially marked balls, often with invisible infrared markings, have been used whenever a player has approached a major record or milestone. On September 5, 2007, Bonds hit his final major league home run—number 762—against the Rockies at Coors Field, but the historic ball was unmarked. Still, under normal circumstances it could have been authenticated on the spot, but because two fans each emerged from the scuffle with a ball in their hands, Major League Baseball officials wanted nothing to do with it.

It turned out that when Bonds stepped to the plate, one of the fans was already holding a ball that he'd caught during pregame warm-ups. That ball, which the fan wisely dropped in order to grab the real home run, was subsequently snagged by a 58-year-old season-ticket holder named Robert Harmon. At the time, there were three weeks remaining in the season; everyone assumed that Bonds would hit at least a few more homers, so no one made a big deal about number 762 or the unnamed fan who grabbed it—until the regular season ended. Then the official manhunt began. One media outlet even issued an all-points bulletin for the owner of the ball to come forward, prompting five phony claims and a follow-up story two months later reporting that the real owner was still at large.

Jameson Sutton, an unemployed 24-year-old from Boulder, Colorado, finally came out of hiding and revealed that he had snagged the controversial ball. Then, thanks to Harmon's unlikely admission that his own ball was a fake, Sutton sent his ball to auction, where it sold for $376,612—money he desperately needed to pay for his ailing father's medical bills. (There was one twist: Sutton had pulled a Jeffrey Maier by reaching out of the stands and interfering with the ball. The play should not have been ruled a home run. Good thing the umpires blew the call.)

HANK AARON'S FINAL HOME RUN

On July 20, 1976, in an otherwise meaningless game between two last-place teams in Milwaukee, Hank Aaron belted his 755th career home run. At the time, no one gave it much thought because there were still two and a half months remaining in the season. The man who snagged the ball even offered to return it to Aaron—for free—under one condition: that he be allowed to meet the future Hall of Famer and hand it over himself. Given the fact that this man, a 29-year-old named Richard Arndt, worked for the Brewers as a part-time groundskeeper, his request could have easily been granted. Well, not only did the Brewers refuse to let Arndt meet Aaron, and not only did they fire him the next day for refusing to return the meaningful item, but the team also docked him $5 from his final paycheck for the cost of the ball. After the season ended, Aaron tried to buy it from Arndt, who declined the offer, moved to Albuquerque, tucked the ball in a safety deposit box, and wasn't heard from for more than two decades.

At some point in the late 1990s, Arndt snuck the ball into a baseball card show and handed it to an unsuspecting Aaron, who autographed it and handed it right back. Soon after, as the ball was headed to auction, Aaron's representatives contacted Arndt and made a lowball offer. Arndt once again refused, ended up selling the ball to a private collector for $650,000, and donated 25 percent of the proceeds to Aaron's charitable foundation.[4]

SAMMY SOSA'S 62ND HOME RUN OF 1998

Before Mark McGwire bashed all those home runs in 1998, the single-season record belonged to Roger Maris, who went deep 61 times in 1961. Luckily for McGwire, his record-breaking 62nd home run ball was returned to him by a groundskeeper in St. Louis. Five days later, when the red-hot Sammy Sosa eclipsed Maris with a 480-foot blast onto Chicago's Waveland Avenue, the precious ball went to court. What set this case apart from other ball-related disputes was that the plaintiff was a legendary ballhawk named Moe Mullins.

Mullins, a 47-year-old truck driver who had reeled in more than 3,100 baseballs over the previous three

---

[4] Arndt claimed he was pressured into donating the money by Aaron's representatives—that if he didn't make the contribution, Aaron himself was going to challenge the ball's authenticity. Arndt initially agreed to donate 42.5 percent, but Aaron accepted the smaller amount after the ball failed to meet its $850,000 reserve price at auction.

*Waveland Avenue, seen here in the late 1990s,
saw far more home runs before the bleacher
expansion of 2006.*

decades, insisted that he had Sosa's homer in his possession before it was ripped out of his hands by a violent mob. Numerous witnesses backed up his claim, and several local residents painted the number "62" in their driveway along with the slogan, "Give it to Moe." Still, there was no way to prove that the fan who ended up with the ball had acquired it illegally. That fan, a mortgage broker named Brendan Cunningham, said he simply found himself in a pile of people and reached down for the ball when it rolled near him. Mullins dropped the lawsuit two weeks later when Cunningham vowed to return the ball to Sosa.

RYAN HOWARD'S 200TH CAREER HOME RUN

This wasn't your typical lawsuit. No one disputed the fact that Jennifer Valdivia snagged Ryan Howard's 200th career home run ball, but when the Phillies reportedly used shady tactics to get the ball back from her, they ended up getting sued.

Valdivia was only 12 years old when she grabbed the milestone ball on July 16, 2009, at Land Shark Stadium.[5] Because of its additional historical significance—Howard hit 200 homers in the fewest number of games—Valdivia was approached by a Marlins representative and taken to the Phillies' clubhouse with her 17-year-old brother. Once they got there, she was told that if she handed over the ball, Howard would autograph it for her later and that she could come back and meet him after the game.

That never happened.

When Valdivia returned after the Phillies' 4–0 victory, Howard wasn't there, and she was given a different (brand-new) ball with his signature. And when Valdivia's mother was told by her coworkers the following day just how special number 200 was, she took action. First she called the Phillies and asked them to return it, and when the team refused she got a lawyer. The lawyer called the Phillies. The Phillies told him to contact Howard's agent. The agent rebuffed him. So the family filed a lawsuit, and wouldn't

---

[5] Home of the Florida Marlins, previously known as Dolphin Stadium, Dolphins Stadium, Pro Player Stadium, Pro Player Park, and Joe Robbie Stadium—and now named Sun Life Stadium. (And the name will probably change three more times by the time you read this.)

you know it? The ball was returned two days later with a letter of authenticity.

BIG MONEY OPPORTUNITIES

In April 2001, when Reds first baseman Sean Casey hit the first home run ever at Pittsburgh's PNC Park, the ball bounced back onto the field and was then absentmindedly tossed back into the crowd by Pirates center fielder Adrian Brown. A month later, the fan who grabbed that ball sold it for $9,400.

Not bad. But it was nothing compared to a ball that had made history 15 years earlier. You've probably seen the replays a thousand times. It was Game 6 of the 1986 World Series at Shea Stadium. Bottom of the 10th inning. Two outs. Winning run on second. Mookie Wilson hit a weak grounder down the first-base line, and the ball trickled through Bill Buckner's legs. Mayhem. Heartbreak. Jubilation. Right-field umpire Ed Montague retrieved the ball, then handed it to a Mets employee named Arthur Richman, who gave it to Wilson—who signed it and gave it back. Six years later, Richman sent the ball to auction, where actor Charlie Sheen bought it for $93,500.[6] At the time, it was the most that anyone had paid for a baseball, but now it wouldn't even crack the top 10:

---

[6] Sheen outbid Keith Olbermann, who walked away at $85,000.

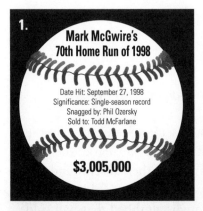

1.

**Mark McGwire's
70th Home Run of 1998**

Date Hit: September 27, 1998
Significance: Single-season record
Snagged by: Phil Ozersky
Sold to: Todd McFarlane

$3,005,000

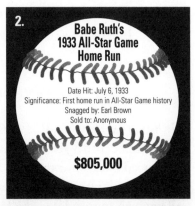

2.

**Babe Ruth's
1933 All-Star Game
Home Run**

Date Hit: July 6, 1933
Significance: First home run in All-Star Game history
Snagged by: Earl Brown
Sold to: Anonymous

$805,000

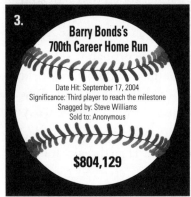

3.

**Barry Bonds's
700th Career Home Run**

Date Hit: September 17, 2004
Significance: Third player to reach the milestone
Snagged by: Steve Williams
Sold to: Anonymous

$804,129

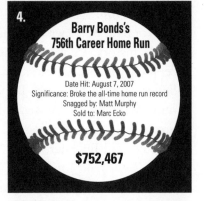

4.

**Barry Bonds's
756th Career Home Run**

Date Hit: August 7, 2007
Significance: Broke the all-time home run record
Snagged by: Matt Murphy
Sold to: Marc Ecko

$752,467

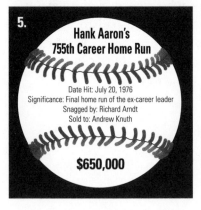

5.

**Hank Aaron's
755th Career Home Run**

Date Hit: July 20, 1976
Significance: Final home run of the ex-career leader
Snagged by: Richard Arndt
Sold to: Andrew Knuth

$650,000

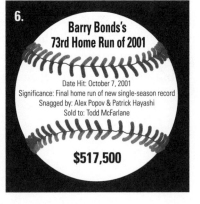

6.

**Barry Bonds's
73rd Home Run of 2001**

Date Hit: October 7, 2001
Significance: Final home run of new single-season record
Snagged by: Alex Popov & Patrick Hayashi
Sold to: Todd McFarlane

$517,500

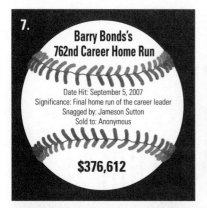

7.

**Barry Bonds's
762nd Career Home Run**

Date Hit: September 5, 2007
Significance: Final home run of the career leader
Snagged by: Jameson Sutton
Sold to: Anonymous

$376,612

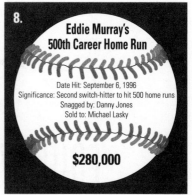

8.

**Eddie Murray's
500th Career Home Run**

Date Hit: September 6, 1996
Significance: Second switch-hitter to hit 500 home runs
Snagged by: Danny Jones
Sold to: Michael Lasky

$280,000

9.

**Mark McGwire's
500th Career Home Run**

Date Hit: August 5, 1999
Significance: Reached 500 home runs in fewest at-bats
Snagged by: Jim Shearer
Sold to: Anonymous

$250,000

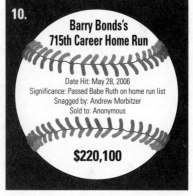

10.

**Barry Bonds's
715th Career Home Run**

Date Hit: May 28, 2006
Significance: Passed Babe Ruth on home run list
Snagged by: Andrew Morbitzer
Sold to: Anonymous

$220,100

CHAPTER 2

FOUL BALL LORE

CONSECUTIVE FOUL BALLS

In the 19th century, foul balls weren't sexy like they are today. For the most part, in fact, they were just plain annoying. Not only were fans forced to return them, and not only was the game delayed each time a foul ball had to make its way back to the field, but the action itself was meaningless. Foul balls were essentially non-events because they didn't count as strikes. As a result, carefree batters intentionally hit fouls in order to wear out the opposing pitcher and wait for pitches they could hammer.

In 1901 the National League made a dramatic attempt to curtail this practice by instituting a rule that turned foul balls into strikes—and it worked. Batters weren't nearly as eager to hit foul balls, and pitchers regained some of their much-needed advantage.[1] The American League adopted the foul-strike rule two years later.

---

[1] In 1894 the mound was moved back more than 10 feet to its current distance of 60 feet, 6 inches, and the National League's batting average

Although foul ball stats were not consistently documented until pitch counts began ruling the sport, there are several known cases of extreme fouls—not surprisingly, from before the foul-strike rule took effect. During a game in 1897, Hall of Famer Billy Hamilton, then a member of the Boston Beaneaters, hit 29 in a row. Later that season, Hamilton led off a game against Cy Young by hitting the first three pitches foul. Young responded by walking toward Hamilton and telling him, "I'm putting the next pitch right over the heart of the plate. If you foul it off, the next one goes right in your ear."

Roy Thomas, a 13-year veteran who began his career with the Phillies in 1899, supposedly fouled off 22 pitches during one plate appearance, but it remains unknown if he hit them consecutively. Jack Dittmer, a second baseman for the Milwaukee Braves in the mid-1950s, is also believed to have fouled off 22 during a single turn at bat. The 21st-century record belongs to Dodgers second baseman Alex Cora, who fouled off 14 straight pitches on May 12, 2004, and punctuated his effort with a home run. But the true master of the mis-hit—the Duke of Deflection, the Sultan of Slap—was Hall of Famer Luke Appling.

"No batter could ever frustrate a pitcher more than ol' Luke," said Dizzy Trout, whose Detroit Tigers faced Appling's White Sox more than 200 times in the 1940s. "He would stand there and nonchalantly foul off your best pitches—10, 12, or more—until he finally got the one he was waiting for." One time, after Appling fouled off a

increased 29 points to .309. By 1900 the leaguewide average had dropped to .279, and in 1901, the first season of the foul-strike rule, the average plummeted an additional 12 points to .267.

Luke Appling was a foul ball–hitting machine.

dozen of Trout's 0-2 pitches, Trout threw his glove at him and yelled, "Hit *that* foul!"

On another occasion, Appling hit two dozen balls into the crowd to get even with his own team. Why he did it, however, is unclear. One account suggests he was angry because the owner wouldn't provide free tickets for his friends; a different (and better) story claims Appling took his course of action because the team wouldn't give him baseballs to autograph and hand out to the fans. According to the latter version, Appling's requests for baseballs were never denied again.

Appling himself claimed to have hit foul balls at least

once for his own amusement. During a game against the Yankees in 1940, the White Sox were so far behind that Appling decided to mess with Red Ruffing, the opposing pitcher. "I started fouling off his pitches," he said. "I took a pitch every now and then. Pretty soon, after 24 fouls, old Red could hardly lift his arm, and I walked. That's when they took him out of the game, and he cussed me all the way to the dugout."

And then there was the peanut vendor who made the mistake of laughing at a fan who had gotten hit by one of Appling's foul balls. "I'll fix him," Appling declared, then stepped back into the batter's box and drilled the guy in the head with the next foul. The vendor had to be carried out of the stadium.

LIGHTNING STRIKES TWICE

Hall of Famer Richie Ashburn was so good at hitting foul balls that a teammate once approached him with an odd (and rather disturbing) request to use his batting skills. The teammate was angry at his own wife, who was sitting in the left-field stands, and asked Ashburn to hit her with a foul ball. Ashburn refused to do it, but on another occasion he accidentally sent a different female fan to the hospital.

That fan was Alice Roth, the wife of Earl Roth, sports editor of the *Philadelphia Bulletin*. On August 17, 1957, she took her two young grandsons to a game at Connie Mack Stadium and made the mistake of momentarily looking away from the action to fix one of the boys' caps. At that very instant, Ashburn fouled off a ball that whacked her in the face and broke her nose—but that was just half of Mrs. Roth's ordeal. As she was being tended to by medical personnel and carried off on a stretcher, Ashburn stepped back into the box and fouled off another ball that hit her again.

"I didn't mean to do it," insisted Ashburn. "When I saw what happened, I felt terrible."

Ashburn felt so bad about it that he visited Roth in the hospital, and the team gave her grandsons free tickets and a clubhouse tour. Back then, people didn't sue when they got hit by a ball, and in the end all was forgiven.

NICE "CATCH"

Norm Zauchin, a hulking first baseman for the Boston Red Sox and Washington Senators in the 1950s, might

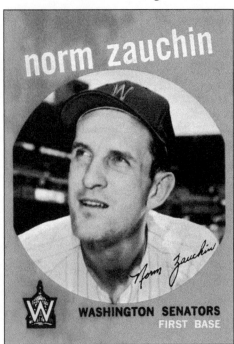

not be a household name, but he made the great-est "catch" of all time on a foul ball. It was a Sunday afternoon in 1950—the year before his major league debut—and Zauchin was playing for the Birmingham Barons at Rickwood Stadium. At one point

Norm Zauchin hit 18 home runs for the Senators from 1958 to 1959.

in the middle innings, Zauchin ran into foul territory to chase a pop-up, reached far over the railing to make a catch, and tumbled into the crowded front row. He happened to land in the lap of a pretty young woman named Janet Mooney, whose parents knew the usher in their section.[2] Back in those days, it was customary for families to welcome players into their homes for Sunday dinner, so the usher finagled an invitation for Zauchin. He and Janet started dating, and the two were married the following season.

HECKLE *THIS*!

According to Joe Cronin, Red Sox manager from 1935 to 1947, Ted Williams once tried to silence a heckler by hitting foul balls at him. Williams later admitted it in his autobiography—the notorious incident taking place in 1942—but there was a discrepancy in the two men's tales. Cronin claimed that Williams hit 17 foul balls at the fan and never missed by more than six feet. Williams said he "aimed three or four fouls in this spot behind third, but never got close enough."

Who's telling the truth? Who cares? If the heckler had brought a glove, Williams would've been doing him a favor.

DON'T MESS WITH CAL RIPKEN JR.

Toward the end of his celebrated career, Cal Ripken Jr. drew heavy criticism whenever he fell into a slump. The

---

[2] As the story goes, it was love at first sight.

future Hall of Famer was in the process of playing in a record 2,632 consecutive games, and lots of people believed that the streak was wearing him out. One of his critics was *Baltimore Sun* columnist Ken Rosenthal, who suggested that Ripken voluntarily take a day off for the good of his team. (The Orioles were actually sort of almost in contention at the time.)

Not long after the column ran, Ripken responded with his bat, sending a foul ball flying back toward Rosenthal in the press box at Camden Yards. Rosenthal ducked out of the way, but the ball smashed and destroyed his laptop.

LYNYRD SKYNYRD

In 1964 a teenager named Ronnie Van Zant stepped up to the plate in a youth baseball game and ripped a foul ball down the first-base line. Two of his schoolmates were in attendance, one of whom got hit in the head by the ball and was briefly knocked unconscious. The kid's name was Bob Burns. His friend was Gary Rossington. Van Zant didn't know them well at the time, but the unnerving incident brought them closer together. All three of them, it turned out, were aspiring musicians, each playing in various garage bands, and in the following days they got together for some jam sessions.

Later that summer, Van Zant and Rossington formed their own band called The Noble Five. The following year, Burns joined them, and they changed their name to My Backyard. The band, which included other members, ultimately became known as Lynyrd Skynyrd. Van Zant was the lead singer (until his untimely death in 1977), Burns was the drummer (until he quit in 1974), and Rossington played the guitar. The group was inducted into the Rock and Roll Hall of Fame in 2006.

BANNED FROM BASEBALL

Forget about Pete Rose and the 1919 Black Sox. The most outrageous gambling scandal in the history of professional baseball (as far as this book is concerned) involves an ex–major leaguer named Joe Tipton, who got banned for life from the minor leagues for hitting foul balls.

In the late 1950s, speculation arose that numerous players in the Class AA Southern Association were intentionally hitting fouls to help gamblers. (Gamblers had an easier time convincing individual players to hit harmless foul balls than paying off entire teams to throw games. The gamblers then sat in the stands and bet with the fans at just the right time that the batter would hit the next pitch foul.) An investigation was launched, and everyone who was questioned denied involvement—everyone except Tipton, who admitted that while playing for the Birmingham Barons in 1957 he had accepted two payments—one for $50 and another for $75—to hit foul balls. Tipton had appeared in his final major league game three years earlier, and he'd already retired from the minors by the time he confessed, yet he still received a lifetime ban.

In the 1960s it was revealed that the gamblers' foul ball scheme had infiltrated the sport decades earlier. Wally Kimmick, a major league infielder whose career had ended in 1926, recalled a bizarre incident in which a fan he vaguely recognized asked him if he could hit foul balls. Kimmick insisted that he could, but when the guy doubted him he was compelled to prove himself. "I could hit 10 in a row," Kimmick told the man. "Naturally I wouldn't try it if there were men on base, but if I come up with nobody on, you just watch." Kimmick found out later that the man made $10,000 betting he'd hit foul balls, and he never saw the man again.

GREAT BALLS OF FIRE

It figures that a guy named Burns was responsible for a foul ball that started a fire. In August 1915, Tigers first baseman George Burns worked a full count against Red Sox starter Dutch Leonard and fouled the next pitch into the stands. As the fans jockeyed for position to make the catch, the ball hit a man's coat and ignited a box of matches in his pocket. Then, when the fire began to spread, a soft drink vendor rushed over, opened up a bottle of soda, and poured it on the guy to douse the flames.

HAPPY MOTHER'S DAY

Mother's Day 1939 didn't turn out the way Bob Feller had envisioned it. His family made the trip from their home in Iowa to watch him pitch against the White Sox at Comiskey Park, and he arranged for them to sit in box seats along the first-base side. The seats were particularly close to the action, and in the bottom of the third inning things went horribly awry. Sox pinch hitter Marv Owen slashed a vicious foul ball into the crowd that hit Feller's mother in the face, broke her glasses, and opened a deep cut over her right eye that required six stitches. Feller, who had thrown the pitch, raced over to the stands and discovered that although his mother was bleeding and in serious pain, she was at least conscious.

"I felt sick," he later recalled. "I saw the police and ushers leading her out of the stands so they could take her to the hospital. . . . There wasn't anything I could do, so I went on pitching."

Feller, incredibly, not only stayed in the game but went the distance for a 9–4 victory. The Hall of Famer then visited the hospital, and his mother ended up making a full recovery.

FAMILY AFFAIR

It wasn't Mother's Day, and no one went to the hospital. It didn't even involve a future Hall of Famer, but at a game at Camden Yards in 2006 a foul ball nonetheless left a family up in arms. Orioles designated hitter Jay Gibbons fouled one straight back over the protective screen and into the family section, where it smashed his own wife in the ribs. Fortunately, she wasn't seriously hurt, but Gibbons was furious. As the team's player representative, he had asked Orioles management to raise the screen long before she got hit—he and his teammates felt it wasn't tall enough to provide adequate protection for their families—but his request was denied. Management had claimed that a taller screen would disrupt the sight lines of fans sitting behind the plate, but team officials finally relented and raised the screen in 2007.[3]

---

[3] Gibbons isn't the only player to have struck a member of his own family with a foul ball. During a Spring Training game in 2010, Twins out-

THAT BALL IS . . . GONE!

It sounds impossible, but this story, reported by Sergeant A. D. Hawkins, a Marine Corps combat correspondent during World War II, comes straight from the archives of the Hall of Fame. The featured foul, as you might already be guessing, wasn't hit at a major league stadium, and in fact this incident didn't even take place during a game. The ball was hit during batting practice in the South Pacific by a player on a First Marine Division regimental team, so you know it had to be something special.

Marine Private First Class George E. Benson Jr., a 20-year-old soldier from Dawson, Iowa, yanked a high foul ball that sailed behind third base and smashed through the windshield of a small Grasshopper airplane that was gliding 40 feet off the ground toward a nearby airstrip. But that's not all the ball did. It broke the pilot's jaw and briefly knocked him unconscious. Marine Corporal Robert J. Holm, a passenger with no flying experience, instinctively pulled back on the dual controls and prevented the plane from crashing, and when the pilot recovered he took over and landed safely at another airfield 15 miles away.

Benson had seen the impact after following the flight of the ball, but a few of his teammates hadn't noticed and went looking for it.

"Once I broke a high school window with a foul ball," he said, "but I never thought this would happen to me."

---

fielder Denard Span sliced a wicked liner that hit his mother in the chest. (Don't worry. She was okay.)

Grasshopper airplanes were not designed for combat—or for absorbing the impact of foul balls.

CHAPTER 3

DEATH BY BASEBALL

DANGEROUS GAME

Remember that scary moment during the 1999 American League Division Series when Kenny Lofton dove violently into first base and dislocated his shoulder? Or the regular-season game in 1995 when Ken Griffey Jr. crashed into the center-field wall and broke his wrist? Or the incident during the 2001 All-Star Game when the 73-year-old Tommy Lasorda got knocked on his ass by a flying broken bat? Fortunately, Lasorda was okay, but the fact remains that there are many ways to get hurt on a baseball field. In addition to the obvious, waiting-to-happen accidents like catchers getting bowled over while blocking the plate, shortstops getting spiked while covering second base, or first basemen falling down the dugout steps while chasing foul pop-ups, there are unexpected hazards everywhere. Players don't necessarily have to dive headfirst or slam into walls to land on the disabled list. After a Cubs victory in 2009, Ryan Dempster broke his right big toe and missed three weeks after tripping over the dugout railing in an attempt to run out onto the field with his celebrating teammates.

What do all these misfortunes have in common? None of them are directly linked to the ball. Sure, the bat that hit Lasorda had been broken by the ball—and it was the ball that Griffey had hoped to catch when making his fateful dash to deep center field—but these guys were not hurt by the ball itself. Ball-related injuries are a whole other story. There've been enough to fill an encyclopedia,

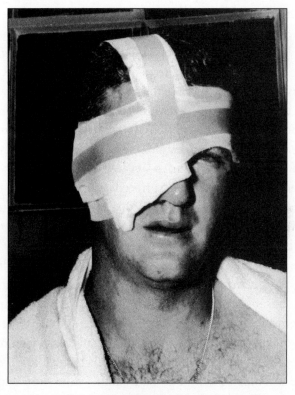

Herb Score was never the same after getting hit in the face by a line drive.

and with all due respect to Mariners reliever Josias Manzanillo, who needed testicular surgery in 1997 after taking a 107-mile-per-hour Manny Ramirez liner to the groin, any discussion of them needs to start with Indians pitcher Herb Score.

A 23-year-old phenom in 1957, Score was struck in the right eye by a wicked line drive off the bat of Yankees shortstop Gil McDougald. The impact broke several bones in his face, permanently affected his vision, and ruined what was shaping up to be a Hall of Fame career. Score had been named the minor league player of the year in 1954 and was voted the American League Rookie of the Year in 1955. The following season he won 20 games while striking out 263 batters and posting a 2.53 ERA. In the five years that Score pitched after his injury, he won a total of 17 games and had a forgettable 4.43 ERA.

Because Score was so young and gifted, and because he played during baseball's golden age, he remains the poster boy for devastating injuries—even though Cardinals right fielder Juan Encarnacion suffered one that proved to be much worse. On August 31, 2007, while standing in the on-deck circle at Busch Stadium, Encarnacion got hit in the face by a foul ball that shattered his left eye socket and caused severe trauma to his optic nerve. The Cardinals' head physician said it was the worst injury he'd ever seen on a baseball player's face and compared the mangled socket to a disintegrated eggshell. Fifteen months later, the *St. Louis Post Dispatch* reported that Encarnacion had "not yet recovered enough vision in his left eye to drive, let alone attempt to play baseball again." And sure enough, his career was over.

There've been lots of other notable ball-related injuries

over the years. In Game 4 of the 2001 American League Division Series, A's right fielder Jermaine Dye fouled a ball off his leg that shattered his fibula. During batting practice in 1988, Mets first baseman Keith Hernandez yanked a foul ball that ricocheted off the batting cage and broke his nose. In Game 7 of the 1960 World Series, Yankees short-stop Tony Kubek suffered a bruised larynx when a ground ball took a bad hop and hit him in the throat. Prior to the 2007 season, Giants catcher Mike Matheny was forced to retire because of all the concussions he'd suffered from get-ting whacked by foul tips. During a regular-season game in 1996, home plate umpire Ed Rapuano sustained a broken collarbone and was taken off the field on a stretcher after getting struck by a foul ball. On Opening Day in 1954, Hall of Fame baseball writer H. G. Salsinger lost his vision in one eye after being nailed by a foul ball in the Briggs Sta-dium press box.[4]

Then there are the untold number of batters who have sustained serious injuries from being hit in the face or on the head, the most notorious cases including Tony Conigliaro, Dickie Thon, Andre Dawson, Kirby Puckett, Ron Santo, Joe Medwick, and Hall of Famer Mickey Cochrane, who in 1937—four years before batting helmets were first used—suffered a fractured skull, remained unconscious for 10 days, and never played again. Incredi-bly, in the history of Major League Baseball, only one player has ever died from being hit by a pitch. That player was Ray Chapman.

---

[4] Tiger Stadium, home of the Tigers from 1912 to 1999, was named Briggs Stadium from 1938 to 1960. The ballpark was known as Navin Field before that.

RAY CHAPMAN

Raymond Johnson Chapman was born in Beaver Dam, Kentucky, in 1891. He made his major league debut with Cleveland in 1912 and quickly established himself as the team's everyday shortstop. If there had been All-Star Games back then, Chapman probably would've played in a few; in 1915 he hit 17 triples and scored 101 runs, in 1917 he stole 52 bases and hit 67 sacrifice bunts (a single-season record that still stands), and in three of his last four seasons he batted .300 or higher.

That final season was cut short by tragedy.

The date was August 16, 1920. The Indians were in New York, facing Yankees superstar pitcher Carl Mays, a fiery competitor who exploited a batter's fear as well as anyone. Not only had he led the American League in hit batsmen just three years earlier, but his repertoire included an erratic spitball, and his submarine-style delivery made all of his pitches tough to see.

By the time Chapman stepped to the plate in the top of the fifth inning, he faced two additional challenges that reduced his visibility. First, the late-afternoon sun was casting shadows on the field, and second, the ball itself was dirty. *Very* dirty. In 1920—the season before Reuben Berman's successful lawsuit—the same ball would be put back into play repeatedly, batter after batter, even inning after inning, until it was scuffed, misshapen, and discolored. But it wasn't just the routine wear and tear that darkened the ball; pitchers often spat tobacco juice on it and rubbed it with dirt to make the horsehide as dark as possible.

No one's sure what type of pitch did Chapman in. It

might've been a spitter, it might've been a fastball, but whatever it was, he didn't see it. He didn't even flinch as the ball cracked him on the left temple. The sound of the impact was so loud that Mays thought the ball had hit Chapman's bat, so he fielded it and threw it to first base. Chapman, meanwhile, was sprawled on the ground with a fractured skull and blood pouring out of his ear. He was rushed to the hospital and died 12 hours later. The spitball, along with other doctored pitches, was banned the following season, and umpires were instructed to take dirty baseballs out of play.[5]

MIKE COOLBAUGH

Back in the old days, ballplayers were more concerned with being tough than being safe. Thus, after Chapman's death, it took 21 years before a major league team was willing to experiment with batting helmets—and then it took an additional three decades for helmets to become mandatory. But change came about much sooner after a wayward line drive struck and killed minor league first-base coach Mike Coolbaugh in 2007. Starting the following season (with predictable resistance from a handful of old-school guys), every first- and third-base coach in professional baseball was made to wear a helmet.

Coolbaugh, a former major league third baseman, was

---

[5] The 17 pitchers who had depended on the spitball in 1920 were allowed to continue throwing it for the remainder of their careers. The list of grandfathered pitchers included three future Hall of Famers: Stan Coveleski, Red Faber, and Burleigh Grimes, who threw the last legal spitball in 1934.

hired on July 3, 2007, by the Tulsa Drillers, the Rockies' Double-A affiliate. Nineteen days later, while standing in the first-base coach's box during a game in Arkansas, he was hit in the neck by a line drive off the bat of Drillers catcher Tino Sanchez. The impact crushed Coolbaugh's left vertebral artery and caused a severe brain hemorrhage that killed him almost instantly.

The incident was particularly tragic because Coolbaugh left behind a pregnant wife and two young boys, who had prompted him to take the coaching job because they loved seeing him in uniform on a baseball field. Later that season the family got a much-needed boost, both emotionally and financially, when the Rockies clinched the National League Wild Card and unanimously voted to give Coolbaugh's widow a full share of their playoff money. That bounty rose to $233,505.18 as the Rockies swept the Phillies and then the Diamondbacks to reach the World Series.

FAN FATALITIES

When the National League was founded in 1876, none of the ballparks had protective screens in place to shield fans from foul balls—and guess what? It didn't really matter. Back then, the pitcher's job was simply to help start the action by giving the batter an easy pitch to hit; pitchers were forced to throw underhand, and batters could request a high or low pitch. It wasn't hard for batters to hit the ball into fair territory, nor was there any strategic advantage in wasting pitches by intentionally hitting them foul. But over the next few seasons, as the rules evolved and pitchers gained the right to throw hard, there was a surge in the number of foul balls and fan injuries. The section of the grandstand located directly behind home plate became known as the "slaughter pens" because of all the injuries that were taking place there, and in 1878 the Providence Grays became the first team to do something about it. They put up a screen in their home ballpark, the Messer Street Grounds, and by the turn of the century most ballparks offered similar protection.

Nowadays, despite the fact that protective screens are a given and fans get warned repeatedly about the danger of foul balls, there are still a disturbingly large number of injuries at professional baseball games—more than 300 every season that are severe enough to send fans to hospitals. Most of these accidents take place in the minor leagues (where there are more games and where fans sit closer to the field), but there've been plenty of gruesome injuries at the major league level. There was a two-year span when Tigers fans were hit especially hard—in 1999 at Tiger Stadium a woman lost her left eye after getting struck in the face by a foul ball,[6] and in 2000 at Comerica Park a young boy suffered a fractured skull and developed a life-threatening hematoma after getting drilled by a line drive—but every team's fan base has fallen victim to the ball. One of the best-known incidents took place in 1982 at Fenway Park, when a six-year-old boy sitting behind the dugout was literally saved by Hall of Famer Jim Rice after a foul ball fractured his skull. While everyone in the stands waited helplessly for medical personnel to arrive, Rice

---

[6] She was reaching for her boyfriend's popcorn and didn't see the ball coming. She later sued the Tigers for $10 million, but because of the "assumption of risk" and printed disclaimer on the back of her ticket stub, she collected just $5,000—the maximum amount that the Tigers' insurance policy permitted. Injured fans often sue, but rarely win.

stepped out of the dugout, reached into the crowd, cradled the boy in his arms, and rushed him to the trainer's room inside the clubhouse.

Incredibly, with all the stadiums and teams and games and defensive two-strike swings, only one fan in the history of Major League Baseball has ever been killed by a foul ball. That fan was a 14-year-old boy named Alan Fish, who was hit behind and above the left ear by a Manny Mota line drive on May 16, 1970, at Dodger Stadium. The impact knocked Fish unconscious and caused a hairline fracture, which in turn caused an intracerebral hemorrhage—part of his skull was pushed into his brain and caused it to bleed—but no one realized the severity of his injury at the time. That's because Fish regained consciousness after a minute, and although he was disoriented at first, he said he felt okay and stayed in his seat. Then, when he was taken to a first aid station later in the game, the doctor examined him quickly, gave him two aspirins, and sent him on his way. Fish felt fine for the rest of the game and even chased another foul ball at one point, but by the time he got home he was feeling dizzy and shaky. His parents (who had not attended the game) rushed him to the hospital, where his condition quickly deteriorated. It was only then that he was properly diagnosed, but the emergency surgery was too late to save him, and he died several days later.

The only other ball-related death in major league history was the result of an errant throw from a player who probably shouldn't have been in the majors in the first place.[7] On September 29, 1943, in the first game of a twi-

---

[7] No, this is not a story about Yankees second baseman Chuck Knoblauch, who hit Keith Olbermann's mother in the face with a bad throw in 2006. (She survived.)

night doubleheader at Griffith Stadium, Senators third baseman Sherry Robertson fielded a routine grounder and airmailed Mickey Vernon across the diamond. (Robertson was a mediocre hitter and an even worse fielder, but he lasted in the major leagues for a decade as the nephew of team owner Clark Griffith.) The ball sailed into the front row of the stands and hit a man named Clarence D. Stagemyer on the head. Stagemyer, a 32-year-old Civil Aeronautics Administration employee, initially shook off the injury but was convinced by the Senators' physician to go to the hospital. It turned out that he had suffered a concussion and a fractured skull, but it was too late to save him, and he died the next day.

While flying baseballs pose a constant threat, far more fans have been killed in fights or by falling off escalators or—as was frighteningly common in the old days when ballparks were made of wood and overcrowding was prevalent—by entire sections of the grandstand collapsing. Just as players have to deal with an array of safety hazards, the same is true for fans. There has even been a case of a fan getting hit and killed by a car outside a stadium. Granted, it wasn't a major league stadium—it happened in March 1988 at the Pirates' Spring Training facility in Bradenton, Florida—but the tragic event still deserves an honorable mention because the man, a 42-year-old named Daniel McCarthy, was hit while chasing a foul ball that had flown out of the stadium.

FOWL BALLS

On June 11, 2009, the outcome of the Royals-Indians game at Progressive Field was determined by a bird. With runners on first and second, a flock of seagulls dawdling in shallow center field, and the score tied at 3–3 in the bottom of the 10th inning, Cleveland's Shin-Soo Choo ripped a line drive up the middle that deflected off one of the birds and skipped past center fielder Coco Crisp to plate the winning run. Everyone was able to laugh about it later because the stunned gull had managed to fly away, but there've been several other games in which birds were not as lucky.

The incidents that have caused the least uproar involved pigeons that were killed by batted balls. That's because it was always assumed to be an accident and—let's face it—because no one likes pigeons, at least not in New York City, where the birds lurk everywhere and poop on everything. It was in New York that a pigeon was famously killed in 1987 by an otherwise routine fly ball hit by Atlanta's Dion James. As Mets shortstop Rafael Santana gingerly picked up the carcass and handed it to the ball girl, the only thing upsetting to Mets fans was that the bird had caused the ball to drop in front of left fielder Kevin McReynolds, allowing James to motor into second base with a double. There've been other pigeon fatalities, including one at Fenway Park in 1974 thanks to a foul ball hit by Tigers left fielder Willie Horton, but again, no one really cared. You want uproar? Enter Dave Winfield.

It was August 4, 1983. Winfield, then playing center field for the Yankees, was just finishing his fifth-inning warm-ups in Toronto, and when he fired the ball back in, it struck and killed a seagull that had been walking across the field. Yankees manager Billy Martin later joked about it, saying it was the first time that his outfielder had hit the cutoff man all year, but it was no laughing matter to the peaceful people of Canada. Many of the 36,684 fans in attendance believed that Winfield had done it on purpose and immediately began pelting him with debris. After the game, Winfield was arrested for animal cruelty, a charge that could've brought a six-month jail sentence had it not been dropped the next day.

Twenty years later, during batting practice at a minor league stadium in Daytona Beach, Florida, a teenaged pitcher named Jae Kuk Ryu intentionally threw several balls at an osprey that was perched on a utility crossbar above the field. Witnesses claimed that Ryu hit the bird on his fourth attempt, causing it to plummet onto the warning track 25 feet below. The bird was blinded in one eye and died six days later. Ryu received numerous death threats and was demoted to the lowest level of the minor leagues; he turned his career around, however, and earned a major league call-up in 2006.

Then there was the unfortunate dove that crossed paths with a Randy Johnson fastball. (There are video clips of the incident online; do a search for "randy johnson bird" and you'll find them.) It happened on March 24, 2001, during the seventh inning of a Spring Training game in Tucson, Arizona. Just after Johnson unleashed a mid-90s heater, the bird swooped in front of catcher Rod Barajas, took a direct hit, and exploded in a puff of white feathers. The ball (in addition to the bird) was called dead, and the play was ruled "no pitch."

CHAPTER 4

STUNTS

SUCH GREAT HEIGHTS

During Spring Training in 1915, Brooklyn Robins[1] manager Wilbert Robinson attempted a feat that was thought to be impossible: catching a baseball dropped out of an airplane. He might have succeeded if not for the fact that a grapefruit was dropped from the plane instead.

Aviation pioneer Ruth Law made the historic flight and circled her biplane hundreds of feet above the field—that much we know—but there are two different versions of the grapefruit portion of the story. It has been widely reported that Casey Stengel, then an outfielder with the team, made the fruity substitution, either as a practical joke or to protect his manager from the destructive force of a rock-hard baseball. Some historians, however, claim that Stengel wasn't even in camp at that point, and Law herself stated years later that no one had put her up to the switcheroo—

---

[1] The Brooklyn Dodgers changed their name in 1914 and were officially known as the Robins until 1932.

she simply dropped the grapefruit because she had forgotten to take a ball. Regardless, as the speeding grapefruit descended, its force became so great that it splattered all over Robinson and knocked him on his back.

"Help me, lads!" shouted Robinson. "I'm covered with my own blood!"

Even after discovering that his body was intact, Robinson still wasn't happy because he'd lost his chance to enter the record books. In 1908 Senators catcher Gabby Street had become the first person to catch a ball dropped from the top of the Washington Monument—555 feet above the ground. Never mind that Street was 25 years old and still needed 13 attempts to make the catch (in large part because the wind blew the balls all over the place); the overweight, 51-year-old Robinson was inspired by the stunt and wanted to one-up him.

After Street earned his place in baseball lore, he said, "The ball I caught hit my mitt with terrific force, much greater than any pitched ball I have ever caught, and I have caught some pitchers who are given credit for having wonderful speed. Though my mitt is three or four inches thick, the force of the ball benumbed my hand."

According to a story published the following day in the *New York Times*, it was estimated that the ball had been traveling "slightly over 140 feet a second," or a shade above 95 miles per hour, when Street caught it—an estimate, given the lack of technology at the time, that was remarkably precise. More than 80 years later, in his seminal book *The Physics of Baseball*, Yale University's Sterling Professor of Physics Robert K. Adair proved, among many other things, that "the terminal velocity of a ball dropped from a great height is but 95 mph."

Street wasn't the first person to attempt to catch a ball

dropped from a great height, and Robinson wasn't the last. Paul Hines, an outfielder who debuted in 1872 with the Washington Nationals, could have become the first to catch a ball dropped off the Washington Monument, but he chickened out (perhaps because baseball gloves were not yet in vogue) shortly before the stunt was supposed to take place in 1885. Nine years later, Chicago Colts catcher Pop Schriver made an unpublicized attempt to catch a ball dropped from the Monument, but was quickly chased away by police after two failed tries. For years after the fact, there were inconsistent reports that Schriver had made the catch, but his teammate and accomplice, Clark Griffith, who had dropped the balls from high above, eventually admitted that they had not succeeded.

In 1910 White Sox catcher Billy Sullivan caught several balls that had been dropped and thrown from the top of the Washington Monument, although it took two dozen attempts before he snagged the first one. In 1925 another White Sox catcher, named Ray Schalk, caught a ball dropped from the newly constructed 462-foot Tribune Tower in downtown Chicago. The following summer, in a stunt that took place at an army aviation field in New York, Babe Ruth caught a ball that was dropped from an airplane flying at an altitude of 250 feet and a speed of 100 miles per hour. (Can you imagine Derek Jeter attempting this?) In 1930 Cubs Hall of Fame catcher Gabby Hartnett bested Ruth and set a record that still stands: catching a baseball dropped from the greatest height. The Cubs were in Los Angeles for a preseason game when Hartnett grabbed a ball that was tossed from a blimp 800 feet above the field. In 1938 Frankie Pytlak and Hank Helf—both catchers on the Indians—caught balls dropped from Cleveland's Terminal Tower at a height of approximately 680

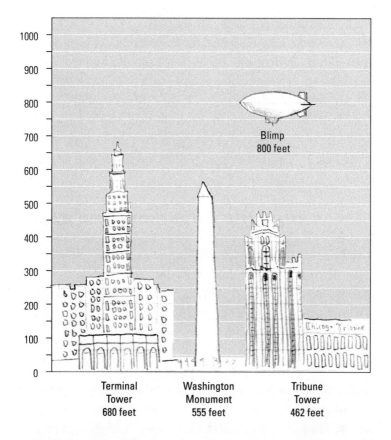

feet. They still hold the record for catching balls dropped from the highest structure.

Among all the successful attempts, there've been numerous failures, but none worse than that of Joe Sprinz in 1939. A former catcher whose brief career had ended with the Cardinals six years earlier, Sprinz agreed to participate in a publicity stunt at the World's Fair in San Francisco. The baseball was supposed to be dropped from an airplane flying more than 1,000 feet high, but it ended up being released from a blimp at 800 feet instead. Sprinz, to his credit, managed to get his glove on it, but the force of the ball smashed his glove into his face. The impact broke his jaw, knocked out several teeth, severely cut his lips, and caused him to drop the ball—and to make matters worse, the mishap discouraged future generations from attempting anything similar.

Why did Sprinz agree to do it in the first place?

"All the other players refused and walked off the field," he recalled. "But I said to myself, 'God hates a coward.' "

KNOCKING THE COVER OFF THE BALL

Ever since Robert Redford's character in the 1984 movie *The Natural* literally knocked the cover off a baseball, people have wondered if such a feat is actually possible. Twenty-three years later, a TV show on the Discovery Channel called *Mythbusters* attempted to find out once and for all.

The two hosts, Jamie Hyneman and Adam Savage, tested the myth by firing balls at a "static bat" from an air cannon. In other words, the bat wasn't being swung; it was held in place by a mechanical arm. And therein lay the first of two problems: the experiment, as interesting as it was, degenerated into an exercise in *bunting* the cover off the ball.

As Hyneman and Savage increased the speed at which the balls were fired, something unexpected happened at the 200-mile-per-hour threshold. The bat snapped in half, but the ball remained intact.

"It's obvious to me," said Hyneman to his co-host, "that knocking the hide off a ball is way beyond the capability of a human pitcher or batter." (Even guest star Roger Clemens.)

The test concluded with Hyneman and Savage cranking up the cannon full blast and shooting a brand-new ball 437 miles per hour into a padded backdrop. That did the trick and caused the cowhide cover to fly off the twiny core—but that's where the second problem arose. There were several unanswered questions: What's the slowest speed at which the ball would've broken apart? What exactly made the cover rip off at top speed? Was it the jolt of 150 pounds per square inch from deep inside the cannon's long barrel? Or was it the air resistance once the ball escaped?

The most important question might be: would it have been possible to knock the cover off an old and slightly worn-out ball, like the one used in *The Natural*? Probably not, but the circumstances were favorable. The scene took place in 1939, when umpires weren't nearly as anal about discarding used balls—and in the moments before Redford unleashed his sensational swing, a close-up of the ball in the pitcher's hand revealed a small imperfection on the stitches.

Still, Hyneman and Savage are probably right: myth busted.

PUNK'D BY PETE ROSE

Pete Rose did not perform well in All-Star Games. He played in 16 of them and batted just .212 (7-for-33), but at the 1978 contest in San Diego he used a different approach to help the National League.

Long before the game took place, Rose devised a plan to psych out the American League. He knew that Japanese baseballs travel farther than major league balls because they're made smaller and wound tighter, so he secretly arranged for Mizuno to ship dozens of balls to the stadium.

"I brought the balls in for the National League's batting practice," said Rose. "It was all for psychological warfare."

With his teammates in on the trick, Rose visited the American League clubhouse and convinced a bunch of players to watch BP.

"Everyone was hitting them out of the park," recalled Phillies second baseman Larry Bowa.[2] "I even hit a couple out in BP—something I never did before. It made me feel like Babe Ruth."

Rose and Bowa and the rest of the National League All-Stars put on quite a show, then made sure to gather every ball before clearing the field and watching the American League take their cuts.

"They were just barely hitting them to the outfield wall," said Bowa. "It was normal stuff, but after the way our balls were flying way up into the stands, the American Leaguers looked like Little Leaguers."

Rose's plan worked. The National League beat the American League, 7–3, for its seventh straight win.

OUTER SPACE

Ceremonial first pitches have come a long way since President Taft started the tradition in 1910. There've been comical first-pitch mishaps, like the time Olympian Carl Lewis made an inconceivably wimpy throw that nosedived 30

---

[2] Bowa finished his 16-year career with a total of 15 home runs and a .320 slugging percentage.

feet in front of the mound and rolled to home plate, or when Cincinnati mayor Mark Mallory flung one so far off the plate that one of the umpires jokingly ejected him, but there've also been historical triumphs. In 1995, before Game 5 of the World Series got under way at Cleveland's Jacobs Field, NASA astronaut Ken Bowersox became the first person to throw a first pitch from outer space. His antigravity toss inside the space shuttle *Columbia* was transmitted via satellite to the scoreboard at the stadium and viewed by a national audience on ABC-TV. The seven-member crew, spending time in space to conduct a microgravity research mission, had taken two baseballs aboard the shuttle—one from each league—and then signed them after the mission. One of the balls was sent to the Hall of Fame. The other was displayed at the NASA Glenn Visitor Center.

Michael Lopez-Alegria, a member of Bowersox's crew, teamed up with a fellow astronaut (and die-hard Red Sox fan) named Suni Williams in 2007 to throw the second ceremonial first pitch from space. This time it took place at the International Space Station before a regular-season Yankees–Red Sox game at Fenway Park. One year later, as the same two teams prepared to face off in the Bronx, NASA astronaut (and lifelong Yankee fan) Dr. Garrett Reisman threw another ceremonial first pitch at the space station.

THE MOTORCYCLE TEST

Before radar guns were invented, there was no way to measure exactly how fast a pitcher could throw. That didn't stop Major League Baseball officials from trying, along with a team of scientists, two cameramen, a stunt driver, the Chicago Police Department, and Bob Feller.

The experiment took place during the 1940 season. The police blocked off a street near Lake Michigan, and two paper "targets" were set at a distance of 60 feet, 6 inches, from Feller. The plan called for him to throw a baseball toward one target at the exact instant that a speeding motorcycle flew past him toward the other.

Feller, just 21 years old at the time and widely regarded as having the best arm in baseball, was instructed to pitch from the stretch in order to time his release. But instead, he used a full windup so that he'd throw as hard as possible, and as a result, the motorcycle raced past him a fraction of a second too soon. The motorcycle was supposedly traveling 86 miles per hour, and the scientists estimated that Feller's pitch gained 13 feet on the bike during its brief flight. Therefore, it was believed that he had thrown the ball 104 miles per hour.[3]

DOES A CURVEBALL REALLY CURVE?

Since the early days of professional baseball, countless people have questioned whether a curveball really curves, suggesting instead that its irregular flight is merely an opti-

---

[3] Sometime later, at the Aberdeen Ordnance Plant in Washington, D.C., Feller was reportedly clocked at 107.9 miles per hour by a primitive speed-measuring device. In recent years, stadium radar guns (often believed to give exaggerated readings for entertainment's sake) have recorded speeds as high as 105 miles per hour, but the official Guinness world record for the fastest pitch belongs to Hall of Famer Nolan Ryan, who was clocked at 100.9 miles per hour during a game in 1974.

cal illusion. (These doubters all have one thing in common: they've never tried to hit one.) "Study Finds Curveballs Do Curve," proclaimed the *New York Times* in 2009 after a Bucknell University professor wowed a group of neuroscientists and psychologists with new findings on the subject. In 1982 a study conducted by physicists at the Massachusetts Institute of Technology confirmed that curveballs are very real. Going back even further, two of America's biggest magazines—*Look* and *Life*—made the same conclusion in 1941 by using stop-action photography.

Yawn.

No one's sure who threw the first curveball, but Fred Goldsmith, a pitcher who debuted in 1875 with the New Haven Elm Citys,[4] was definitely the first person to prove that a curveball really curves, and get this—he did it as a 14-year-old in 1870. The demonstration, which took place in front of a large crowd at the Capitoline Grounds in Brooklyn, New York, began with a 45-foot chalk line being drawn on the ground. (That was the distance at the time from the pitcher to the batter.) Two 8-foot poles were then driven into the ground at each end, and a third pole was set up in the middle. The right-handed Goldsmith, baseball in hand, took his position on the left side of the line at one end. His goal was to throw the ball from the left side of the first pole, make it hook around the right side of the middle pole, and return to the left side of the line before reaching the far pole. Not only did Goldsmith suc-

---

[4] Yes, that was a major league team. Sort of. It was in the National Association. That was the only "major" league at the time. Historians are still debating whether to count it as part of the Major Leagues. The stats, meanwhile, are on MLB.com, so you can make your own decision.

ceed, but he performed the feat half a dozen more times. Henry Chadwick, a legendary baseball pioneer and writer, was on hand for the event and provided what should have been a definitive account the next day in the *Brooklyn Eagle*: "That which had up to this point been considered an optical illusion and against all rules of philosophy was now an established fact."

THE BRASS GLOVE AWARD

Hecklers sometimes yell *"Clank!!!"* when a fielder drops the ball, as if to suggest that his glove is made of metal. During batting practice before Game 1 of the 1964 World Series, Cardinals backup catcher Bob Uecker literally made some clanking noises when he brought an unusual piece of equipment onto the field—and the hometown fans couldn't have been happier. Uecker was standing in left field, not too far from three Dixieland bands that were there for the pregame festivities. When the musicians took a break and left their instruments behind, Uecker walked over and picked up a tuba. He briefly considered playing it, but then his baseball (and comedic) instincts took over and he attempted something even funnier: he tried to catch a fly ball with it.

Uecker, a notoriously bad player, missed the first ball, then caught the next one in the mouth of the tuba, and dropped another. His teammates were laughing. The crowd was cheering. He finished by booting a couple of balls and catching one more—not a great fielding percentage, but he'd put on quite a show. The only person who didn't appreciate it was the tuba's owner; the baseballs had dented the instrument, and the Cardinals later received a bill for $250.

JUST SAY NO

This isn't your typical stunt. In fact, no one was supposed to know about it. On September 25, 1980, a drug-sniffing German shepherd at Chicago's O'Hare Airport alerted customs officials to a suspicious package that had arrived on Air France from Sialkot, Pakistan. Mike Streicher, a special agent for the federal Drug Enforcement Agency, opened the package and found an assortment of sporting goods, including 18 baseballs, which further attracted the dog. Agents carefully dissected the balls and discovered that each of the cork centers had been replaced with two ounces of pure heroin. The entire shipment had an estimated street value of $2.5 million.

"We had to get the balls sewn back up," Streicher told the *St. Louis Post-Dispatch*. "Unless the suspect tried to open the balls, we would have no case against him."

Streicher recruited three Rawlings employees to construct a batch of baseballs with the original Pakistani covers stitched on top. One of the balls was left with one gram of heroin in it—just enough to prove criminal possession—and the package was returned to the Air France claims desk. After weeks of surveillance and stakeouts, it was traced to a customer of the National Bank of Pakistan in Chicago—a man named Arshad Ali Malik, who'd gotten busted four months earlier on a heroin charge.

Malik and his accomplice were arrested and held in jail pending bond. It turned out, though, that they hadn't actually cut open the baseballs, so the case against them was weak. Fortunately, they told another prisoner about their smuggling operation; that prisoner happened to be an FBI informant, and the pair were convicted and sentenced to 15 years in a federal penitentiary.

CHAPTER 5

FOUL BALLS
IN POP CULTURE

MOVIES AND TV SHOWS

There's a Stephen King novel called *Under the Dome* in which a character gets bludgeoned by a golden baseball. There's a *Star Trek* character named Benjamin Sisko who receives a baseball from an alien and keeps it in his office on the space station. There's a song by Rodney Carrington, a country music artist, about his grandfather getting hit by a Joe DiMaggio foul ball in 1952.

What do we learn from all of this? First, that the baseball is part of America's DNA, and second, that it can be helpful to do a little fact-checking; Joe DiMaggio retired after the 1951 season.

Want more culture?

There've been too many foul ball–themed TV commercials for even the Elias Sports Bureau to count, and they're all pretty much based on the same premise. In most cases, there's either some dude in the stands who catches a ball because he used the advertised product, or there's a guy who gets hit by the ball because he didn't—so let's not even go there.

Foul ball scenes in movies and TV shows, while sometimes just as predictable, are more fun to dissect because they're more complex. Here are some examples, none from baseball movies, which would be redundant in this book.

FERRIS BUELLER'S DAY OFF—1986

THE PLOT Ferris Bueller, in the process of playing hooky from school, attends a game at Wrigley Field and catches a foul ball. After making the bare-handed grab, he jumps around in celebratory fashion, causing the TV cameras to zoom in on him. Somehow he doesn't get noticed by his bumbling principal, who's looking for him in a pizzeria and briefly turns away from the TV as the action unfolds.

THE CRITIQUE Although Bueller's dorky fist pumps (and attire) belie the athleticism required to make a bare-handed catch in a crowded section of presumably rowdy Cubs fans, the scene is very realistic. It begins as the dozens of extras react to the ball entering the stands—an obvious detail that often gets overlooked—and continues with Bueller's snag. First he experiences the rush of obtaining the souvenir. Then, after a few seconds, the pain sets in and he shakes his left hand. Upon closer inspection, his girlfriend Sloane can be seen ducking with her right hand covering her head, while his best friend Cameron quickly looks to the side as if he's trying to see who ended up with the ball. The only flaw is that when the TV camera follows the initial flight of the ball, two relief pitchers can be seen warming up along the left-field foul line, but when the field is then shown from Bueller's perspective, the bullpen mound is mysteriously empty. That said, writer-director

John Hughes expertly blended actual game footage with his own attention to detail in the stands.

BIG—1988

THE PLOT Thirteen-year-old Josh Baskin makes a wish that he could be big, then wakes up the next day in an adult's body. As he learns to embrace his new identity, he lands a great job in New York City, moves into a sweet apartment, and meets a beautiful young woman. Life, for the moment, is more fun than ever for Baskin as a kid in a grown-up world. A 90-second montage shows him dropping a water balloon off his fire escape, skateboarding and playing basketball in his spacious loft, getting a pinball machine delivered, impressing his boss with his childlike enthusiasm, boxing with an inflatable dinosaur, and, most importantly, helping his best friend Billy snag a foul ball at Yankee Stadium.

THE CRITIQUE Baskin, seated with Billy in the front row along the right-field foul line, grabs his small friend around the waist and lowers him over the short wall, enabling him to snatch the foul grounder off the warning track. This is a common ball-snagging maneuver, and the two actors execute it with precision. The whole scene lasts just five seconds and looks sharp at first glance, but there are two subtle mistakes that are noticeable in super-slow motion. First, in the snippet of actual game footage that shows the batter making contact, it's clear that the ball is not going to be the foul grounder that Billy then snags, but rather a fly ball to right field; both the batter and umpire start to look up (to track its flight) as soon as the batter makes contact. Second, the background reveals the scene to have been filmed before the game started; as the two boys rise to their feet, the scoreboard behind them is filled with zeroes—no runs, no outs, no balls, no strikes—and has a blank spot in the "at bat" column where the batter's uniform number is normally displayed. In addition, as Billy reaches for the ball, there's a uniformed security guard standing in the distance on the warning track, just in front of the first-base dugout. Security personnel never stand on the field during games—only during commercial breaks and pregame warm-ups. Still, it's a fairly realistic scene that captures the joy of getting a foul ball.

SEINFELD—March 25, 1992
(Season 3, Episode 20: "The Letter")

THE PLOT George, Elaine, and Kramer are given tickets to a Yankees game and discover that their seats are in the second row of the owner's box right behind the dugout. One of the owner's friends notices that Elaine is wearing a cap of the visiting Baltimore Orioles—a blatant sign of disrespect in his mind. He asks her to take it off, and when she refuses, he summons a security guard to have her removed from the stadium. As George reluctantly agrees to leave with her, Kramer climbs awkwardly into the front row and gets whacked on the head with a foul ball.

THE CRITIQUE This scene is completely unrealistic. At Yankee Stadium, when fans are courageous enough to support the visiting team, they get punched and *then* ejected. Beyond that (and not surprisingly), the main problem lies with the extras' nonreaction as the ball enters the stands. Not only do they neglect to duck or flinch or make an attempt to catch it, but they all appear to be staring aimlessly in various directions. Why even hire extras? Why not fill the seats with cardboard cutouts? Finally, in the moments leading up to the foul ball, there's a continuity error involving the sporadic clips of game footage. It starts when a left-handed batter on the Orioles is shown taking a called strike on the outside corner. The *Seinfeld* crowd then cheers boisterously as if it were strike three, and just 20 seconds later another clip shows a right-handed batter hitting a weak grounder up the middle. Why is this a problem? Because the first batter hadn't really struck out. The called strike was a harmless first strike; the batter can be seen backing away casually from the plate as the umpire points to the side with his right index finger extended. One finger equals one strike. Come on.

I LOVE LUCY—October 1, 1956
(Season 6, Episode 1: "Lucy and Bob Hope")

THE PLOT Lucy disguises herself as a hot dog vendor at Yankee Stadium in order to get near Bob Hope, who she thinks has ignored her husband's offer to join him in a commercial venture. With comedic insensitivity, she keeps trying to convince Hope to buy a hot dog and ultimately gets to talk to him when two hungry fans in his row call her over. Hope becomes so distracted by the transactions that he turns his attention away from the game and gets hit on the head by a foul ball.

THE CRITIQUE Though the fan-getting-bonked-by-ball concept has become a cliché, *I Love Lucy* deserves credit for leading the way. The extras in this scene do a half-assed job of tracking the "flight" of the ball, the word "flight" being in quotes because the camera only shows a close-up of the spectators, and the ball has obviously been dropped from just outside the frame. The scene accurately portrays the commotion that typically occurs when a fan gets hit;

the unrealistic aspect lies in Lucy's ability to harass Hope without being stopped by stadium security. Of course, that's what makes it funny.

SESAME STREET—May 14, 1998
(Season 29, Episode 3,784: "The Emperor's Invisible Mishaps")

THE PLOT Mr. Johnson brings his glove to a baseball game and finds himself in the perfect seat to catch a foul ball. On three separate occasions, as he's about to catch one that's heading his way, he gets tackled by Grover the hot dog vendor, who's trying to protect him. A fourth ball begins to fly toward Johnson, but he's too busy scolding Grover to notice. It ends up hitting him on the head and bouncing into Grover's hands.

THE CRITIQUE This entire four-and-a-half-minute scene was done exclusively with puppets, so let's forget the technical inaccuracies and focus on the stuff that works. Grover as a meddlesome vendor? Perfect casting. Most fans have encountered a vendor who thinks he's bigger than the game, and Grover nails it. As for the fans in this scene, they're aware that baseballs are flying into the stands, and they're all trying to catch them—all except for one character who's sleeping in the background. The reactions of the first three fans who catch balls are funny and realistic, ranging from surprised ("I got it!") to elated ("Oh yeeeeah, baby!") to uber-competitive ("In your *face*! Ha-ha-ha!! *Woo!!!*"). Perhaps the most unrealistic moment of this scene occurs at the end when Grover celebrates his snag—stadium employees are not allowed to keep balls—and then shouts, "Hot dogs on the house!" Fans should be so lucky.

SEX AND THE CITY—June 6, 1999
(Season 2, Episode 1: "Take Me Out
to the Ball Game")

THE PLOT After Carrie's recent breakup with her boyfriend, she and the other three main characters—Miranda, Samantha, and Charlotte—attend a game at the old Yankee Stadium. Miranda, the only true baseball fan in the group, rattles off stats about the Yankees and drops a foul ball that is hit right to her. Carrie grabs the ball when it bounces under her seat and ponders her own relationship stats.

THE CRITIQUE This scene is an embarrassment to the national pastime. For starters, Carrie and her friends are sitting well beyond foul ball range, so there's no chance that a ball would've reached them in the first place. (Stock footage from their vantage point at Yankee Stadium indicates that they're at the top of the upper deck behind the right-field foul pole, and Samantha backs this up by bitching about their sucky seats.) Secondly, after Carrie comes up with the ball, Miranda asks incredulously, "Do you know what the odds of catching a fly ball are?!" One word: duh. A baseball-savvy fan like Miranda should know the difference between a fly ball and a foul ball. (Outfielders catch fly balls. Fans catch foul balls, or at least they try, and Carrie didn't "catch" hers. She picked it up off the ground. There's a difference.) Third, the set doesn't look anything like the old Yankee Stadium. The staircase is way too wide, the upper deck is not slanted nearly enough, and the puny stadium lights look like they belong on a high school football field. Fourth, Carrie is smoking a cigarette throughout the scene. Security guards at Yankee Stadium are militant about enforcing every single rule, including the smoking ban, even in the back rows of the upper deck. Fifth, Carrie and Samantha are both drinking out of big, red, frat-like plastic cups. At baseball games, beers are either served in plastic bottles or poured into clear plastic cups (and in the unlikely event that the ladies were drinking soda, it would've come in a tacky souvenir cup). Finally, there are general continuity errors, the most obvious being the changing position of the fans in the background. When Carrie reaches down to grab the ball, there are two kids standing right behind her, but when the camera angle switches, the kids are back in their seats in the last row. On a positive note, when Carrie briefly holds up her prize, it does appear to be an official American League ball.

KING OF QUEENS—April 20, 2005
(Season 7, Episode 20: "Catching Hell")

THE PLOT Doug gets taunted by a boy sitting near him at Shea Stadium, responds with juvenile threats, and gets scolded by the boy's mother. Doug gets even by reaching out and snaring a foul ball right in front of the kid's outstretched glove. He then laughs in the kid's face, makes him cry, and gets booed by everyone in the section. And then he's ejected from the stadium.

THE CRITIQUE The set is realistic, and the extras do a good job of tracking the flight of the ball. Inexplicably, however (and to the dismay of many a ballhawk), the ball is fake. The camera zooms in on it as soon as Doug makes the bare-handed catch, and yes, it's a cheap prop and not an official ball. Another baffling error is that the crowd noise shifts pointedly while the ball is in midair, starting with a typical "Ohhhh!!!" and changing to an unusually loud cheer. Overall, not bad, not great.

THE SIMPSONS—April 29, 2007
(Season 18, Episode 18: "The Boys of Bummer")

THE PLOT Bart Simpson, playing shortstop for the Springfield Isotots, drops a pop-up that costs his team the Little League championship and turns the whole town against him. His mother secretly arranges for the game to be replayed in order to give him a shot at redemption. Unfortunately for Bart, who moves to third base for the makeup game, his subsequent attempts to catch the ball go awry. After flat-out dropping the first pop-up, he gets hit on the head by a line drive and watches helplessly as the next ball fatally strikes a bird. Bart then gets nailed by another liner, sees a fly ball get struck by lightning, and loses his chance to catch a foul pop-up when Homer reaches out from the stands—à la Steve Bartman—and robs him.

THE CRITIQUE Bart is left-handed. Left-handers don't play third base, at least not in the Major Leagues, but this is Springfield, and it's a cartoon, so anything's possible. Still, one must consider that if a left-hander *were* going to play third base, he'd have to be the best athlete on the team—or else, why bother? And yet Bart is the worst. There are other questionable details, but do they really matter? Who cares that the sky is blue when the lightning strikes, or that the police don't chase Moe when he streaks onto the field, or that the mound becomes higher toward the end of the scene? The only issue, if judged by its real-life equivalent, is that Homer—unlike Bartman—actually catches the ball. At least the two guys look alike: Homer is sporting the same type of Walkman headphones that Bartman was famously wearing during the original incident.

IT'S GARRY SHANDLING'S SHOW—
October 1, 1986
(Season 1, Episode 4: "Foul Ball")

THE PLOT Garry's best friend Pete takes his Cub Scout pack to Dodger Stadium and gets hit in the face by a foul ball. As a result of his clumsiness, Pete gets teased by the kids and mocked by a local sportscaster who features the mishap on the evening news. Pete's son Grant is so ashamed of his dad that he plans to withdraw from an upcoming father-and-son athletic competition—until Garry concocts a creative plan and saves the day.

THE CRITIQUE Meh. This one-shot scene takes place on a generic set without any stadiumlike characteristics. The ball seems to come out of nowhere, as if tossed by the cameraman, and given Shandling's earlier on-air joke about the show's low budget, that might have been the case. While the kids do a decent job of reaching for the ball with their gloves, the other fans barely react; none of them flinch or attempt to snag it. Pete doesn't flinch either, but only because he doesn't see the ball—or does he? At the last second, he appears to lean a couple inches to his left in order to make the ball hit him squarely in the face. At least the scene is mildly amusing. As Pete frantically tilts his head back and holds his nose, Garry is standing beside him, absentmindedly combing his magnificent hair.

*ACCORDING TO JIM—*September 20, 2005
(Season 5, Episode 1: "Foul Ball")

THE PLOT Jim sneaks his son Kyle out of his first day of kindergarten and takes him to Wrigley Field for his first game ever. Kyle, sitting in the front row between his dad and his uncle Andy, gets hit in the face with a foul ball and ends up with a black eye. This leaves Jim with the difficult task of explaining the boy's injury to his wife.

THE CRITIQUE Why are the Wrigley Field ushers wearing red? Why doesn't Kyle cry when he gets hit by the ball? Why does Andy wait 28 seconds to reveal that he snagged it? In spite of these puzzling elements, the scene is still pretty good. The extras react convincingly to the ball, and the set is extremely realistic, but then again, there's a small and revealing mistake that proves that it is in fact just a set. (It's the kind of detail that you'd only notice if you're looking for mistakes and watch it 20 times, but still.) Jim's cup of beer is sitting on top of the short wall that separates the field from the stands; when the Cubs player lunges into the crowd to try to make the catch, the beer sloshes around, but not because the cup itself gets hit. The cup moves because the wall is bumped, proving that it's not the actual brick-and-concrete barrier at Wrigley, but rather a flimsy prop in a studio. The player, meanwhile, is wearing "19" on the back of his uniform, but in 2005 the Cub with that number was an outfielder named Matt Murton. Why is this a problem? Because Jim's seats are near the dugout— not exactly an outfielder's territory. One nice touch is that there are several Cardinals fans sitting in the packed stands. It almost makes you willing to overlook the fact that the ball doesn't actually hit Kyle's nose.

ROOMMATES—1995

THE PLOT Michael Holzcek, a newly orphaned five-year-old, moves to Pittsburgh to live with his feisty grandfather Rocky. They help each other cope with the loss of their loved one by spending lots of time together and attending a baseball game. Michael copes exceptionally well by scrambling for a foul ball—but just as he grabs the would-be souvenir, an older fan steps on his hand and snatches it. Rocky confronts the bully, and when the guy refuses to return the ball, the old man head-butts him and reclaims it for his grandson.

THE CRITIQUE The scene takes place in 1963, when the Pirates played at Forbes Field. Unfortunately, it was filmed at a minor league ballpark in Indiana called Bush Stadium (oops), but everything else is solid. The pitcher looks up to follow the flight of the ball. The right fielder chases after it and ends up near the stands. The fans rise in unison, and there's a man who alertly hustles up the steps to get as close to the ball as possible. It looks like real action at a real game. The one sketchy detail is that the ball rattles around in the crowded stands for six seconds before Michael gets his hand on it. Though not impossible, such a duration is highly unlikely.

CSI: NY—May 11, 2005
(Season 1, Episode 22: "The Closer")

THE PLOT On the same day that a prominent sports agent named Margo Trent is mysteriously struck and killed by a truck, a blue-collar Red Sox fan named Gilbert Novotny is found dead in his car at Yankee Stadium. As the investigators look for clues in these seemingly unrelated tragedies, they find a game-used baseball in Novotny's car that has one of Trent's hairs on it. Television footage from the game reveals the connection: the two were sitting near each other, and Novotny had bumped her while catching a foul ball. Meanwhile, Novotny's autopsy proves he had died from internal injuries after being hit by a baseball, and a search of Trent's apartment indicates there'd been a physical altercation; her bathroom door had been smashed by a baseball. After determining that the ball would've had to have been thrown more than 90 miles per hour in order to break the door, the investigators watch additional footage and spot a free-agent pitcher named Ruben DeRosa sitting between Trent and Novotny. They track him down at a try-out, see him topping out at 94 miles per hour on the radar gun, concoct a plan to obtain a sample of his DNA, and ultimately charge him with murder.

THE CRITIQUE What's with all these scenes being filmed at bogus locations? The game is supposed to take place at Yankee Stadium, but the establishing shot shows San Francisco's Candlestick Park, and the episode was taped at the L.A. Coliseum. Director Emilio Estevez let some other dubious details slip through, but the plot is so clever and elaborate that they hardly matter. As it turns out, the foul ball is the murder weapon. (How cool is that?) In a misguided attempt to be funny, Novotny had leaned over and kissed DeRosa when their section was shown randomly on the JumboTron; after the game, DeRosa got his revenge by grabbing the ball from Novotny in the parking lot and firing it at his abdomen. Good detail: the stitches of the ball leave an imprint on Novotny's skin. Bad detail: Trent's hair, barely clinging to the ball in the car, would have flown off when the ball was thrown. Good detail: the investigator who finds the ball swabs it with a Q-Tip and says, "Mud. Delaware River mud, to be exact" (see page 188). Bad detail: the ball doesn't actually appear to have any mud on it. Good detail: the crowd's reaction to the foul ball looks authentic. Bad detail: the foul ball is clearly animated—CGI at its worst. Good detail: the detective gets DeRosa's DNA by entering the stands and catching a home run ball that the pitcher had rubbed with his saliva. Bad detail: the batter facing DeRosa's mid-90s heat isn't wearing a helmet. Good detail: none of the balls yield reliable fingerprints because of all the people who had touched them. Bad detail: the balls all have horrendously fake, non-official logos. Perhaps the goofs do matter after all, if only to the obsessive minority.

B.C., *a long-running comic strip based on prehistoric times, depicted the first foul ball ever.*

CELEBRITY BALLHAWKS

Over the years, there've been lots of fans who became famous for snagging baseballs at games. Here's a smaller collection of fans who were already famous when they caught one—or at least tried.

JERMAINE JACKSON

Hall of Fame announcer Vin Scully has called some incredible moments during his legendary career. There was Don Larsen's perfect game in the 1956 World Series, Hank Aaron's 715th career home run in 1974, and Jermaine Jackson's foul ball snag at Dodger Stadium in 2009. No, not the Jermaine Jackson who played five seasons in the NBA—the other Jermaine Jackson who shared lead vocals in The Jackson 5. The namesakes, however, were irrelevant to Scully, who simply remarked, "Nice catch by a fan directly behind the dugout."

The catch really *was* nice. Rafael Furcal had just lunged at a 1-2 changeup from Braves starter Jair Jurrjens and blooped it toward the outfield end of the third-base dugout. Jackson, wearing a glove on his left hand, stood up, leaned back, reached deep into the crowd, and made a backhanded stab high over his head (which he then celebrated with a series of fist pumps). But there was more to it. At the instant that he caught the ball, the man seated directly behind him was ducking for cover; Jackson saved that guy from getting hit on the head, but unfortunately robbed another fan—a young boy with a glove—in the process.

RICKEY HENDERSON

In 2007, four years after his Hall of Fame career ended, Rickey Henderson attended a Mets-Giants game in San Francisco and caught a foul ball in the stands. The story made national headlines because he kept the ball for himself instead of handing it to a young fan sitting nearby.

Henderson was quoted as saying, "Everybody was asking me for the ball. I said, 'You're not getting this ball. I always wanted to get a foul ball. This one's going on a shelf at home.' "

Henderson made it up to the kid by autographing a different ball.

CHARLIE SHEEN

Charlie Sheen really likes baseballs. Four years after he spent $93,500 for a ball, he paid $6,537.50 just to try to catch one. It was April 19, 1996, the Detroit Tigers were in

Anaheim, and Sheen bought 2,615 outfield seats at an Angels game to increase his odds of snagging a home run ball.

"I didn't want to crawl over the paying public," he said afterward. "I wanted to avoid the violence."

Sheen accomplished one of his goals—he didn't get hurt—but ultimately went home empty-handed. Still, for his determination to catch a ball, and for his willingness to make a fool of himself in the process, he deserves to be acknowledged as a "celebrity ballhawk." (Perhaps "honorary ballhawk" or "wannabe ballhawk" would be more appropriate.)

JIMMY CARTER

Starting with William Howard Taft in 1910, every U.S. president except Jimmy Carter has opened at least one season with a ceremonial first pitch. But Carter is one of just two presidents to have caught a foul ball at a game—George H. W. Bush is the other, having accomplished the feat as a kid at Yankee Stadium—and it happened in Atlanta on the same day as Sheen's shenanigans. Carter, 71 years old at the time, was sitting in the front row near the third-base dugout and made a bare-handed catch on a foul ball hit by the Padres' Ken Caminiti. The crowd responded with a standing ovation, and the president later received praise from one of the players.

"He showed good hands," said Braves catcher Javy Lopez.

MARK McGWIRE

Mark McGwire accomplished two great feats in 1998. Not only did he hit the most valuable baseball in history, but he also caught a foul ball during the World Series—as a spectator in the stands. McGwire's Cardinals had failed to reach the postseason, so the slugger was available to throw out the ceremonial first pitch before Game 4 got under way at Qualcomm Stadium. In the top of the fourth inning, Yankees leadoff man Chuck Knoblauch swung a bit early on a pitch from Padres starter Kevin Brown and bounced the ball into foul territory down the third-base line. McGwire, who was sitting in the front row, effortlessly bare-handed it. Then he stood and smiled, held up the ball, and flipped it into the crowd behind him.

BEN AFFLECK

Memo to Ben Affleck and anyone else who's privileged enough to sit in the front row: when a foul pop-up is about to land in your lap, the fielder is allowed to reach into the stands to catch it, but you have every right to go for it as well. And when that fielder is on the visiting team, it's not just your right to snag the ball—it's your duty.

Affleck, seated in the front row beside the Red Sox dugout at Fenway Park on July 30, 2006, bungled his foul ball opportunity and got booed by 36,000 fans. That's because the ball was hit by a Sox player and Affleck's lame attempt to snag it—in front of his wife Jennifer Garner no less—enabled Angels first baseman Howie Kendrick to run over and make the catch.

Two weeks later, in a segment on *Access Hollywood,* Affleck received a surprise birthday gift. Kendrick had autographed the ball and sent it to him with a videotaped message that said, "Sorry I didn't let you have that foul ball, but I have a job to do, y'know. Nice try, though, even for a Red Sox fan, so here ya go."

GEORGE BRETT

Offense has a way of overshadowing defense. Take George Brett, for example. You know that he had over 3,000 hits and that he won the batting title in three different decades, right? But did you know that he was a Gold Glove third baseman in 1985? Or that he caught a foul ball at Game 2 of the 2002 World Series?

Brett was sitting six rows behind the third-base dugout when Angels designated hitter Brad Fullmer blooped a check-swing pop-up in his direction.

"I just put down my beer with my left hand and reached up and caught it," recalled the Hall of Famer. "Then I took a bite of my fish taco."

It was a solid play, but Brett committed an egregious error later on.

"I lost the ball getting into the car after the game in the parking lot," he said. "It slipped out of my jacket pocket."

DOUG FLUTIE

According to *Sports Illustrated,* football Hall of Famer Doug Flutie snagged a foul ball at a Red Sox–Devil Rays game at Fenway Park in May 2004. Unfortunately, the Rays didn't actually visit Boston that month—but they made the trip in late April, so let's assume that's when it happened. As the story goes, Flutie was sitting in the front row of seats outside a suite on the first-base side; sometime around the seventh inning, Kevin Millar hit a foul ball that sailed over Flutie's head, ricocheted off some Plexiglas, bounced off a man's hands two rows behind him, and plopped into his lap.

Fairly standard stuff. But here's where it gets interesting. On April 14, 2005, Flutie snagged another foul at Fenway, this time off the bat of Tino Martinez. It was a line drive that hooked down the right-field foul line. Flutie, seated in the third row, caught the ball on the fly and later told a reporter from the New England Sports Network (NESN) that it was the fourth consecutive game at which he'd gotten a ball.

What made headlines, however, was not the incredible ballhawking feat itself, but rather the fact that Flutie—a professional athlete!—had used a baseball glove to achieve it. Sports radio hosts were so critical, and the topic received so much airtime, that *Sports Illustrated* referred to it as a controversy.

"That's just Doug. He's a big kid," his wife Laurie told the magazine. "He won't go to a baseball game without bringing his glove."

"No way," agreed Flutie. "Now I just have to hide it in my bag."

JUSTIN BIEBER

In 2010, at the delicate age of 16, Justin Bieber became the youngest male solo artist with a number-one album in 47 years[1]—but his legacy wasn't fully cemented until he snagged a foul ball six weeks later at U.S. Cellular Field.

"Awsome [*sic*] time at the whitesox game," tweeted the teen idol soon after the final out. "Caught a foul ball and gave it to a fan. Oprah tomorrow. Cheahhhh."

To clarify, Bieber was in fact in Chicago to tape an interview with Oprah Winfrey—he also got to throw out the ceremonial first pitch at the game—but he didn't actually make a clean catch. No sir. The ball, fouled off by White

---

[1] Stevie Wonder was 13 when his album *Recorded Live: The 12-Year-Old Genius* was released in 1963.

Sox first baseman Paul Konerko with one out in the bottom of the third inning, bounced into Bieber's luxury suite after deflecting off another fan's fingertips. Bieber then gave the ball to the fan and later autographed it.

That fan, a high school senior named Alex Rittel, put his souvenir to good use.

"I took the ball to school today to show everyone," he said. "So many girls were jealous. So many girls."

Justin Bieber knows what's up.

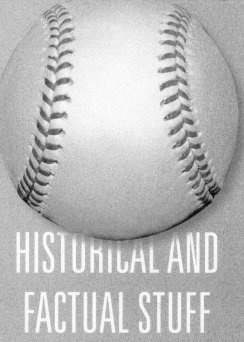

PART TWO

HISTORICAL AND
FACTUAL STUFF

*There is no getting away from the fact that the
ball is quite lively this year . . . there are too many
home runs and long, drawn-out games.*
—Ban Johnson, American League president, 1925

CHAPTER 6

THE EVOLUTION OF THE BALL

When it comes to the baseball itself, many fans know the basics—or at least they think they do. They'll tell you that it weighs five ounces ("give or take") and that the cover is made of horsehide ("or . . . wait, is it cowhide?") and that there's some kind of corkish rubbery thing in the middle with yarn wrapped around it ("the balls *are* machine-made, right?") and that the balls come from Haiti ("or Costa Rica or China or Taiwan or one of those places").

When you consider that the ball has gone through more changes than any other piece of equipment in the history of baseball, it's easy to see why people—even die-hard fans—aren't always sure how it's made. But history isn't solely responsible for the confusion; check out Major League Baseball's current rule book and you'll see that the specifications aren't all that specific. Rule 1.09 states: "The ball shall be a sphere formed by yarn wound around a small core of cork, rubber or similar material, covered with two strips of white horsehide or cowhide, tightly stitched together. It shall weigh not less than five nor more than 5¼ ounces avoirdupois and measure not less than nine nor more than 9¼ inches in circumference."

This murky rule raises more questions than it answers: What kind of yarn? How small a core? What materials are considered "similar" to cork and rubber? What the hell does "avoirdupois" mean?[1] And most important, how tight should the stitches be? Too loose and the ball will be dead; too tight and it'll be flying all over the place.

Most fans are aware that there've been some controversies in recent years about the balls being too lively, but the juiced-ball debate goes back much further than McGwire and Sosa, Mantle and Maris, and even Babe Ruth. It began in 1867 when the Nationals of Washington, an experienced team made up of government employees, drubbed several opponents by using a hopped-up ball that favored their own potent offense. At that time, the home team was responsible for providing the ball—there was quite a variety of balls from which to choose—but even after the ball was standardized, manufacturing techniques continued to develop.

For the better part of the 20th century, the evolution of the ball threatened the integrity of the sport by skewing the delicate competitive balance between the pitcher and batter. During some seasons, the number of home runs suggested that the batters had an edge, while in other seasons it seemed as if 1–0 games were the norm. The biggest statistical aberrations led some folks to denounce the ball, while others (especially executives in the ball manufacturing industry) defended it and blamed everything else.

———

[1] "Avoirdupois" comes from Old French and literally means "goods of weight." The word was first used in baseball's rule book in the 1870s and for some reason still remains there.

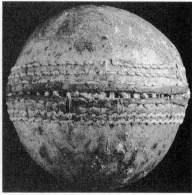

Early baseballs, such as the "lemon-peel" ball (left) and the "belt" ball (right), were stitched differently.

But let's go back even further, to the early 1840s, when the first baseballs began taking shape. The earliest balls weighed as little as three ounces, but because the specs were so loose, the size and composition varied dramatically. Some were even larger than the balls in use today. Balls were homemade, often assembled hastily before neighborhood pickup games. Just about any small, hard object—like a walnut, rock, or bullet—was used as the core. String (perhaps from an old fishing line) or yarn (possibly from an unraveled sock) was then wrapped around it until the sphere was palm-sized. Finally, a piece of dark brown leather (typically cut from old shoes) was used for the cover and sewn on, often in a one-piece "lemon-peel" style but occasionally as a two- or three-piece "belt" ball. Some balls were very lively because they had a melted rubber center; teams that used them sometimes scored over 100 runs per game.[2]

---

[2] In 1846 the rules changed so that the first team to score 21 runs was the winner. Eleven years later, the rules changed again and the length of the game was set at nine innings.

Here's how the baseball—as well as the sport itself—continued to evolve:

1847 A physician named Daniel "Doc" Adams was elected president of the New York Knickerbockers, one of the primary and dominant teams in the early years of organized baseball. Before long, Adams voluntarily began making all the balls for most of the teams in and around New York City. Simply owning a baseball was such a big deal that some teams raised the stakes of their competitions by playing for the ball itself. Each ball had to last for the entire game, and at the conclusion it was awarded to the winner. The Knickerbockers used a particularly large ball that weighed as much as 6.5 ounces and measured 11 inches in circumference. Adams was the first ball maker to discover that the tighter a ball was wound, the livelier it would be, but the balls he made remained dead and generally light in weight—so light that his outfielders weren't able to throw the balls all the way back to the pitcher. They needed to relay the balls to a teammate, and by the end of the decade the shortstop position was born.

1848 John Van Horn, a player on Brooklyn's Baltic Base Ball Club, started getting paid by the team to make balls. A shoemaker who initially produced just 50 to 60 balls a year, Van Horn is recognized as the first commercial manufacturer of baseballs.

1853 The typical ball was small but dense, measuring 2 inches in diameter and packed with 1 to 2.5 ounces of lead in the center. Knitting yarn was wound tightly around the core, and the ball was covered with chamois skin.[3] These

---

[3] A chamois is a goat-antelope. In the 19th century, chamois leather was commonly used for gloves—not baseball gloves, just regular gloves—for both men and women.

skins were always brown, but ranged in shade from medium to dark.

1854 The three main teams in New York—the Knicker-bockers, Gothams, and Eagles—had a meeting and decided to make the ball bigger: 5.5 to 6 ounces with a diameter between 2.75 and 3.5 inches. This was supposed to be *the* new ball, but the specifications (which placed no restriction on the amount of rubber) didn't last long.

1857 Sixteen teams from New York formed the National Association of Base Ball Players (NABBP), held a convention, and voted to tweak the specs once again. The new ball (which was to be stitched only in lemon-peel fashion) weighed between 6 and 6.25 ounces and measured 10 to 10.25 inches in circumference.

1858 At the second annual baseball convention, everyone agreed that the composition of the ball had to be regulated. The core would be made of india rubber, wrapped with yarn, and covered with leather—but these new specs served more as a guideline than a rule; at a game on May 31, 1858, members of the visiting team insisted on using their own rubberless ball. They'd made it by wrapping yarn as loosely as possible around a bullet so that the ball would be the right size. Not only was the ball hard to catch, but several players had their fingers twisted and suffered other nasty hand injuries. The "bullet" ball was never seen again. Meanwhile, a man named Harrison Harwood founded Harwood & Sons in Natick, Massachusetts, and opened the first baseball factory, a three-story building with more than 9,000 square feet. Harwood was the first manufacturer to stitch the ball with a figure-eight cover, a design often credited to Ellis Drake, despite his failure to patent it. Drake, whose father was a shoemaker, claimed to have come up with the idea in school in the

1840s and made a prototype with scraps of his father's leather. Some historians believe, however, that the figure-eight cover was invented by Colonel William A. Cutler.

1859 The dimensions of the ball were reduced to 5.75 to 6 ounces with a circumference of 9.75 to 10 inches. Around this time, John Van Horn was dominating the New York ball-making business.

1860 The weight of the ball was further reduced to a maximum of 5.75 ounces.

1861 The NABBP shrank the dimensions yet again, by a quarter-inch and a quarter-ounce. Baseballs started being made with lighter-colored covers. This helped the fielders to see them coming off the bat against the dark wooden backdrops of old ballparks.

1862 Henry Chadwick denounced the ball as "overelastic."

1863 Balls started being widely manufactured. In New York the three biggest ball makers were John Van Horn, Daniel Adams, and Harvey Ross—men who personally handcrafted every single ball—but there were many lesser-known ball makers whose materials and manufacturing techniques varied. As a result, some balls were lively, others were dead, and games were often determined by the type of ball selected by the home team. Visiting teams with great hitters often found themselves playing with a dead ball, and vice versa. Even if the type of ball was agreed upon beforehand, that first ball might "accidentally" get lost and a different ball would conveniently be offered as a replacement.

1864 One of the most significant rule changes of the era was instituted: the one-bounce catch no longer counted as an out. Prior to this, no one wanted to use a ball that was so lively that it would've bounced over the fielders' heads, but once this rule was abandoned, ball makers began producing even livelier balls. The result? More errors, more injuries, longer games, and a sloppy style of play that ruled the sport for the remainder of the decade.

1866 The ball was supposed to weigh exactly 5.75 ounces and measure 9.75 inches in circumference.

1867 The Nationals of Washington went on a huge baseball tour and got embroiled in the first major juiced-ball controversy in baseball history. The only team to beat the Cincinnati Red Stockings in 1867, they were accused of playing with a lively ball that helped their own talented hitters and proved difficult for opposing fielders to catch. (Baseball gloves hadn't yet been invented.) Speaking of lively baseballs, John Van Horn was making balls by cutting strips from old rubber shoes, balling them into crude spheres that weighed anywhere from 2 to 4 ounces, and heating the rubber until it melted and fused together. He then wrapped cotton yarn around the rubber center and stitched a sheepskin cover on top. Although these "elastic" balls were exceptionally lively, they got hit out of shape within a few innings because the flimsy cotton yarn wasn't resilient enough. Despite the NABBP's new ruling that the baseball had to weigh between 5 and 5.25 ounces and measure 9.25 to 9.5 inches in circumference, Van Horn's balls often weighed more than 6 ounces and had a 10-inch circumference. Harwood & Sons made their balls according to the specifications and sold $150,000 worth that year alone.

1868 Manufacturers were forced to put their names on the balls, as well as figures listing the weight and size. Also, for the first time, the official rules stated that the ball would "become the property of the winning club as a trophy of victory." This keepsake was sometimes painted

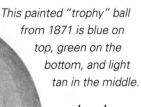

This painted "trophy" ball from 1871 is blue on top, green on the bottom, and light tan in the middle.

and decorated with the date and the score of the game. Teams with good fielders generally used the smallest possible ball with the least elasticity. Alex Waugh, a toy maker from New York City, catered to the slick fielders by introducing a dead ball that was made without any rubber in the core. The amount of rubber had been decreasing anyway because the elastic ball was so dangerous.

1869 At the 13th annual NABBP convention, the Philadelphia Athletics, known for their powerful offense, adamantly opposed a proposal that would have limited the ball's rubber content to 1.5 ounces. The Red Stockings, dominant in every facet of the game, embarked on a historic season-long tour and used balls that may have contained far more rubber than that. (Their balls also reportedly had tan or white stitches.) In the process of compiling a stunning 57-0 record, the team was accused of using balls that were too lively. In retrospect, there's no way to determine if the balls were intentionally juiced, but the Red Stockings' stats were undeniably inflated. Their shortstop—and future Hall of Famer—George Wright played in 52 games, hit 59 home runs, and scored 339 times.

1870 On July 9, 1870, the *New York Clipper* ran an article that criticized the sport and blamed the ball. "A change in the composition of the ball used is necessary to the full development of the beauties of the game," it said. "The record of this season's play thus far presents a catalogue of severe injuries . . . on the ball field, arising from the use of an over-elastic and heavy ball, which calls for a prompt remedy." The article suggested limiting the rubber content to 1.5 ounces, and it encouraged fans to boycott games that were played with lively balls. As public sentiment began to change and people demanded a tighter style of play, some ball manufacturers advertised "dead balls." Later in the season, as another ball-related need manifested—namely, reducing the glare from the sun—several manufacturers introduced red baseballs. One New York–based sporting goods company called Peck & Snyder combined the two trends and ran an ad for its "Dead Red Ball" that said: "Our new Ball is made of the best yarn, covering an ounce and a half of the best Unvulcanized Rubber, and is of a Dark Red color, thereby getting rid of the objectionable dazzling whiteness of the ordinary ball which bothers fielders and batsmen on a Sunny Day." Meanwhile, Harwood & Sons was now filling single orders for as many as 6,000 baseballs. Natick, Massachusetts, the town where they set up shop, was described by the *New York Times* as "the greatest base ball manufactory in the world." Harrison Harwood employed more than 200 women and divided the factory into different areas where groups of them each performed one specialized task. For example, one group cut the figure-eight covers and passed them along to another group that punched the holes around the edges through which the balls were later stitched. The covers, previously made of flimsy sheepskin, were now made of horsehide—a material so durable that before it was stitched onto the balls employees had to roll it up in damp cloths to make it pliable. The best balls were stitched with silk thread; low-end balls got linen thread. All the balls were then left to sit around for a few days to dry out. On November 30, 1870, the weight and size of the ball changed for the last time. The specifications that we have in place today—5 to 5.25 ounces and 9 to 9.25 inches in circumference—were instituted.

1871 The first professional league was formed. It was called the National Association of Base-Ball Players (aka "National Association"), and the ball was supposed to contain exactly one ounce of rubber. Still, some balls were not being manufactured according to the specifications. One New York ball maker boldly advertised: "Our professional dead balls . . . are made of all yarn without rubber and are the deadest balls made."

1872 Manufacturers devised a popular technique for assembling a rubberless ball. A seated worker started by stripping yarn off a wall-mounted pulley and coiling it by hand. When he felt that the wound core had reached the proper size, he placed it in a small iron cup affixed to a wooden platform in front of him. Then, with half the core poking out, he whacked it repeatedly with a wooden mallet and kept rotating it in an attempt to strike it evenly all over. After compacting the core, he added another layer of yarn and whacked it some more. Some manufacturers used wet yarn because it stuck in place better and enabled them to wind the ball tighter. These wet balls ended up too large and heavy, so they were placed in an oven and baked until they dried out and shrank. Naturally, it was hard to achieve uniformity through this process.

1874 The rules governing the composition of the ball changed again. Now, instead of the rubber content being fixed at exactly one ounce, it was limited to *no more than* one ounce. As a result, more rubberless balls were manufactured.

1875 A man named John Giblin patented a seamless ball with a vulcanized rubber cover and a core made with palm leaves. He claimed that it wouldn't get waterlogged or injure players' hands, but the innovation wasn't widely accepted because the lack of seams made it impossible to throw curveballs, which had become popular in the 1860s.

1876 On January 18, 1876, a man named Samuel Hipkiss patented a baseball with a bell in the middle. It was intended to help the umpire make tricky judgment calls (for example, whether the bat had tipped the ball), but the invention never amounted to anything more than a novelty. Three months later, another wannabe baseball pioneer named Wolf Flechter patented one of the first ball-making machines. This, too, failed to gain mainstream acceptance because it eliminated the necessary winding process: two "hemispherical depressions" were simply filled with yarn and then, with the aid of a hinge and a handle, pressed together as if the baseball were a snowball being packed into shape. Later in the season, the double-cover ball was introduced. This was essentially a completed ball with an additional cover stitched on top. It was supposed to be much more durable, but failed to catch on. The year's biggest triumph belonged to Chicago White Stockings pitcher Al Spalding. Not only did the future Hall of Famer lead the newly formed National League with 47 wins, but he founded the Spalding sporting goods company. Spald-

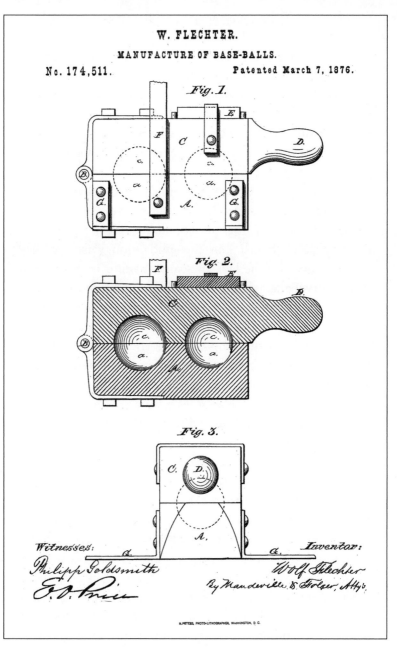

*Patent diagram from 1876; Wolf Flechter designed a machine
that compacted the ball rather than winding it.*

ing didn't yet have a factory—he and his brother simply opened a store in Chicago—so he teamed up with Louis H. Mahn, a well-known ball manufacturer in Jamaica Plain, Massachusetts, who made rubberless balls and agreed to stamp Spalding's name prominently on them. It was essential for these men (and their competitors) to produce baseballs at the proper size and weight; starting in 1876, if an umpire discovered that a ball didn't meet the specs, balls made by that manufacturer were not supposed to be used ever again.

1877 The National League ruled that the ball had to contain exactly one ounce of rubber. Mahn continued to work with Spalding's company to make these new balls—which were evidently juiced. Deacon White, a lifetime .303 hitter whose 15-year career began with the White Stockings in 1876, claimed that when William Hulbert became the National League president in 1877, he decided to make the sport more exciting by using a livelier ball. "A core of elastic rubber was used, around which was wound tightly the highest grade of yarn," recalled White in an interview long after he retired. "In order to put more life into the ball, the maker wrapped this yarn lightly with leather lacing, then pressed the cover on by shrinkage. Our team first ran into that ball at St. Louis about the middle of the '77 season and we knocked it all over the city . . . it was so lively it almost tore our hands off, but we didn't mind when we got to bat." According to White, Hulbert later witnessed a particularly high-scoring game in Chicago. After the final out, the president walked onto the field, cut open one of the balls, and discovered the leather lacing. He then declared that the ball was made against specifications, ordered a recall of all the balls, and told the manufacturer not to use the lacing anymore. Finally, to ensure that

THE LEADING BALL FOR 1878.

The ball manufactured by us and known as "SPALDINGS LEAGUE BALL" enjoys the very hi best reputation among professional and amateur players, as attested by several testimonials received from some of the most prominent players in the country, a few of which we print on the preceding page of this book. This ball is made of the very best of materials, and every one warranted to stand the hardest kind of usage, without ripping or losing its shape. Each ball is done up in tin foil, neatly packed in a box by itself, and sealed, in accordance with the latest League regulations. Beware of counterfeits. None genuine without our trade-mark on the label of each box and ball. In addition to our League Ball, we manufacture a Professional and Amateur Dead Ball, and also a full line of the cheaper grades, which are superior to any others at the same price.

	Per Dozen.	Sample by Mail. EACH.
Spalding's League Ball, - - - -	$15.00.	$1.50.
Spalding's Professional Dead—Red or White,	12 00.	1.25.
Spalding's Amateur " " "	9.00.	1.00.

Spalding's American Club, each. 75c.		Spalding's Eureka, - each, 20c
" King of the Diamond, 50c.		" Rattler, - - " 15c
" Grand Duke, - each, 35c.		" The Boss, - " 10c.
" Boy's Favorite, " 25c.		" Nickel Ball, - " 65c.

Liberal discount to dealers, who will find this new line of Balls the cheapest and best selling goods ever before offered.

Clubs or dealers ordering one-half dozen balls at one time, are entitled to our dozen rates. Address orders to **A. G. SPALDING & BRO.,**
118 Randolph St., Chicago, Illinois.

Spalding's 1878 League Ball was "warranted to stand the hardest kind of usage, without ripping or losing its shape."

proper baseballs were used, Hulbert ordered teams to obtain them through the secretary of the league.

1878 At the age of 28, Spalding retired as a player in order to focus on building his sporting goods empire.[4] A shrewd businessman, he not only provided balls to the National League for free but paid the league one dollar for every dozen balls in exchange for the right to call his balls *the* official balls. Spalding then used the endorsement to market his balls to folks all over the country. Spalding was also given the honor of publishing the National League's official guide, which he used to promote his own sporting goods products. Before long, the guide was selling 50,000 copies a year, and Spalding got the contract to make the league's uniforms. Section 1 of the guide specified the size and weight and materials of the ball. Sections 2 and 3 covered the parties responsible for "furnishing" the ball: the home team for regular games and the secretary of the league for championship games. Section 4 went as follows: "When the ball becomes out of shape, or cut or ripped so as to expose the yarn, or in any way so injured as to be unfit for fair use, a new ball shall be called for by the umpire at the end of an even innings [*sic*], at the request of either captain. Should the ball be lost during the game, the umpire shall, at the expiration of five minutes, call for a new ball." (Henry Chadwick had suggested the time limit two years earlier.) Therefore, it was important for teams to score early in the game because the ball was often in shambles by the end.

---

[4] In 1877, Spalding appeared in 60 games as an infielder, but pitched just 11 innings. The following season, he played just one game at second base, went 2-for-4 with a pair of singles, and committed four errors.

1880 Harry Wright, the older brother of George Wright and player-manager of the 1869 Red Stockings, decided to compete with Spalding by introducing a livelier ball. This ball, which featured a cork center with string and rubber and yarn around it, was used in an experimental game and turned out to be way too lively. As a result, Spalding's balls became even more popular.

1881 Al Reach, a former player in the National Association, also hoped to compete with Spalding. In 1881—four years after starting his own sporting goods company—he teamed up with Ben Shibe, an inventor and fellow manufacturer. Shibe, the future part-owner of the Athletics, was an expert mechanic and the business took off.

1882 A rival league called the American Association played the first of its ten seasons and used the Mahn ball. Meanwhile, the National League rule that prevented the ball from being replaced during an inning wreaked havoc at the Polo Grounds on August 7, 1882. It was a rainy game between the Cleveland Spiders and New York Metropolitans, and a ball that became soggy and severely lopsided couldn't be tossed out of play.

1883 The American Association switched to the Reach ball as its official ball. Reach's assembly line produced one ball every ten minutes; the highest-quality ball made by the company cost 75 cents. But the big news of 1883 was a key rule change: in the National League the umpire became authorized to put a new ball in play whenever he felt it was necessary. On July 17, 1883, Samuel Castle repatented the seamless ball. It was manufactured and marketed by Reach, but tanked once again. In an unrelated incident, a juiced-ball theory surfaced five days later in *Sporting Life* magazine: "It is one of the remarkable freaks of base-ball that when the Chicagoes play at home the balls used are noticeable for their hardness," said the article. "All the outside clubs have noticed this, and the players think that Spalding manufactures an especial ball for home use."

1884 Another rival league called the Union Association played its only season and, according to players and sportswriters, used balls that were extra-lively. These balls were manufactured by Wright & Ditson, a company in Boston that was run by George and Harry Wright. Unfortunately, none of these balls are known to have survived, so no one's sure what was inside of them, but it's believed that the core contained at least two ounces of rubber. At the time, people blamed the ball for inflating offensive numbers—it certainly helped Fred Dunlap, a career .292 hitter, lead the league with a .412 batting average—but the ball didn't seem to have much of an impact overall. The leaguewide batting average was just .245, and aside from Dunlap, only six hitters batted over .300.

1886 Both major leagues started using a ball that contained a thin layer of plastic cement. This not only made the ball somewhat waterproof and more durable by holding the yarn in place but eliminated the need for the double-cover ball. The home team was required to provide two balls to the umpire at the start of the game. As a result, if the first ball got lost, players no longer had to spend five minutes looking for it.

1887 This was a big year with several key advances: Rawlings was founded, the home team was required to provide extra balls if needed, and the rules specified that "the last ball in play" would be awarded to the winning team. Baseballs were still so valuable that Harry Wright, now managing the Phillies, not only kept a log of every ball that his team owned but also noted the condition of each one.

1889 Manufacturers were still eager to make use of new technology, and Ben Shibe and Al Reach developed machinery to wind the ball—two balls at once, in fact. An employee started the process by wrapping old gray stocking yarn once around the rubber core; the machine picked it up from there and wound quickly. When the ball became half-sized, the machine stopped and cut the yarn. The employee then removed the ball and dropped it in a bucket, which, when full, was delivered to another worker at a second machine who repeated the process with half an ounce of worsted yarn. A third machine added a layer of strong white cotton thread, after which the ball received a coating of plastic cement and another half-ounce layer of worsted. The ball was then weighed, and if it was a bit off, the difference was corrected with a thicker- or thinner-than-usual horsehide cover. The machines could be adjusted to wind the yarn tighter or looser, so even though the rubber core was fixed at one ounce, Reach could have easily altered the liveliness of the ball. He had 500 employees at his factory and roughly 40,000 dozen balls in stock, including cheap balls that were made with pressed leather shavings and sold for as little as five cents. Unbeknownst to most people at the time, Spalding secretly bought out Reach but continued to let him run the operation; few people knew about it because Spalding continued stamping Reach's name on the balls in order to create the illusion of competition.

1890 The Players League (later recognized by historians as an official major league) played its only season and tried to compete with the two established leagues by beefing up offense in two ways: increasing the distance from the pitcher's box to home plate by 18 inches, and using a livelier ball. The ball was made by Keefe & Becannon, a sporting goods company in Brooklyn that was founded by two pitchers.[5] On September 12, 1890, these balls were slipped into play at a National League doubleheader by a pair of fans who had hidden them in their coat pockets. Whenever a foul ball sailed into the crowd, these men made sure to get their hands on it as it was passed back to the field. If the visiting Cleveland Spiders were batting, the fans returned the real ball, but when the hometown Chicago Colts were up, they tossed back a livelier ball instead—and it paid off. The Colts swept both games, by scores of 17–2 and 11–4. (Keefe and Becannon may have scoffed at the claim in *Spalding's Official Base Ball Guide* that the Spalding League Ball "cannot be further improved upon.")

1892 Still unaware that Spalding had bought out Reach, people began speculating that there was a difference between the two balls. The fact is that since all the balls were being wound by machines with different settings, there could have been a difference if Spalding wanted one.

1894 Spalding bought out Peck & Snyder.

1895 The National League used 3,800 balls. This amounted to slightly fewer than five balls per game and probably included balls used during batting practice.

1896 A new rule required the home team to provide a dozen new balls per game. Around this time, the National League owners were feuding—and Spalding, who owned the Chicago franchise, was caught in the middle. The other owners got so angry at him that they threatened to take away his National League ball contract and award it to the Overman Wheel Company, a manufacturer that already

---

[5] Tim Keefe, a future Hall of Famer who compiled 342 career wins, pitched in the Players League and went 17-11. Buck Becannon, a guy you've almost certainly never heard of, went 3-8 with a 5.93 ERA in 11 career starts and played his last game in 1887.

made the Victor ball (which was later used by the Federal League). Spalding's response? He bought the Overman factory to protect his contract.

1897 The National League used more than 5,500 balls—a 45 percent increase over the previous two seasons. The average team paid $500 for 40 dozen balls, which, according to league president Nicholas Young, was "quite an item of expenditure for this necessary tool of the trade." Young stored the balls in his home, then weighed and shipped them out whenever an owner or manager wired him to request more. Young also approved a new rule that said that if a player intentionally doctored a ball, the umpire was supposed to remove it from the game and fine him $5.

1898 The St. Louis Browns set a record by using 17 balls in one game.

1899 There were 400 employees at Spalding's Reach factory, plus 700 more who stitched balls in their homes. On a typical day, the company manufactured 1,500 high-end balls (which sold for $1.50 apiece) and 18,000 cheap balls (which sold for as little as a nickel). The good balls were made with rubber in the core, four different types of yarn, and two layers of plastic cement; cheap balls had no rubber and were assembled in the factory's cellar with jute and hemp waste. Machines cut the covers and punched holes around the edges, so for the first time every ball contained the same number of stitches. Cheap balls were made with sheepskin covers; good balls got horsehide and were rolled in a machine that smoothed the surface. Reach made many different types of balls, including the American Association ball, Professional Lively ball, Amateur Lively ball, Youth's Lively ball, Southern League ball, Junior League ball, Junior Professional Dead ball, King of the

Field ball, Cock of the Walk ball, thread-stitched League Ball, catgut-stitched League Ball, Bounding Rock ball, Champion ball, Out of Sight ball, Skyrocket ball, Dandy ball, Patent Seamless ball, and Indoor ball. The factory also manufactured other equipment, including gloves, which ranged in price from 25 cents to $7.50.

1900 Other manufacturers began marketing balls with different stampings and nicknames such as Lula, Rattler, Atlantic, Pacific, Red Dead, Lively Bounder, Prince, King, Monarch, Bingo, Broncho, Liner, Skyscraper, Eureka, Corker, and The Boss. The Corker was probably inspired by Spalding, who experimented with a cork-centered ball, but it failed because the yarn expanded after the ball was stitched. (The cork ball succeeded 10 years later because it had less cork and the core was enclosed with a thin layer of vulcanized rubber.)

1901 The American League played its first major league season and used the Reach ball. People assumed that the ball was juiced—that this latest "outlaw league" tried to lure fans away from the well-established National League by inflating offense—but statistical evidence suggests otherwise. The American League batted 10 points higher (.276 to .266), but hit only *one* more home run (228 to 227). Even if these differentials had been greater, it wouldn't have meant much because the American League hadn't yet

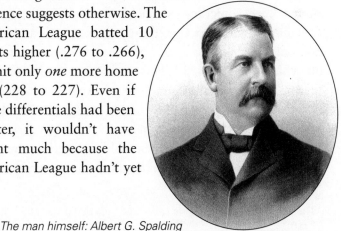

The man himself: Albert G. Spalding

adopted the foul-strike rule. In other news, the National Agreement—a pact governing all of professional baseball—caused an uproar because it stated that minor league teams were required to use a standard, official league ball. Major league executives had pushed for this so they'd be able to evaluate minor leaguers by looking at their stats. Minor league executives wanted to use their own balls because it was cheaper than having to buy them from a big-name manufacturer.

1903 The American League adopted the foul-strike rule, and the average team put four to six new balls into play per game.

1905 As American League hitters adjusted to the foul-strike rule (while also using a ball that was dead by today's standards), only three players finished the season with a batting average above .300.

1906 The *New York Sun* estimated that an average of nine balls per game were used in the major leagues and that some teams used just 40 dozen balls for the entire season.

1908 When a batter hit the ball exceptionally hard, the rubber core sometimes cracked. According to *Sporting Life* magazine, this occurred on a weekly basis and "burst not only the multitude of yarn and wrappings, but the horsehide cover as well." This obviously wasn't a problem for the Cardinals and Superbas[6] on August 4, 1908: the two teams managed to play an entire game at Brooklyn's Washington Park with just one ball.

1909 On June 18, 1909, Ben Shibe patented the cork-centered ball. In his patent application, he wrote, "The

---

[6] The Brooklyn Dodgers were called the Superbas from 1899 through 1910.

object of my invention is to produce a playing ball . . . having a resilient central core . . . upon which the layers of yarn may be wound under greater tension, whereby greater compactness results." Six weeks later, the Reach company (which had worked with Shibe since 1881) was granted the patent.

1910 When the season started, balls with rubber cores were still being used. The public had no idea that the cork-centered ball even existed until Reach ran an ad on May 12, 1910, that said: "Big Improvement Made in Base Balls. A. J. Reach & Company Patents a Cork Core, supplanting the rubber center, and producing the finest ball ever known. More rigid and durable, will absolutely keep its shape. The Perfect Ball at Last." Al Reach was so proud of this new ball—"It is the greatest triumph we have ever achieved," he said—and was so eager to see it in action, that he secretly arranged for the ball to be used in the World Series. Offense suddenly increased. No one knew why. But everyone seemed to like it. The secret was so well kept that American League president Ban Johnson didn't even find out until December 8, 1910. That's when Reach ran an ad in *The Sporting News* that boldly stated: "The Cork Centered Ball Was the Official ball of the World Series."

1911 The cork-centered ball was used by both leagues throughout the season, and the number of .300 hitters doubled from 15 (in 1910) to 30 (in 1911). Because the ball was so lively, pitchers came up with freak deliveries and trick pitches, like the spitball and scuffball, in order to stay competitive. What made the ball so lively was that it was wound tighter. It actually had to be tighter: while the old rubber core was dense and heavy, the new cork core was just as big, yet weighed much less. Therefore, in order to manufacture the new ball according to specifications—it still had to weigh at least 5 ounces but couldn't be bigger than 9.25 inches in circumference—the missing weight from the core was reclaimed by cramming more yarn into the ball. This could only be done by winding it tighter. The public accused Reach of tampering with the ball, but the hitters weren't complaining. When asked about the new ball, Cardinals Hall of Fame catcher Roger Bresnahan said, "You can make a home run in the ninth inning just as easily as in the first." Bresnahan wasn't the only player questioned. On August 28, 1911, the editor of *Spalding's Official Base Ball Guide* sent a letter to every player in the National League, asking them to share their views on the ball. The players were asked these seven questions:

1. Has the ball increased or decreased batting?
2. What percentage is the increase or decrease?
3. Is the ball too lively?
4. Is it well thought of by other players?
5. Is it easier to handle than the old ball?
6. Can it be thrown as far and accurately as the old ball?
7. Can it be thrown more accurately and farther than the old ball?

According to the survey, 98 percent of players thought batting had increased 10 to 15 percent, 95 percent said the ball was not too lively, 98 percent reported that it was well thought of by other players, and 75 percent claimed it was easier to handle and could be thrown farther and more accurately. Tom Shibe, the older of Ben's two sons, correctly predicted that the cork center was "here to stay." Liveliness aside, this was the first season that the National League ball had a combination of red and black stitching; from 1878 to 1910 it had been all black.

1912 Technology had improved so much that a single machine could wind several hundred baseballs per hour. The world's biggest baseball factory, located in Philadelphia, churned out 24,000 balls per day, including balls for the National and American Leagues, dozens of minor leagues, and cheap balls for amateur and recreational use. The covers, however, were still stitched onto the balls by hand. Employees sat at long tables with vises that held the balls in place. Cheap balls were stitched by young women, usually 18 to 20 years old, who completed each ball in eight or nine minutes. High-end balls were stitched by men, who occupied a separate floor and worked slightly faster. The best balls were then sent down to the first floor, where they were stamped by hand, wrapped in tin foil, and packed into pasteboard boxes by a machine. Each major league team used roughly 100 dozen balls this season—a number that was rising because fans were keeping more and more baseballs that flew into the stands. Tom Shibe was well aware of the developing souvenir craze. "The losing of many balls in the stands," he said, "has a decided effect on the number of balls we sell, and therefore is an interesting sidelight on the manufacturing of them."

1914 The Federal League played the first of its two major league seasons and used the Victor ball. The American League hit 148 home runs, the National League 267, and the Federal League 295—so people suspected that the Victor ball (which was made by a company owned by Spalding) was extra-lively. National and American League teams paid $15 per dozen balls and used more than 40,000 over the course of the season (including balls used during batting practice and Spring Training). The Washington Senators paid $1,500 for balls, the least in either league, while the Boston Braves spent the most at $4,675.

1915 On July 21, 1915, a 20-year-old pitcher named Babe Ruth hit a mammoth home run that traveled approximately 470 feet over the right-field bleachers at Sportsman's Park in St. Louis. The ball cleared a major thoroughfare called Grand Boulevard and nearly struck a building on the other side. This home run was one of just 14 long balls hit by the Red Sox all season.

1916 Up until this time, balls had to be removed from their boxes with the seals broken by the umpire in front of the two teams' captains. This rule had made it almost impossible for people to tamper with the balls—to slip "ringers" or phony balls into play—but fans were glad to see it go because the ground behind home plate became littered with boxes after the ump tore them open.[7] Later in the season, Pirates owner Barney Dreyfuss disassembled a Victor ball and discovered that it had a two-ounce rubber core. (This was twice the legal limit, but because the Federal League had folded a year earlier, nothing could be done about it.)

1917 Recent Cubs owner Charles Webb Murphy incorrectly predicted that a material called "ivory nut" (which was used to make buttons) would replace the cork centers in baseballs. Lots of people were speculating about the composition of the ball because the government was starting to commandeer various materials for World War I, including high-grade wool yarn. The Federal Bureau of Standards tested different manufacturers' baseballs to see which ones were best for the army. The Bureau perhaps should have focused on finding better balls for the Washington Senators, who hit just four home runs all season, but

---

[7] Like, duh, hand the trash to a ballboy?

inferior yarn was only part of the problem. Offense also lagged because of all the doctored balls and trick pitches that were being thrown; batters had to choke up on the bat, sometimes as much as 10 inches, and take shorter swings to increase their chances of making solid contact. It also didn't help that most teams played in cavernous ballparks. Braves Field, the first stadium with more than 40,000 seats, was one of the largest at the time. The distance from home plate to the center-field fence was 550 feet.

1918 Offense reached an all-time low, especially in the American League, which combined for 96 home runs and saw four of its eight teams fail to reach double digits. The Senators once again went deep just 4 times, while the St. Louis Browns hit 5 homers, the White Sox 8, and the Indians 9. In the National League, where teams slugged 139 homers, the Brooklyn Dodgers scored just 360 runs and posted a miserable .291 on-base percentage—both major league lows. The Senators, it should be noted, made up for their weak hitting by leading the major leagues with a 2.18 earned run average and finishing the season 16 games over .500. Sadly, but not surprisingly, fans lost interest as pitching dominated the sport, and major league attendance plunged.[8]

1919 The First World War was over, better materials became available for baseballs, and the competitive balance was restored. The American League out-homered the National League for the first time in 13 years, this time by a 240-to-207 margin. Every team in the majors hit at least 17 homers. Attendance more than doubled. Things were going well until season's end, when several White Sox

---

[8] In 1918 the Major Leagues drew 3,080,126 fans, the lowest total since 1900, when there was only one league.

HOME RUNS PER SEASON—1901–1930

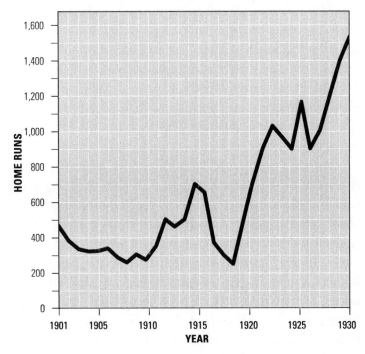

*Offense plunged during World War I when high-quality yarn
was scarce and doctored balls were prevalent.*

players accepted money from gamblers and intentionally
lost the World Series to the Reds. As details of the "Black
Sox" scandal emerged, the public's faith in the sport was
nearly destroyed.

1920 Babe Ruth played his first season in New York and
single-handedly hit more home runs than all but two entire
teams. He finished the year with 54 homers, a staggering
total that nearly doubled his own record and caused ram-
pant speculation that the ball was juiced. When sportswriters began to claim that the ball was responsible for Ruth's
accomplishments, a group of fans banded together in his

support. They called themselves "The Friends of Ruth" and made several successful attempts to snag his home run balls. The fans then sent these balls to the Bureau of Standards to find out if they differed from the 1917 batch. Eventually the Bureau declared a decisive victory for Ruth's fans—the balls had not changed—but there was one small problem: it wasn't true. In 1917 the Bureau had tested brand-new balls; in 1920 they tested game-used home run balls that had probably been batted around for an inning or two and therefore appeared to be deader than they really were. Although this difference may have evened out the test results, the 1920 ball was, by most other accounts, hopped up. Hall of Fame outfielder Edd Roush said the livelier ball forced him to play so deep in the field that for the first time in his career he had to relay the ball to reach home plate. Some people, including Hall of Fame second baseman Rogers Hornsby, insisted that the American League was using an extra-lively ball. Given the fact that the American League hit 108 more home runs than the National League, this theory was hard to disprove. Hornsby said he'd seen a ball from each league get cut open, and he claimed that the contents were different. Other people simply attributed the leaguewide power surge—a 41 percent increase in home runs—to Ruth himself, arguing that his success inspired other players to swing for the fences. But everyone agreed that Ruth's emergence came at the best possible time: in the wake of the Black Sox scandal, it kept fans excited about baseball and pushed attendance to an all-time high.

1921 The juiced-ball debate exploded in 1921 when the number of home runs jumped 49 percent. Halfway through the season, F. C. Lane, the editor-in-chief of *Baseball* magazine, wrote letters to various baseball executives to get their take on it. "In my opinion," replied Jim Dunn, the owner and president of the Indians, "there is no question but what the balls in use this year are much livelier than in former years. I am unable to say whether it is on on [*sic*] account of the superior quality of yarn which is now being used, or an increased amount of rubber, but the fact is that the great increase in hitting is evidence that the ball is livelier." Baseballs were, in fact, being wound with a more resilient grade of Australian wool yarn—a modification that Ban Johnson admitted: "It permits of a firmer winding, a harder ball, and naturally one that is more elastic," he wrote in a letter to Lane. Braves owner George W. Grant believed that offense had increased because of Ray Chapman's death—that the subsequent ban on freak deliveries made hitters more willing to dig into the batter's box. (More Chapman fallout: because the tragedy was caused by a dirty baseball, teams were ordered to keep new balls in play. Pitchers complained that the new balls were too slick, and batters complained that the white horsehide created a glare, so the umpires started rubbing dirt on them. Oh, the irony!) With apparently no glaring differences, National and American League balls were now being made at different factories. After visiting the Spalding factory, National League president John Heydler said, "I found that the methods in use were precisely the same as heretofore. Only the wool yarn was a better quality and in my opinion more firmly bound." Lane visited both factories and reported only one difference between the two: National League balls were made with red and black stitching; American League balls were made with red and blue. In September 1921, *Baseball* magazine ran a feature story called "Has the 'Lively' Ball Revolutionized the

Game?" The subtitle dug deeper and posed the following question: "The Prolonged Batting Carnival—The Slump in Pitching and Base Stealing—Is the Lively Ball Responsible for These Grave Changes?" According to the two manufacturers, the answer was no. A Reach spokesman said, "To explain the great advance in hitting this season you must blame something else beside[s] the baseball in use in either league." Spalding issued a similar statement, suggesting that "the remedy lies rather in revising the rules so as to favor the pitcher." As the debate persisted, another theory emerged: during the war the highly skilled baseball stitchers left their jobs to serve the country; after the war they returned to the factories and made better balls.

1922 Around this time two brothers named Walter and Edward Hubbert, who had once worked for Reach as baseball stitchers, formed a business arrangement with Spalding and began stitching balls in their home in Perkasie, Pennsylvania. It didn't take long before other members of the family began stitching, and eventually the neighbors joined in. After several years there were so many stitchers that the Hubberts built an extension onto the house and later opened their own factory.

1923 Only six pitchers finished the season with an ERA under 3.00, down from 64 pitchers in 1915. While most people were enjoying the offense, others wanted the ball to be deadened.

1924 The National League used 43,224 balls.

1925 As offense soared yet again, *Baseball* magazine denounced the "blind orgy of hitting" in the feature story "Should the Lively Ball Be Abolished?" John Heydler didn't think so. "I do not see how there can be any complaint about this year's baseball," he said. "Every ball which leaves the factory is as perfect as human intelligence can devise." Ban Johnson disagreed with his fellow league president. He conceded that the ball was lively, admitted that there were too many home runs, and suggested zoning the outfield so that the batter wouldn't automatically get credit for a homer just because the ball went over the fence. (This idea was quickly shot down.) Reds president August Herrmann felt that "baseball would be improved if the ball now in use would be made less lively," but Connie Mack disagreed. "I am not at all in favor of having the baseball changed from what it is at the present time," said the legendary manager and owner of the Athletics. "The crowds which turned out to see Ruth is an indication that the people want to see batting, so give them batting." Mack made a valid point—baseball was a form of entertainment—but there were batters who didn't even want to see so much batting. Brooklyn's first baseman, Jacques Fournier, who had led the National League with 27 homers in 1924, said, "I don't think the ball this year is any livelier than it was last season, but it's altogether too lively. It has completely upset baseball standards. The lively ball handicaps fielding and it is sometimes positively dangerous to infielders as well as to the pitcher." As the debate raged on, Heydler arranged for a Columbia University chemistry professor named Harold A. Fales to test three baseballs: one from 1914, another from 1923, and a third from 1925. Fales measured and weighed the balls, dropped them from a height of 13.5 feet, and finally cut them open to inspect the contents. Aside from the fact that the 1923 ball bounced 2.04 inches higher than the other two, and that the two older balls weighed a quarter of an ounce less than the new ball—a result attributed to natural aging and shrinkage—Fales didn't report any significant differences. When the test results were published, an anonymous player was quoted as saying, "They give one baseball to represent a season's output. . . . The chemistry professor cut it open and found rubber and yarn. What did he expect to find, dynamite? Nobody ever said the ball was made of different materials." In November 1925, *Sportlife* magazine ran a huge article titled "Secret of the 'Rabbit Ball' Exposed," but the way the magazine "exposed" the secret wasn't exactly scientific. (In case you're wondering, "rabbit ball" is an antiquated term for "juiced ball.") The reporter, a prolific baseball writer named Frederick G. Lieb, cut two baseballs in half with a circular saw. One ball was from 1912, the other was brand-new, and—surprise surprise!—the stuffing in the newer ball expanded more. Here's how Lieb explained his groundbreaking discovery:

> Any woman, who has handled yarn to any extent, knows the "deadness" of an inferior grade. The housewife has her own way of putting it. She says it doesn't "fluff up" like the superior qualities. By that she means that when a good quality of yarn is compressed and then suddenly released, it will "fluff up" or "spring" far more than the inferior grade. In that "fluffing up" you have the secret of the lively ball.

Julian Curtiss, the president of Spalding, insisted that the balls weren't being made differently. "There has been altogether too much blame placed on the baseball during this home-run epidemic," he said. "Ever since Babe Ruth became the center of the baseball spotlight through his home run efforts it was only natural that the other players would try and duplicate his performances. . . . If the players played as they did in the old days the lively ball charge would die."

1926 The official National League ball could be bought directly from Spalding for $2, and according to the company's catalog it was "warranted to last a full game when used under ordinary conditions." Spalding's cheapest ball was the ten-cent Rocket, which was listed as "a good lively boys' size ball; two-piece cover." In August 1926, with home run numbers down in both leagues, *Baseball* magazine reported that the dead ball had returned: "The sluggers are hitting this new-old ball with all the force at their command, but they find it very difficult to hit it beyond the upturned hands of an awaiting outfielder."

1928 Yellow baseballs were used in a minor league game between the Louisville Colonels and Milwaukee Brewers.

1930 So much for the dead ball. As offensive statistics climbed toward new heights, legendary sportswriter Ring Lardner described the ball as "a leather-covered sphere stuffed with dynamite." The entire National League batted .303, Hack Wilson set the single-season record by knocking in 191 runs, and Wally Berger set National League rookie records with 38 homers and 119 RBIs. Some people proposed shortening the distance from the mound to home plate or removing the gloss from the ball's surface— anything to help pitchers regain their edge. Barney Dreyfuss suggested that batters only be awarded a double when they hit the ball over a fence less than 300 feet away.

1931 The ball was deadened and equilibrium was restored, especially in the National League, where home runs plunged 45 percent and the batting average dropped 26 points to .277. The introduction of the "cushioned cork center"—an extra layer of rubber that encased the core of the ball—made the biggest difference, but there were other factors that helped to trim offense.[9] National League pitchers in particular got an extra boost because the seams were raised on the Spalding ball. "The new ball affords a better grip and this has given my curveball a sharper, downward break," said Reds pitcher Red Lucas, who had posted a career-high 5.38 ERA in 1930. "I couldn't get that result with last year's ball." Hack Wilson also noticed the difference as he slogged through a mediocre season. "If your bat just caught a piece of the 1930 ball," he said, "it might travel into the bleachers. Now, the same shot sends a fly within reach of the fielders." Cubs first baseman Charlie Grimm compared baseballs from 1930 and 1931 by dropping each one twice on a concrete surface. In round one the older ball bounced higher, and in round two he dropped them so they'd land on their seams. "The old one arose vertically," he said. "The new failed to come up true." Just about everyone agreed that the new ball was better—even Pirates third baseman Pie Traynor, whose batting average dropped 68 points in 1931. "The present ball makes for a better game," he said. "Last year there were too many slaughters. . . . Such burlesque performances not only wrecked the mound staffs but they deadened interest." While Spalding and Reach tweaked the major league balls, a man named George Senn patented a practice ball with a core that was intentionally placed off-center. This invention, known as the "Wobble Ball," was designed to

---

[9] Prior to 1931, the batter was credited with a sacrifice fly (and therefore not charged with a hitless at-bat) when a runner tagged up and advanced from any base; starting in 1931 a sac fly was awarded only if the runner scored. And that's not all. Prior to 1930, the batter was credited with a home run if he hit a ball that bounced over the outfield fence; the American League changed these would-be homers to doubles in 1930, and the National League followed suit one year later.

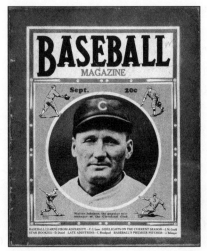

The September 1933 issue of Baseball *magazine featured new Indians manager (and 417-game winner) Walter Johnson on the cover.*

help pitchers throw better curveballs and make fielding more of a challenge.

1933 There was widespread speculation that the National League ball was deader—and had been for years. In its September 1933 issue, *Baseball* magazine supported this theory by pointing out that there'd been "brilliant moundsmanship" even during the 1920s when the ball was supposedly livelier than ever.

1934 The National League ball switched from red-and-black stitching to all red.

1935 Jumping on the bandwagon, the American League changed the stitching on its ball from red and blue to all red. This was also the year that the Hubberts' stitching operation expanded from their home to a factory.

1936 Aside from their logos, Spalding and Reach balls were proclaimed identical. The core weighed ⅞ of an ounce and consisted of a small cork sphere surrounded by two layers of rubber—one black and one red. The core was wrapped with 71 yards of ⅛ white woolen yarn followed by 41 yards of ⁴⁄₁₅ white woolen yarn. Then, after receiving a layer of rubber cement, the ball was wrapped with 41 yards of ⁴⁄₁₅ blue-gray woolen yarn and 100 yards of ²⁰⁄₂ fine cotton yarn. At this stage the ball was supposed to weigh 4.625 ounces and measure 8.875 inches in circumference.

A second coating of rubber cement was applied, and then the alum-tanned horsehide cover was stitched on with red thread. The cover was 1⁄20 of an inch thick and weighed half an ounce.

1938 On April 27, 1938, yellow baseballs staged a comeback and were used in a college game at Bakers Field between Columbia and Fordham. On August 2, 1938, the Dodgers and Cardinals used yellow balls in the first game of a doubleheader at Ebbets Field, which Brooklyn won, 6–2. The balls, which were known as "stitched lemons," made the players' hands yellow, and winning pitcher Freddie Fitzsimmons complained that the balls were too slick. In other colorful news, the Middle-Atlantic League—a Class C minor league with such teams as the Dayton Ducks and Johnstown Johnnies—used balls with white stitches throughout the season. League president Elmer Daily thought the stitches were better for night games, but no one agreed, and the balls weren't used again. Meanwhile, as the National League outpitched the American League by a full run in the ERA column, players grumbled about the balls and insisted there was a difference. "In order to pitch a curve in the American League," said Yankees pitcher Monte Pearson, "the leather must have been in the game a little while. . . . With the National League ball you can do things right off. The cover feels thicker, looser. The stitching is raised and gives you a chance to put on your stuff, and control is better." Naturally, the Bureau of Standards got involved and tested the balls at Griffith Stadium. H. L. Dryden, the head of the Bureau's Division of Mechanics and Sound, built an air gun that used ballistic pendulums to shoot a one-pound piece of wood 200 feet per second into the ball. Designed to re-create the force of a batter making contact, the device sent balls flying at an average distance of 367 feet. Dryden concluded that there wasn't much of a difference between the balls—that the covers and stitching had little to do with the liveliness. "The science of the home run is hard to pin down," he said. "Give me two baseballs and I can prove almost anything. The emphasis should be on the batter, not the ball." Dryden's statement didn't deter a group of two dozen players and baseball executives from conducting their own unofficial experiment at Oriole Park. With roughly 500 fans on hand, the players took batting practice—and took aim for the bleachers—with balls from both leagues. A reporter named Randall Cassell noted the difference: "Both will travel over the fences when hit properly. However, the N.L. ball has a distinctly 'dead' sound coming off the bat."

1939 The lemon ball hadn't yet been deemed a total lemon, and the Dodgers used yellow balls for three games. Meanwhile, in a feat of innovation still with us today, Athletics third base coach Lena Blackburne began selling mud to professional teams (see chapter 8 for more). When rubbed onto the balls, the mud reduced the glare and improved the grip without scratching the covers or making them too dark.

1941 Another world war meant another shortage of materials. On December 11, 1941—four days after the attack on Pearl Harbor—the U.S. government prohibited the use of crude rubber in baseballs. Spalding and Reach claimed they had enough rubber in stock to manufacture all the balls for 1942, but there was serious concern about what would happen beyond that. The manufacturers experimented with plastic cores, which seemed to be adequate, but then the government banned plastic as well.

1942 As the rubber supply dwindled, offense declined, baseball executives panicked, and Spalding falsely claimed that the balls weren't being manufactured differently. High-quality horsehide was no longer being imported from Belgium—cheaper domestic horsehide was now being used to cover the balls—and the crude rubber in the core had been replaced with less resilient reclaimed rubber. As word leaked out and the controversy grew, Kenesaw Mountain Landis, the sport's first commissioner, formed a special committee to investigate alternative materials for baseballs. The best solution? Golf ball pills. Baseball wasn't the only sport affected by wartime shortages; the government also banned the use of rubber thread in golf balls, which effectively prevented the balls from being manufactured at all. It just so happened that 720,000 golf ball pills—tiny cores made of a non-elastic rubber called balata—had already been manufactured, and on September 9, 1942, the rubber and rubber products branch of the War Production Board approved the use of these pills as baseball cores for the 1943 season. Spalding manufactured sample balls and, with further permission from the government, padded each pill with 0.42 ounces of vulcanized scrap rubber. Several teams tested the balls in practice and said they were okay.

1943 The balata balls turned out to be dead. Seriously dead. All four games on Opening Day resulted in shutouts, and the first home run wasn't hit until the 12th game of the season. (It also didn't help that many of the sport's biggest stars were off fighting in the war.) Commissioner Landis vowed to bring back the rabbit ball. Reds general manager Warren Giles threatened to use his own type of ball. Something had to be done. With baseball hugely responsible for raising the morale of a war-weary public, it was crucial to regain the competitive balance that made the sport so exciting. On April 22, 1943, the manufacturers tried to distance themselves from the debate by arranging for a representative to publicly cut open one of the new balls. Big mistake. The dissection revealed that the yarn was damp and loosely wound. No one knew how it happened, but the theory was that the new ball was susceptible to the weather and somehow absorbed the moisture of the spring air. Lou Coleman, the vice president of Spalding, issued the following statement:

> The official 1943 baseball as adopted by the major league committee is inherently satisfactory. The shipment of baseballs sent out for the opener of the season, unfortunately, did not measure up to standard. Investigations have been made and the reason discovered. In the manufacture of baseballs a layer of rubber cement is applied between layers of wool. Under war conditions this cement is made from reprocessed rubber. The cement used on the baseballs turned out by the factory in recent shipments has proved of inferior quality. Instead of providing resilience the cement hardened to a point where the wool was affected. This deadened the ball.

Spalding announced that it needed two weeks to prepare a new batch of balls, and once they were ready, National League president Ford Frick made sure that every team started using them on the same day. Ultimately both leagues rounded up enough prewar balls to finish the season, but the statistical damage was done. There were fewer runs scored per game than in any season from 1919 to 1968.[10]

---

[10] 1968 is known as "the Year of the Pitcher." Bob Gibson posted a microscopic 1.12 ERA, and Denny McLain became the last 30-game winner.

1944 To the great joy of all involved, the government lifted its ban on cork and rubber, and Spalding resumed normal production of baseballs.

1947 With the real ball back, the National League hit 886 home runs—the highest total since 1930 and more than double the amount from 1943. Edward Hubbert, still stitching for Spalding, told *The Sporting News* that the 1947 ball was juiced. "It is the fastest, liveliest ball made," he claimed, "and if records aren't broken, it will be because there are no Ruths, Gehrigs or Foxxes around." Hall of Famer Stan Musial, then playing his sixth season in St. Louis, agreed that hitters had an edge. "The ball definitely is livelier. It goes farther," he said. But Phillies manager Ben Chapman, whose team hit a National League–worst .258 in 1947, wasn't convinced that the ball had changed. "Take one look at the batting averages on my club and you won't say the ball is any livelier," he quipped.

1948 Indians owner Bill Veeck secretly froze some baseballs and pitched them to Hall of Famer Hank Greenberg, just for fun. Greenberg, who had retired the previous season, reportedly couldn't hit the balls past shortstop and had no idea why—until he felt one of them. Meanwhile, as both leagues combined to surpass the previous season's home run total, the juiced-ball debate continued. Yankees manager Bucky Harris said, "They have done something to the ball. Men who used to find it tough to drive a ball 350 feet now send it 450 feet." Connie Mack, still managing the Philadelphia Athletics, defended the manufacturers. "There is nothing wrong with the ball," he insisted. "It has not been changed. They raise that cry every spring."

1949 While some rules became more relaxed—the home team was no longer required to provide an exact number of balls, and the winning team was no longer officially awarded the final ball—other rules were put into effect. For the first time, the rule book stated that the ball had to "meet the approved resiliency standards," which was great except for one thing: these standards had not yet been established. In May 1949, George Reach, the 81-year-old son of Al Reach, gave a candid interview to the *Philadelphia Evening News* about the ball's resiliency. He admitted that during his tenure in the family business, the Reach factory had made the balls livelier some years and then deadened them when they got too lively—but he didn't specify when these adjustments had taken place. When asked about 1911, the first full season that featured the cork center, Reach said, "The ball was the liveliest it has ever been. In fact, we had to tone it down. We were making infielders out of outfielders." There was, of course, a reason why Reach never squashed the lively ball debate. "We thought the arguments were wonderful," he said. "Look at all the advertising we got. Why, some papers used to run stories on the front page about the rabbit ball."

1950 Major league teams combined for more than 2,000 home runs—quite an expense considering that balls cost $28 per dozen. As the annual juiced-ball debate got under way, one writer suggested using lively balls only in big ballparks. *The Sporting News,* however, didn't think the ball was responsible for the inflated offense and ran the following front-page headline: "It's Putrid Hurling, Not Rabbit in Ball." Spalding moved from Pennsylvania to Massachusetts, and the Hubberts stayed in business by turning their attention to softballs.

1953 Max Kase, the sports editor of the *New York Journal-American,* asked Joseph S. Ward, the head of the Materials Testing Laboratory at Cooper Union College, to test American League balls from 1952 and 1953. Ward accepted the challenge and, with help from a colleague named Joseph M. DeSalvo, detected two key differences. First, when dropped from a height of 26 feet, 8 inches, the 1953 ball bounced 8.1 percent higher, and second, when squashed with a 100-pound load, the 1953 ball compressed 7.4 percent less. Ward estimated that the aging factor deadened the 1952 ball by 1 percent at most—so in other words, the new ball was significantly harder and livelier. Proving him right, the number of home runs increased by 22 percent. And in other news, the Wiffle Ball was invented.

1954 In December 1954, the rule that required the ball to meet resiliency standards was eliminated. The composition of the ball, however, became more clearly defined, and the now-famous clause about the ball being "a sphere formed by yarn wound around a small core of cork" was added to the rule book.

1955 Rawlings was bought out by Spalding and began manufacturing baseballs in St. Louis.

Peanuts *strip from April 6, 1955*

1956 Prior to a Spring Training game in Wichita, Kansas, the White Sox and Cardinals played around with a new invention called the Glo-bal. This novelty baseball, which glowed even during the day and was supposedly easier to see, was a hit with the players, but never found its way into an actual game. During the regular season, visibility wasn't a problem as the National and American Leagues each hit more than 1,000 home runs for the first time ever. Of course, this got the media riled up for another juiced-ball controversy, and the manufacturers and league executives denied responsibility. In May 1956, Spalding vice president George Dawson met with Warren Giles, then the president of the National League, and issued the following statement: "Mr. Giles said he had reports that there was more jackrabbit in the ball. I informed him that the 1956 baseball is being made of the same materials we have been using for a long, long time." In early June, scientists at the Franklin Institute in Philadelphia conducted a series of experiments that proved that the 1956 ball wasn't livelier than the 1955 ball. On June 22, 1956, the National League issued a press release titled "Lively Ball?—Bunk!— Why not give slugger his due!" The release urged people to stop complaining about lively balls, and it suggested that there were simply more power hitters than in the old days. "Players are *NOT* hitting *MORE* home runs," it said. "*MORE* players are hitting home runs!" The press release pointed out the fact that players had gotten bigger over the past 20 years: in 1956 the average first baseman was 6-foot-2½ and 203 pounds—3 inches taller and 24 pounds heavier than the typical first baseman in 1936. Players at every position were bigger, including pitchers, who were throwing harder than ever before. The league claimed, "It's axiomatic that the faster a pitch is thrown, the farther it will travel upon impact."

1958 Harwood & Sons published its own newsletter and facetiously claimed to have "used sufficient materials during its one hundred year operation to use the world as a core and make a giant baseball of it." The company shipped baseballs to all 48 states of the continental United States, as well as to the Arctic region and U.S. armed forces bases all over the world. The average major league team used roughly 700 dozen balls this season, and Spalding began winding them in a temperature- and humidity-controlled environment. The inside of each ball contained enough material to circle the bases three times: 121 yards of course gray yarn, 45 yards of smoother white wool, 53 yards of fine gray wool, and 150 yards of fine white cotton.

1961 The juiced-ball controversy intensified as Roger Maris took aim at Babe Ruth's single-season home run record. In early August 1961, Spalding president Edwin L. Parker tried to settle the issue with a 1,500-word statement. It didn't work. "Don't tell me it isn't a rabbit ball," said Reds pitcher Jim Brosnan. "I can hear it squealing every time it goes over the fence." Hall of Famer Satchel Paige agreed, adding, "It's livelier, all right. No two ways about it. That's why you have to be careful when you're handling it." On August 14, 1961, the *New York Times* published a 3,200-word article called " '61 Ball May (or May Not) Account for Homers." The newspaper had arranged for a group of chemical engineers from Foster D. Snell, Inc., to test three different baseballs—one from 1927 (when Ruth had set the record), another from 1936, and a third from 1961—and as the title of the article suggests, the results were inconclusive. But hey, at least the engineers tried. They had used a "vernier caliper" to measure compressibility and an "explosive-driven Remington Arms Ram" to shoot the balls in the air (in Central Park) in order to test the rebound coefficient. They had also dissected the balls and recruited a "rubber technologist" to study the innards. Snell's director of engineering concluded that the 1961 ball was slightly larger, lighter, and livelier than the 1927 ball, but he acknowledged that the aging factor might have affected the results. Two weeks later, *Sports Illustrated* ran a feature story called "YES It's Livelier—and Here Is the Proof." Joseph S. Ward and Joseph M. DeSalvo, the guys from Cooper Union who'd tested the balls in 1953, re-created their original experiments with the 1961 ball, thereby eliminating the aging factor. They claimed that the new ball was 2 percent livelier (an increase that would've added six feet to a 300-foot fly ball) and 8 percent harder. Ward and DeSalvo also reported that the average 1961 ball, weighing in at 5.29 ounces, was heavier than the rule book specifications permitted. Commissioner Ford Frick denounced their findings. "I haven't the slightest doubt that the ball has been the same year after year after year," he said. "The Spalding people would not make a change in the ball without an order from me. I have issued no such directive." On August 29, 1961, Parker appeared at a news conference and declared, "Today's ball and the one that Ruth hit are identical. Period." Spalding's chief seamstress, a 49-year-old woman named Beryl Gauthier who hadn't even heard of Roger Maris, said, "The ball is just the same as it ever was."

1964 Spalding used cork from Spain and Portugal, rubber from the Malay Straits, and horsehide that came from dog food companies. "They're more careful with their skinning process and therefore can offer us a much finer grade of hide," said Lewis J. Corneliusen, the assistant advertising manager at Spalding's factory in Massachusetts. Before the cover was stitched onto the ball, the thread was treated with chemicals so it wouldn't deteriorate when it touched the solvents that tanned the horsehide. Once the ball was completed, it had to pass through the "go-no-go" contraption. That's what Corneliusen called the factory's wooden board with two round holes, the first measuring 9 inches in circumference and the second 9.25. If the ball fit through the first hole it was too small; if it failed to pass through the second hole it was too big. Despite Spalding's meticulous manufacturing techniques, the media still came up with new ways to scrutinize the ball. In August 1964, *Baseball Digest*'s feature story was "Case for the Dead Ball: Should It Be Revived After 43 Years?" Bill Veeck said that the lively ball was ruining the sport, and White Sox manager Al Lopez agreed. "The ball is too lively," he said. "The other day a pop foul struck concrete in the stands. No one was near and the ball bounced clear up to the roof. Atmospheric conditions may make a ball livelier or balls may dry out in storage. Whatever the reason, the emphasis on the home run has changed the game and not for the better." There were several players, however, who thought the ball was fine. Yankees Hall of Fame pitcher Whitey Ford said, "With a dead ball it'd be so hard to make runs that the fans would fall asleep." Ford's batterymate Elston Howard added, "The ball doesn't seem lively to me. It acts mighty dead when I'm in a slump."

1965 The Astrodome opened on April 9, 1965, and offered a brief respite from the juiced-ball controversy. Instead, the roof caused the controversy. That's because it originally had glass panels, which were designed to let in sunlight for the natural grass field; the sun caused a severe glare that impaired the fielders' visibility. The Astros had 10 dozen baseballs dyed yellow, orange, and cerise and practiced with them to see if the colors made a difference. Ultimately the glare was fixed with a coating of paint on the glass, and when the grass died from the lack of sunlight, it was replaced with an artificial surface that became known as AstroTurf. Soon enough, the focus went back to the balls. Shortly after the All-Star break, during a high-scoring four-game series in Detroit that saw 19 home runs, Al Lopez complained that the Tigers' baseballs were too dry. The following week, during a low-scoring, homerless five-game series in Chicago, the Tigers accused the White Sox of using frozen balls. "All the balls were cold, ice cold," said Tigers starter Hank Aguirre after losing 1–0. "Freeze a baseball and it sure won't go anyplace." Lopez denied the accusation, but that didn't stop the *Detroit News* and *Chicago's American* from conducting experiments, not only on frozen baseballs (which of course were dead) but also on oven-baked balls (which were much livelier than anyone expected). The *Detroit News* simply

The Astrodome was not the easiest place to keep one's eye on the ball.

administered an in-house drop test from an unexciting height of eight feet. *Chicago's American,* on the other hand, was much more resourceful, first recruiting Dr. Herbert Weinstein, a professor of chemical engineering at the Illinois Institute of Technology, to dissect a ball and determine the correlation between temperature and resiliency, and then arranging for two White Sox players—Pete Ward and Dave Nicholson—to take batting practice with frozen and heated balls at Comiskey Park. Not only did Chicago have the better team in 1965, but it had a better newspaper too.

1968 Of all the wild theories about slumps, 1968 rang in the most outrageous. As offense plunged to historic lows, people went nuts trying to figure out why. One theory that emerged was that the balls were less lively because the yarn was less resilient because a metallic chemical element called molybdenum had been introduced to the diet of sheep in order to prevent a specific type of skin ailment and had therefore made the wool less fluffy. (Seriously.) The theory was shot down by Dr. Harold P. Lungren, chief of the Wool and Mohair Laboratory of the U.S. Department of Agriculture. Although the doctor admitted that wool could occasionally be affected by too much molybdenum or too little copper, he insisted that it was easily corrected with dietary changes. While the "molybdenum ball" controversy was taking place, Spalding got caught up in a government antitrust investigation and was forced to sell Rawlings.

1969 On March 13, 1969, Major League Baseball experimented with a livelier ball during a Mets-Tigers Spring Training game in Lakeland, Florida. Made by Spalding and nicknamed the 1X, this new ball was supposed to be 10 percent livelier. Commissioner Bowie Kuhn was one of several executives on hand to witness the effects. "I like the action it creates," he said. "I notice a big difference on balls that are grounded into the infield. They shoot through. There has been concern expressed for the well-being of the pitcher, but I really don't think that's a problem." Mets outfielder Ron Swoboda also noticed a difference but simply stated, "Those balls are up and away, man." The Tigers hit three home runs in the game—the Mets none—but no one knew if the ball was responsible because the wind had been blowing out to right field. Tigers starter Denny McLain, who surrendered three singles in four scoreless innings, liked the 1X. "The seams on the ball are higher than they are on the regulation ball," he told a group of reporters. "It helps a pitcher throw a better breaking ball." Two days later, the 1X was used during an Angels-Giants game in Phoenix, Arizona. Once again the teams combined for a modest total of three home runs, but according to the *New York Times,* which had covered both contests, "line drives sprayed over the fields as if shot from cannons and Gaylord Perry, the Giants pitcher, ducked every time he released the ball." Players on both teams acknowledged that the 1X was livelier. Hall of Famer Willie Mays, then in his 18th season with the Giants, said, "Baby, I hope they legalize that ball before I retire." Angels shortstop Jim Fregosi suggested that "with this ball the pitcher should have a standing appointment with his dentist." Kuhn never did authorize the 1X to be used during the regular season. Not only did he decide that it was a bit too lively, but Spalding had only made 15 dozen of the balls for the experiment; the company wouldn't have had enough time to manufacture a big enough supply by Opening Day, and Kuhn didn't want to introduce a new ball midseason. On April 10, 1969—the third day of the regular season—Mets center fielder Tommie Agee hit two home runs, including a monstrous blast that reached the cross-aisle of Shea Stadium's upper deck.[11] Because Agee, the Mets' leadoff hitter, stood just 5-foot-11 and had hit a mere five home runs the previous season, the juiced-ball debate instantly reignited. On September 29, 1969, the 1X ball was secretly used in the Mayor's Trophy Game between the Mets and Yankees at Shea Stadium. Since the game was an exhibition, albeit one that drew 30,000 fans and established bragging rights while raising money for charity, Kuhn slipped the ball into play in order to get an honest reaction from the players. The 1X was never used again—MLB instead restored the competitive balance by lowering the mound five inches after the 1968 season—but a similar ball did find its way into several minor league games. Eastern League president Tommy Richardson admitted that he'd secretly used a ball called the Five Triple X, which was supposed to be 5 percent livelier.

1970 The two leagues combined for a record 3,429 home runs. After the season, Cubs Hall of Fame manager Leo Durocher said, "The ball not only seemed smaller and lighter than the 1969 ball, but the pitchers tell me that the stitching was tighter and the seams weren't as raised."

1971 A beeping baseball was used at Fenway Park, not in an actual game, but in a demonstration during which a

---

[11] Shea Stadium, which closed after the 2008 season, had four seating levels: field, loge, mezzanine, and upper. The upper deck was so high that just a handful of foul balls reached the front-row seats behind home plate each season. According to Greg Rybarczyk, founder of the seminal home run–measuring website Hit Tracker, Agee's shot traveled 450 to 475 feet.

visually impaired 17-year-old named Bobby Verette played catch with Hall of Famer Carl Yastrzemski and swung a bat at underhanded pitches. The ball was designed by a nonprofit charitable organization called the Telephone Volunteers of America and sold for $38.

1972 Baseballs with cowhide covers were used in blind experiments during Spring Training.

1973 Oakland Athletics owner Charlie Finley briefly used orange baseballs in Spring Training. Designed to reduce the glare, the best thing they did was generate publicity for the team. Later in the season, Spalding moved part of its operations from Massachusetts to Haiti.

1974 Major League Baseball officially switched from horsehide to cowhide, and the new covers first appeared in a regular-season game in Cincinnati on April 4, 1974. The reason for the switch was simple: horsehide had become scarce and more expensive; changing to Eastern European cowhide saved each team roughly $2,000 per season. By August 1974, home runs were down 9 percent, and people began speculating. Pitchers said the new balls were easier to grip. Bill Singer, a 20-game winner for the 1973 Angels, said some balls had soft spots. Hall of Fame catcher Johnny Bench (who was known to have unusually large hands) said, "I could almost peel the cover off them. If you grip them hard enough and twist, the seams seem to give. And the dirt scuffs it easier."

1975 Spalding took the Reach name off American League baseballs. (National League balls were already stamped with "Spalding" at the time, as they had been since 1878.)

1976 Late in 1976, Rawlings took over the major league ball contract from Spalding. The new balls were wound in

Haiti, then shipped to Taiwan and stitched at a cost of 10 cents apiece.

1977 Rawlings baseballs replaced Spalding balls in both leagues, and home runs increased by a whopping 63 percent. Granted, American League expansion helped to bolster offense—there were two new teams and 162 additional games—but everyone blamed Rawlings. In May 1977, executives from both leagues wanted to have the balls tested. "If the baseball is a cause, we want to know it. We want the truth," said Bob Fishel, the assistant to American League president Lee MacPhail. Rawlings cooperated, but asked that the location of the experiments not be revealed. The company didn't want the media to make a spectacle of it and, with Major League Baseball's approval, quietly chose a midwestern university. After the tests were conducted with hundreds of unused balls from 1974 to 1977, Fishel said, "We're told by Rawlings that the baseballs this year are made exactly to the same specifications as those made by Spalding. . . . We've noticed one difference, though. The glue that is being used to coat the ball after it's wound and before it's covered with cowhide is holding them together much better. In Spring Training in '76 we had trouble with balls falling apart, the covers coming off. That's no longer the case."

1980 Around this time, major league teams were paying $3 per ball and an average of $47,500 per season. The 26 teams combined to spend more than $1.2 million.

1983 The Dodgers used approximately 16,000 balls over the course of the season: 500 during Spring Training, 10 dozen for each home game, and 6 dozen for batting practice before every road game. The Indians used 3 dozen new balls in batting practice every day and mixed them with the old ones. The Yankees, not just big spenders when it came to free agents, used 12 dozen new balls every day in BP.

1986 Haitian president Jean-Claude Duvalier was overthrown by a massive uprising, prompting Rawlings to look for a more stable country where it could relocate its ballmaking operations. The company considered China, which would have been the cheapest option, but picked Costa Rica instead because of the strong workforce there. For several years Rawlings continued manufacturing major league balls in Haiti while setting up its new factory. Meanwhile, former player and Hall of Fame announcer Tony Kubek was convinced that the balls were juiced. "I throw batting practice once in a while," he said, "and you can hear it in the way balls whistle over your head. . . . The balls are livelier. Oh, I know the baseball company will deny it." Kubek was right—that is, about the denial. "He doesn't know what he's talking about," said Rawlings president Bob Burrows. "The balls are the same, but that idiot Kubek keeps on complaining about it."

1987 A rookie named Mark McGwire hit 49 home runs, a utility man named Larry Sheets hit 31, and an uberconsistent singles machine named Wade Boggs tripled his previous career high by going yard 24 times. What was happening?! Howard Johnson, a 5-foot-11 infielder on the Mets, also tripled his career high by hitting 36 balls out of the park, and on two separate occasions he slugged such prodigious blasts that his bats were confiscated and X-rayed. Were they corked? No. So why were all these homers being hit? Was it expansion? No. The major leagues hadn't added any teams for a decade. Was it the strike zone? Possibly. Umpires *had* pretty much stopped calling anything above the belt. Was it the weather?

Maybe. According to experts who study these things, there *had* been a season-long barometric abnormality. Was it the baseball? Yes, of course, it had to be, and Yankees pitcher Tommy John offered a suggestion: "After all this Oliver North stuff is over, Congress should take a look at the ball." Congress never did get involved, but shortly after the All-Star break, both leagues arranged for the balls to be tested by the Science and Aeronautics Department at the University of Missouri–Rolla, and they eventually issued the following joint statement: "The test results indicated that the 1987 baseballs are totally within the parameters of major league standards." Bobby Bonds, then a 41-year-old coach for the Indians, swore the balls were juiced. "I've taken batting practice and I've hit those balls," he said. "I've hit the ball as far as I did when I was 25 years old. . . . I don't need tests on some machine. I go by contact." Hall of Fame manager Sparky Anderson agreed. "I know this: they are winding those babies differently," he insisted. "If this is the same ball the majors has always used, they've added some gasoline to it. I don't know who they're trying to kid." Scott Smith, a high-ranking Rawlings executive, vehemently denied the juiced-ball charges. "We take a great deal of care in manufacturing our baseballs and we do a great deal of testing and so I can say with a great deal of confidence that the baseballs are the same as they were." Case closed.

1990 Rawlings officially moved into its new factory in Costa Rica.

1993 In addition to supplying baseballs for the Major Leagues, Rawlings also provided balls for the California and Pacific Coast Leagues. This was the last season that Wilson Sporting Goods supplied balls for the rest of the minors.

1994 Rawlings moved the assembly of its low-end baseballs to China. Prior to this, the company had 1,900 employees in Costa Rica, more than half of whom stitched the cheap balls in their homes. Rawlings was supplying approximately 720,000 balls per season to the Major Leagues, a number that was considerably lower this year because of the strike-shortened schedule. During the season the number of home runs had increased dramatically, with several players on pace to break Roger Maris's single-season record. Not surprisingly, there was another juiced-ball debate. When Twins slugger Kent Hrbek was asked about it, he said, "Why are you asking me? Do my grounders to second look a little harder?"

1995 Major league teams paid $50 per dozen balls, including shipping.

1996 "Fifteen years ago," said Sparky Anderson, "if you took a new ball and rubbed it with your hands—and I'm not a guy with strong fingers—you could wrinkle the cover. You can't do that today." Anderson was asked about the ball because there was, of course, another controversy. This time, with home runs on the rise yet again, people began to wonder if Major League Baseball had secretly instructed Rawlings to make the ball livelier in order to create more home runs and help to draw fans back after the strike.

1997 Orlando Hernandez became the first player to visit the Rawlings factory in Costa Rica. He was allowed to stitch his own ball, and he proudly kept it as a memento even though it didn't turn out too well. "The boss said to me, you may be a good ballplayer, but you don't know anything about making baseballs," he said through an interpreter.

1999 In the wake of Mark McGwire's 70-homer season and the inevitable juiced-ball allegations, Rawlings and

Major League Baseball gave $400,000 to the University of Massachusetts–Lowell to open a baseball research center.

2000 There were 931 home runs hit in April 2000, a record for the season's opening month. Major League Baseball executives responded by scheduling a tour of the Rawlings factory for May 22, 2000—a visit that happened to take place one day after hitters blasted 6 grand slams and 56 homers overall. "Those weren't bad baseballs. Those were bad pitches," said Sandy Alderson, the executive vice president of operations for Major League Baseball. Alderson also said that during the tour he and his crew hadn't found anything wrong with the balls, and that MLB was considering raising the mound from 10 to 16 inches. On May 24, 2000, Bob Duffy of the *Boston Globe* wrote, "Even the bat boys seem to be on a 40-homer pace in this season of the sonic boom as baseballs dot the sky like snowflakes." Blue Jays closer Billy Koch became a key player in the juiced-ball debate, first by cutting open a ball during a game in Oakland and claiming that the core was "like a Super Ball," then by comparing it to a 1999 core with a series of drop tests in the Blue Jays' clubhouse at Sky-Dome. The newer core, on average, bounced several inches higher every time. "I saw on ESPN that they're talking about making some changes," Koch said, "like raising the mound. Why? You got a guilty conscience? If they changed the ball, why not just say they changed the ball?" Rawlings president Howard B. Keene insisted there hadn't been a change. "This place would literally have to shut down for weeks," he said, "until we figured out how to make balls that were easier to hit over the fence. Even if [Major League] baseball asked us to change something, we'd have to look at each step of our process to figure out how we could accomplish it." The baseball research center at the

University of Massachusetts–Lowell finally got involved. A group of mechanical engineers tested dozens of balls from 1999 and 2000 by firing them with a pitching machine against a piece of white ash that was mounted on a concrete wall. James Sherwood, the director of the center, reported that the 1999 ball was "marginally livelier," but according to Koch, the 2000 ball still favored the batter. He contended that the seams weren't as high, a claim that was proven to be true by Diamondbacks pitching coach Mark Connor, who stuck his hand into a bucket of balls and, without looking, could tell the difference between 1999 balls and 2000 balls every time. Another hitter-

The MLB logo on the newly redesigned ball may have favored the hitters.

friendly theory emerged about the 2000 balls: after the 1999 season, the entire logo of the baseball had been redesigned; starting in 2000, the words CUSHIONED CORK CENTER were replaced by a dark MLB logo that supposedly made it easier for batters to detect the spin on pitches.

2001 With help from a local radio station, Dennis Hilliard, the director of the crime lab at the University of Rhode Island, got five different fans to donate foul balls that they'd caught at major league games between 1963 and 2000. He and his team cut the balls open with band saws and scalpels, then dropped the cores from a height of 182 inches. The three oldest cores (from 1963, 1970, and 1989) bounced an average of 62 inches. The two newer cores (from 1995 and 2000) bounced an average of 82 inches—a 32.3 percent increase. "It's very hard to control for age," said Hilliard.[12] "Without more tests, we can't say anything conclusive." Hilliard and a group of textile scientists did make a notable discovery about the yarn inside the 2000 ball: it appeared to contain a higher percentage of synthetic fibers than the rule book allowed.[13] In other words, since the artificial wool was more durable but less resilient, Billy Koch and James Sherwood were both right: while the core from the 2000 ball that Koch bounced was livelier, the entire ball that Sherwood tested was not.

2002 In an attempt to limit the number of home runs at Coors Field, the Rockies began storing their baseballs

---

[12] Really?!

[13] The rules capped the synthetic fiber content at 18 percent. Hilliard's team gathered the shredded yarn windings and placed them in a heated bleach solution. This caused the natural woolly fibers to dissolve while leaving the synthetic fibers intact. The team then determined that the synthetic portion may have accounted for as much as 21.6 percent.

in a humidor (see chapter 8 for more). Down near sea level, a mini-juiced-ball debate broke out after Game 2 of the World Series in Anaheim. The Angels had beaten the Giants, 11–10, and the teams had combined for six home runs. In keeping with history, several players whined about the balls being too lively, and league executives denied it.

2003 Rawlings was acquired for $84 million by K2 Inc., a Los Angeles–based sporting goods manufacturer (which decided to leave the Rawlings name on the balls). Meanwhile, the hard work of the Costa Rican baseball stitchers was going somewhat unnoticed. Cubs All-Star pitcher Mark Prior thought the balls were entirely machine-made, as did most other players who were interviewed by the *Chicago Tribune*—but to be fair, the factory workers didn't know a whole lot about the Major Leagues. Yunerth Garcia, the supervisor of the stitching area, had never heard of Barry Bonds.

2004 Rawlings manufactured approximately 2.2 million major league baseballs and sold an estimated $35 million worth of baseballs overall.

2007 Universal Systems, Inc., a company based in Solon, Ohio, performed a CT scan on Mark McGwire's 70th home run ball from 1998 and declared that it was juiced. According to company president David Zavagno, there was a mysterious synthetic rubber ring around an enlarged core that helped the ball travel farther—30 feet farther, to be specific—than the balls in use when Hank Aaron retired. "Bonds' home run record," said Zavagno, "along with other home run milestones by different players of his generation, should have an asterisk next to their statistics: 'achieved with league-approved juiced baseball.' " Bob DuPuy, the president and chief operating officer of Major League Baseball, dismissed the claim. "All of our balls are subject to rigorous quality control standards and testing conducted by Rawlings," he said. "No changes have been made to the core of the ball through the entire time they have manufactured it."

2009 Not all ball-related controversies are buried beneath the stitches. After suffering a late-season 6–1 loss in Cincinnati, Cardinals manager Tony La Russa accused the Reds of providing mud-free baseballs—and accused their starter Bronson Arroyo of using pine tar to get a better grip on them.[14] Reds manager Dusty Baker didn't appreciate the accusation. "Where I come from, man, you call somebody a cheater, you better know what you're talking about," he said after being told about it by a

———

[14] This wasn't the first time that La Russa accused an opposing pitcher of using pine tar. In Game 2 of the 2006 World Series, Tigers starter Kenny Rogers was seen with a mysterious brown smudge on the palm of his hand; one inning after La Russa reported it to the umps, the smudge mysteriously vanished. But let's not be too quick to call La Russa a complainer, and let's not put all the blame on Rogers and Arroyo. There've been countless examples throughout baseball history of pitchers doctoring the ball. Bobby Mathews, a diminutive right-hander who began his professional career in the late 1860s, is believed to have invented the spitball. Tommy Bond, a curveball pioneer in the 1870s, used glycerin to add extra movement to his pitches. Red Faber and Eddie Cicotte, star pitchers for Chicago around the time of the Black Sox scandal, threw the shineball by using an oily substance that teams sprayed on the field to prevent the dirt and dust from blowing around. Lew Burdette, a two-time All-Star in the 1950s, used the sweat from his forehead and eyebrows to gain an edge. Hall of Famer Gaylord Perry, a champion spitballer from the 1960s to the 1980s, threw a "puff ball" late in his career by using powder from the rosin bag behind the mound. And so on. There have also been lots of big-name pitchers who have scuffed the ball in various ways, including Hall of Famers Whitey Ford, Don Sutton, and Phil Niekro.

reporter. La Russa, as it turned out, had made his claim based on hard evidence: he had several balls in his possession from the game that were not rubbed up. Sure enough, Reds clubhouse attendant Mike Dillon (who was in charge of rubbing mud on the balls) acknowledged that something was fishy, although he personally denied responsibility. "That is all just stupid," insisted Baker. "Nothing went on. News to me. I don't believe in cheating."

2010 Rawlings sold major league baseballs through its website for $18.99 apiece.[15]

2011 The idea of using one baseball for an entire game seems insane. Today the average life span of a major league ball is less than six pitches—kind of funny considering the balls are better than ever and could last a whole lot longer.

---

[15] Plus $6.99 for shipping and handling.

CHAPTER 7

THE RAWLINGS METHOD

(DE)CONSTRUCTING THE BALL

It's hard to take apart a baseball. The cover is perfectly smooth. The stitches are deceptively tight. There's nothing to grab on to, no easy way to get inside. You need tools—sharp tools—and a whole lot of patience. Nail clippers work best, at least at the start. You basically have to pick at one of the stitches until it starts to loosen and fray. This is the toughest part. It might take a minute or two, especially if you take extra care not to damage the cover, and then you'll have to repeat the process a few more times, cutting each stitch as you go. Eventually, you'll be able to wedge the tip of the clipper's nail file underneath the seam. Wiggle it around. Twist it back and forth. Pry up the cover. Try to peel it back and poke a fingertip inside. The ball will put up a good fight—the stitches will cling to the cover like weeds grip the earth—but you can beat it. Continue cutting the stitches—or better yet, simply undo them by pulling the thread out through the tiny holes.

Once you remove the cover, you'll have a rock-hard ball

Dismantling a baseball is much harder than you'd think.

of thin, white string. It kind of looks like dental floss, but feels much softer. Find the end and start unraveling it. Keep going. And going. And going. And then keep going some more. There's an unbelievable amount of string and yarn inside each ball—so much, in fact, that for a moment, you might think it'll never end.

Like a layer of vanilla ice cream giving way to a scoop of chocolate underneath, a darker color will emerge as you work your way deeper toward the core of the ball. Gray yarn—that's what it is. It's much thicker and coarser than the white string, so don't bother saving it. It won't make a good scarf. The same is true for the tan yarn underneath it, as well as the even thicker gray yarn underneath that.

Finally, after unraveling all four layers, you'll be left with a hard, reddish rubber sphere that's slightly smaller than a ping-pong ball. Hold it tight (ideally in a vise or with an adjustable wrench) and carefully cut it open. There are two thin layers of rubber—one red, one black—surrounding an even smaller black ball made of something that vaguely resembles cork. This is your "cushioned cork center."

To say that major league baseballs are "made" in Costa Rica isn't entirely true. The fact is that all the materials—the cork, rubber, yarn, stitches, and cowhide—get shipped to the Rawlings factory from North America.[1] It's more accurate, therefore, to say that baseballs are "assembled" in Costa Rica. Here's a closer look at each part of the manufacturing process.

THE PILL

The red rubber sphere, officially known as "the pill," is made by a company called Hultec in San José, Costa Rica. Hultec gets the rubber from Goodyear. Goodyear gets it from Indonesia. And like all the other materials inside the ball, there's a specific amount that gets used. The red layer measures $\frac{1}{10}$ of an inch thick, and the black layer underneath it measures 0.15 inches—that much we know, but its composition remains a mystery. During the process in which the rubber gets melted, Hultec adds a bunch of secret powders and other ingredients.

The tiny dark gray ball at the very center of the pill, aka "the pellet," consists of rubber and finely granulated cork. These two materials are compressed into a sphere that

---

[1] That's why Rawlings removed the words COSTA RICA from the ball in the early 1990s; import-export rules didn't require it.

The four pieces inside the pill

measures $^{13}/_{16}$ of an inch in diameter. Hultec gets the cork from a company called Maryland Cork, which imports it from Portugal. The inside of the pill consists of four separate pieces that get assembled by hand.

In addition to the pellet, the black layer is made of two halves, and there's a thin, red rubber ring that looks like a washer. The pellet is placed into one of the halves, the ring fits snugly around it, and the other half is placed on top to encapsulate it. This entire four-piece unit then gets put into a cooker of sorts that molds the outer red layer around it. That's your pill—and Hultec, on average, trucks more than 40,000 of them per week to the Rawlings factory in nearby Turrialba.

MISSION: IMPOSSIBLE

It's not easy to find the Rawlings factory, and it's even harder to get inside. For starters, it's a two-hour drive from

San José, beginning on a major highway and ending up in what might feel like the middle of nowhere. The smaller roads, paved but often unmarked, snake past mountainous farmland and unfenced livestock. GPS devices? Not all that helpful. The factory does not have an official street address; its location is known simply as "behind the Rafael Camacho Stadium."

If you're lucky enough to find the factory, you'll have to settle for photographing it through a barbed wire fence. The place is guarded 24 hours a day, and it's absolutely, positively, definitely not open to the public. It's not even open to the media, for the most part, and the entrance is so secure that high-ranking Rawlings executives visiting from the United States must present their passports just to enter the parking lot.

The one-story factory—78,016-square feet in all— looks rather ordinary from the outside. It's an off-white

Outside the Rawlings baseball factory in Turrialba, Costa Rica

building. There are several large Rawlings logos on the wall. There are also a few palm trees scattered about. So why all the fuss? It's because Rawlings has an exclusive (yet temporary) contract to supply the official major league baseball. That's the only type of ball made at the factory in Costa Rica, and some of the manufacturing techniques are top secret.

THE WINDING ROOM

There's one room in the factory that's completely off-limits to photographers—a place so restricted that most visitors don't even get to see it. It's called the winding room, and as the name suggests, it's where the yarn (which comes from Rhode Island) and thread (which comes from Canada) get wound around the pill.

The room isn't huge, at least in terms of what you might expect inside a factory that churns out more than 8,000 balls per day. Nevertheless, it's big enough for several dozen employees and a two-day supply of yarn, stacked in spools around the edges on metal shelves from floor to ceiling. Because it doubles as a storage unit, the room is kept at 70 degrees Fahrenheit with a relative humidity of 50 percent.

"If this room was not air-conditioned, a hot day would dry the yarn and a rainy day would moisten it," said factory manager Alejandro Cotter. "Costa Rica is a tropical country, so we want to make sure the weather does not influence the ball."

The main attraction of the winding room is the machinery—48 individual winding machines that were built by Rawlings engineers and therefore don't exist anywhere else in the world. The machines are arranged in groups of six—two for the inner layer, one for each of the middle layers, and two more for the outer layer of the "center." That's what the ball is called during this phase of the manufacturing process. The room essentially has eight work stations (though one remains unused as a backup); each station has six machines, and every two machines are operated by one employee.

It's noisy inside the winding room, a constant whirring and hissing of mechanical parts. Many employees wear protective headphones, and some also use surgical masks to guard against the faint smell of fumes. The fumes come from the pills, which are coated with a latex adhesive in order to help the first layer of yarn stick.

Here comes the really cool part.

At each work station, the employee at the first machine wraps the end of the yarn around the pill and places it on a tiny platform with a narrow opening at the back. Then, with the push of a button, the pill twirls furiously as the machine pulls yarn all around it from a spool below. Within seconds, the pill gets covered with a one-inch-thick layer of four-ply gray yarn, and the machine shuts itself off automatically.[2] The employee then cuts the yarn, weighs the center on a digital scale, and measures its circumference with a thin, metal tape ruler.

Each phase of the winding process has its own specifications, and the parameters are astonishingly small. After the

---

[2] The exact measurement of each layer is proprietary, but it all adds up to 330 yards' worth of yarn and thread. The innermost layer measures roughly 220 feet. After that, there's approximately 65 feet of three-ply tan yarn followed by 150 feet of three-ply gray yarn and 555 feet of white poly/cotton thread.

Cross section of a major league baseball

first layer, the weight of the center must not vary more than
.02 ounces. In case you're bad at math, that's $\frac{1}{50}$ of an
ounce, and the specs get even tighter from there; after each
of the outer three layers, the margin of error shrinks to $\frac{1}{100}$
of an ounce. Meanwhile, the circumference of the first two
layers can vary as much as $\frac{1}{2}$ of an inch, and the outer two
layers have a slightly bigger target at $\frac{1}{16}$ of an inch.

The measurements aren't always perfect right away, but
that's not a problem. If, after any of the four winding
phases, the center weighs a fraction of an ounce too much,
the employee snips a tiny piece of yarn off the end and puts
the ball back on the scale. This is actually a common

occurrence, so by the end the day, each employee is left with a bucket of useless yarn clippings.

Then there's the issue of yarn tension.

"If you wind something at zero tension, it's gonna feel like a sponge," said Cotter. "If you wind something very tight, it's gonna be rock solid, so we want to get between those two and be as consistent as possible."

Therefore, each work station has a computerized Tension Meter that monitors the force with which the yarn and thread get pulled from the spools. It's basically a small black box with four digital displays. The meter is programmed to shut down the machines if the tension—measured in grams—slips outside the parameters, but that hardly ever happens.

Finally, there's an inspector who brings his own scale and tape measure into the room once a day. He randomly selects a center from each machine and charts the measurements. Then, after the data is processed, the employees receive personalized graphs with the results so they can see how they're doing.

THE COWHIDE

Let's get something straight: cows are not killed to make baseballs. They're killed because people like to eat them, so don't accuse MLB of animal cruelty. One of the many by-products that comes from cows just happens to be the hide, and there's a company called Tennessee Tanning that prepares it exclusively for Rawlings.

Tanning an animal hide is a complex process. There's bacteria to be killed, fat and muscle tissue to be scraped off, and hair to be removed as well. The hide gets cured and soaked with a whole lot of chemicals, and in Raw-lings's case, it has to be whitened with a potent aluminum-sulfate compound. It also has to be cut horizontally (like a bagel would be sliced) in order to achieve the proper thickness. MLB's specs require the cowhide to measure between .046 and .056 inches—a differential of $\frac{1}{100}$ of an inch—and only the outer part gets used on the balls.

By the time the cowhide arrives in Costa Rica, it doesn't even look like cowhide. It comes in bed-sized sheets of dry-ish white leather, often bearing imperfections that make certain areas unusable. There are wrinkles, stretch marks, rough patches, and sometimes more specific flaws; if a cow bumps into a barbed wire fence or gets bitten by a tick, the hide will have a blemish that must be avoided. Employees carefully work around these spots with two pieces of equipment. The first is a small hydraulic press that hovers two inches above a sturdy countertop. The second is kind of like a figure-eight-shaped cookie cutter with 108 prongs around the inner edge.

At each of the five work stations, an employee places the cutter on the hide, presses a couple buttons to lower the press—and that's it. The result is a perfectly formed figure-eight piece of cowhide with 108 stitch holes conveniently punched in place.[3]

The soon-to-be baseball covers are then weighed and manually stamped with a six-letter code. Cut open any ball

---

[3] Speaking of numbers, it takes about five square feet of cowhide to make a dozen balls. Each sheet of hide represents half a Holstein cow—that's the breed that gets used—and yields about 25 square feet of leather. To make a year's worth of major league baseballs, it takes about one million square feet of cowhide (roughly 35 percent of which ends up getting scrapped) or roughly 20,000 cows.

A small strip of cowhide beside the hydraulic press; note the figure-eight-shaped cutouts.

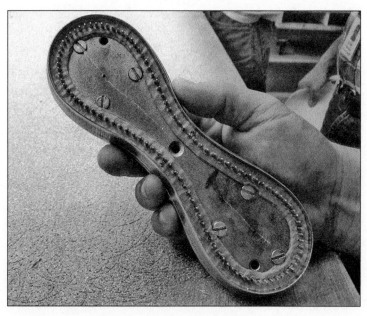

The tool that cuts the figure-eight pieces from the cowhide; note the 108 prongs around the edge.

and you'll see it. It's Rawlings's secret method of tracking the date and leather batch in case there were ever a problem. The covers are also measured for thickness—there's a machine that can shave them slightly thinner if necessary—and fed through small metallic rollers that apply an adhesive on the underside. This helps the leather stick to the center of the ball. Finally, in order to make the cowhide more pliable during the stitching process, the covers get rolled up in damp towels and stored in coolers.

THE STITCHING PROCESS

You would not believe how hard it is to stitch a baseball, so consider this: it's so hard that machines can't even do it. The thread can tear or get tangled. The cowhide can get scratched or smudged. The sewing needles can break or stab you if you're not careful. And even without these mishaps, there's the challenge of getting the first stitch started—and then hiding the last one from sight. For a new trainee, it can take an hour to stitch a ball that won't ever leave the factory; for experienced employees, it takes about 14 minutes, and even then there's no guarantee that it'll pass the first inspection.

The stitching room is huge, about as big as a large gymnasium. It has to be, because 350 people work there—actually a bit more if you count the supervisors and inspectors and material handlers. The room has a slanted tin roof that measures 23 feet high at its peak. There are low-hanging fluorescent lights and dozens of industrial-strength fans mounted above the work area on exposed metal beams.

It's a raw space with a no-nonsense atmosphere and

The stitching room

pleasant conditions. There's no dress code. The stitchers are allowed to wear headphones and listen to music. And because the stitching process is strenuous, the factory employs a full-time safety and health engineer who guides the workers through a stretching program every morning.

"Every person also gets their chair modified according to their size and build," said Cotter. "You'll see some that are different heights. It's because that person is different."

The chairs are arranged classroom-style in 14 rows of 25. Each one has a small desk attached to the front, along with a vise that clamps the ball in place. To get the first stitch started, the needles get poked through the center and pulled up through the first two stitch holes in order to anchor the cover. The strenuous part has to do with making the stitches tight; with one needle in each hand, the stitcher yanks his (or her!) arms back like a butterfly opening its wings, except the motion is much more violent. It's almost as if he's trying to smack two people who are peeking over his shoulders. And then he does it 107 more times, pausing every so often to rub the thread with a small block of wax so it won't slacken and get tangled.

The last stitch is executed much like the first. With help from a pair of pliers, the needles get pushed through the center and tugged back out through the seam. It might sound easy, but this maneuver requires great precision. Don't forget how narrow the seam is. It's really just a hairline gap between the two pieces of leather, so if the stitcher's aim were even 1/16 of an inch off, the tip of the needle would puncture the cover and render the entire ball worthless.

This happens on occasion. Roughly half of 1 percent of all the balls get scrapped for various reasons, and that's okay. Rawlings understands that human error is part of the process, and yet the company still strives for perfection. That's why there are so many quality control checks—and why the most talented stitchers get rewarded.

"The more you make, the more you get paid," said Cotter. "That's how we motivate them."

In addition to their base salary (which is slightly above the minimum wage), the stitchers earn per-ball bonuses if they complete more than 160 within a single week. Those who reach the 175-ball plateau can stop work for the week and still get paid as if they were there—or they can keep stitching and continue to earn bonuses for as many as 200 balls. Every week, approximately 30 percent of the stitchers make it that far, at which point they get sent home with full paychecks.

Quality, of course, is more important than quantity; once a ball is completed, it has to pass three different visual inspections, starting with a quick glance in the stitching room.

The 350 stitchers are grouped into seven teams of 50. Each team has a material handler (who provides the centers and covers) and an inspector (who constantly roams the floor). Whenever a stitcher completes a ball, he places it in a plastic bag hanging from the side of his desk. After a bunch of balls have accumulated, the inspector collects them. If a ball has a defect that can easily be fixed, he'll hand it back to the stitcher. If a ball looks good, he'll stamp it with invisible ink, toss it in a barrel, and punch a ticket to track the stitcher's productivity.

FINISHING TOUCHES

Don't let the title of this section fool you. The balls still have a long way to go, and it starts in a small room called "the racks." As soon as the balls are brought in from the stitching room, they get dumped onto a dropcloth covering a wooden table with raised edges. Two inspectors then carefully examine every single ball for these six correctable flaws:

1. **Beginning and End Stitches** If they're visible, that's a problem.
2. **Misaligned Stitch** Every double-stitch must meet in the middle to form a perfect *V* shape.
3. **Borders** The two cowhide pieces can't overlap or have too much space between them.
4. **Loose Stitch** Every stitch must be pulled tight (but not too tight because that causes other problems).

5. **Incorrect Method** For every stitch, the left-hand needle must be poked through the hole first, followed by the right-hand needle.

6. **Straight Stitch** The stitches must form *V*s, not straight lines across the seam.

The inspectors have six rolls of stickers hanging above their table, each with a different number that corresponds to the six flaws. Whenever they spot a flaw, they place the appropriate sticker beside it and send the ball to the nearby black light station. Remember the invisible ink? Every stitcher has a stamp with a personalized code. That's how the stitching room inspectors mark the balls, and yes, the ink only appears in ultraviolet light.

The black light worker writes the codes on Post-it notes with regular ink and then, with the notes attached, sends the defective balls back for repair.

Now, it doesn't happen often, but the tip of a sewing needle can break off and get lodged beneath the cover. Therefore, the balls that don't have flaws get passed through a metal detector before being sent to the rolling machine—a clunky yet effective device that sits in a glass case in the corner of the room. Its purpose is simple: make the stitches uniform by pressing them flat. The machine has a solid metal wheel, roughly three feet wide and three inches thick, that spins flat like a frisbee above a wooden platform. The platform has a track, just wide enough for a baseball, that spirals inward toward a hole in the center. In order for the machine to do its thing, an employee needs to feed the balls into it. The balls then get rolled around under 40 pounds of pressure, and after half a minute, they reach the center hole and drop into a plastic crate.

At this point, the cowhide is still damp so the balls get

Inspectors at work inside "the racks"

loaded onto metal racks (hence, the name of the room) to dry overnight.

Each rack is a floor-to-ceiling unit with 120 gutterlike rows. Each row is long enough to hold 40 balls. And since there are six racks, there's way more than enough space for the factory's daily output.

Once the balls have dried, they get rolled again and sent to another room for the final inspection. Symmetry, stitch alignment, roundness, color, stains, scars, and even faint traces of insect bites on the cowhide—that's what the inspectors look for. They also weigh and measure the balls and wipe them with a cleaning solvent to remove any excess wax or oil. (In some cases, the solvent removes the invisible ink as well, so if you examine your own baseballs under a black light and some don't have the secret code, that's why.) Finally, the inspectors sort the balls into three categories based solely on their appearance; the balls that make it this far are all within the specs for weight and circumference, so it's just the minuscule cosmetic defects that determine where they end up. Perfect balls are approved for game use, while those that are ever-so-slightly off will end up in one of two places. They'll either be designated as practice balls and offered to teams at a discount, or they'll get sold commercially in retail stores.

Next stop: the stamping machines. Two of them sit just across the room from the inspectors, and they look rather intense. There are plastic tubes, metal cylinders, and colorful switches and buttons and warning lights. It's like a maze of robotic parts—a mad scientist's dream—but the actual stamping process is fairly simple. Each machine has three rubber heads positioned above three different ink plates, and each plate is embossed with a different portion of the logo. (The top portion says "Rawlings," the one in the middle features the commissioner's signature, and the bottom section has the MLB silhouette.) Just below the plates sits a cup-shaped holder. An employee has to place a ball there every two seconds. That's how long it takes for each automated stamping cycle. The heads get lowered to the plates simultaneously. Then they come back up for a split second before going back down to the stamp the ball. Then they come back up. Then they touch the plates. Then they come back up. Then they stamp the ball. Then the plates. Then the ball. Plates. Ball. Plates. Ball. Get the picture? The machine is programmed to operate at that pace, so the challenge lies in keeping up with it and positioning the balls just right. If the employee doesn't place a ball in time, it's no big deal. The stamping heads will simply come down and whiff, and the cycle proceeds uninterrupted. Meanwhile, a second employee removes the freshly stamped balls and places them on a conveyor belt that passes through a heated area. Thirty seconds and 200 degrees Fahrenheit later, the ink is dry.

The balls are pretty much done after this. All that remains is a grueling two-part testing process in the factory's quality lab. First, a compression machine tests the hardness of a random sample of balls by measuring how much weight it takes to squash them ¼ of an inch. Second, a pitching machine fires a different batch of balls 85 feet per second against a wall of northern white ash—the same type of wood that most bats are made of. The balls must bounce back at 54.6 percent of the original velocity, plus or minus 3.2 percent. In fancy terms, the rebound speed is known as the "coefficient of restitution" or COR, the key factor in determining how lively the balls are. As a backup, Rawlings conducts these same two tests at a facility in St. Louis, Missouri, as does Major League Baseball at its research center in Lowell, Massachusetts.

But before the baseballs reach the States, they have to be packaged. This takes place at a long table near the stamping machines. Retail balls are placed in individual plastic cubes, while team balls get wrapped in tissue paper and boxed by the dozen. Then they're ready to be shipped. From the factory, the balls are trucked to Limón, a province on the eastern coast of Costa Rica. From there they go by boat to Port Everglades, Florida, and by rail to the Rawlings distribution center in Washington, Missouri. After that, it's just a matter of sending them to teams and stores. On average, a major league baseball will make its way into a game two to three months after leaving the factory.

COMMEMORATIVE BALLS

Snag a ball at one of Major League Baseball's premier events and you'll notice something different about your souvenir: the logo has an artistic flair. Balls from the All-Star Game, Home Run Derby, and World Series—even from regular-season games that take place at first-year stadiums—all have special commemorative designs in place of the standard MLB logo. Howard Smith, the senior vice president of licensing at Major League Baseball, oversees the design process and granted an exclusive interview for this book:

Who designs the commemorative logos?

"Major League Baseball has an in-house design department that works with the particular Club to design the ball, with input coming from Rawlings as well."

How does the process work?

"Once a specific design is approved, Major League Baseball will work with the Club to decide when and where the baseball will be used. Some baseballs are used on-field during each of a Club's 81 regular-season home games, while others will appear as a ceremonial first pitch."

Are some teams more proactive?

"I don't think it's really a question of being proactive. Each Club might just have different ideas of exactly how they wish to celebrate these events or achievements. For example, one Club might choose a commemorative baseball while another goes the route of an on-field ceremony."

How far in advance do you start planning the logos?

"It's never too early to start planning for a given year, but we do require that the Clubs submit an approved logo prior to the start of Spring Training."

Can a team approach you with a logo idea at any point?

"On-field baseballs are set for the year prior to the start of each season, but we will work with our Clubs to accommodate requests for ceremonial first-pitch baseballs within a given season."

Are there any rules about the logos themselves?

"You'll notice that any special ball must have a Club mark or a silhouetted batter mark. Additionally, the third panel is always the location for the event logo."

Is there a size restriction?

"There isn't a specific size restriction per se, but we are always conscious of the way in which the logo shows up on the ball and whether or not that logo would make the ball more or less visible to batters."

Does it cost extra to make commemorative balls?

"No."

How come the World Series logo stayed the same for so many years and then started changing every season?

"We heard from our fans that they wanted the logos refreshed each year, and we obliged."

Although commemorative balls are highly coveted among collectors, casual fans often aren't aware that they exist. Whether or not you fit into either category, here are some photos of balls that you may never have seen:

*First commemorative
ball ever (This one
was stamped
with red ink.)*

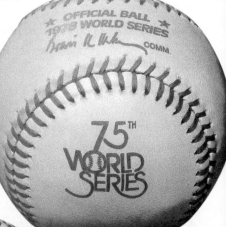

*First
commemorative
All-Star Game
ball—Seattle
hosted; note the
tiny Mariners
logo.*

*First commemorative
regular-season ball,
used at Comiskey
throughout the season*

First All-Star ball with multicolored stitches—orange and blue for the Padres, who hosted

First game-used ball with a commemorative logo recognizing an individual player

First commemorative ball for a regular-season series outside the United States and Canada

ANNIVERSARIES

Jackie Robinson, the first black player in the modern era, debuted on April 15, 1947.

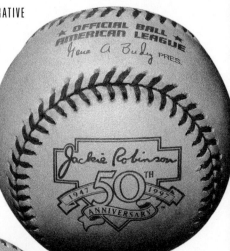

Hank Aaron became the all-time home run leader with blast number 715 on April 8, 1974.

The American League became a major league in 1901.

ANNIVERSARIES

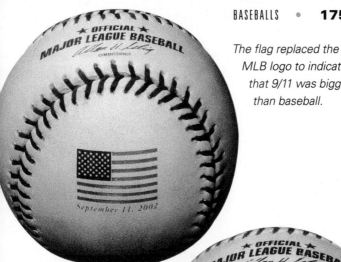

The flag replaced the MLB logo to indicate that 9/11 was bigger than baseball.

The Yankees were known as the Highlanders when they moved to New York in 1903.

Many commemorative balls never see game action—like this one, made for Larsen's perfecto.

Joe DiMaggio Day took place on September 27, 1998. (This ball has navy blue stitches.)

Exactly one year after the Yankees honored DiMaggio, Tiger Stadium saw its last game.

Simple and gorgeous. The stars are on a blue background; the stripes are red and white.

MLB has used several different Opening Day logos since 2000. This was one of them.

SkyDome's name change warranted this, the last red-stamped ball.

Exhibition games don't count; the new Busch Stadium opened for real on April 10, 2006.

POSTSEASON

The World Series logo switched back and forth from red to blue from 1978 to 1999.

Commissioner Bart Giamatti died before the '89 Series, but his name was left on the balls.

From 1996 to 1999, the first two rounds of the playoffs each had their own baseballs.

The 1999 ALCS featured the last American League ball that was ever used.

World Series balls started being stamped with gold logos in 2000.

The words FALL CLASSIC first appeared on the 2009 World Series ball.

INTERNATIONAL

MLB played Spring Training games in Mexico, Venezuela, and the Dominican Republic.

In 2003 and 2004, the Expos played a total of 44 "home" games in Puerto Rico.

American All-Stars took on Japanese All-Stars biennially from 1986 to 2006.

MLB's first trip to China featured two Spring Training games between the Padres and Dodgers.

The WBC logo isn't terribly exciting, but the gold stamping makes up for it.

More Asia. More Spring Training. This time the Dodgers faced a professional Chinese team.

MISCELLANEOUS

Enron Field?! This silver-stamped ball should be ashamed of itself.

Red stamping. Red and navy blue stitches. And so much ink that the hitters may have had an edge.

U2 won five awards at the '06 Grammys; John Legend, Mariah Carey, and Kanye West each won three.

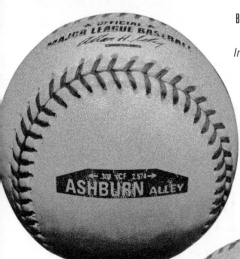

In 2006 the Phillies used these balls during BP to honor Hall of Famer Richie Ashburn.

The Home Run Derby logo changes every season. This was the one used at AT&T Park in 2007.

2K Sports, a partner of MLB, was allowed to advertise on these BP-only balls.

CHAPTER 8

STORAGE, PREPARATION, AND USAGE

STRIVING FOR UNIFORMITY

Let's go back to 1965 for a moment, to the five-game series at Comiskey Park when the Tigers accused the White Sox of using frozen baseballs. Even though this wacky incident was never settled, it served an important purpose: for the first time ever, people suggested that balls be stored under uniform temperature and humidity. It was a great idea. The only problem was that no one did anything about it.

Four years later, when Commissioner Bowie Kuhn experimented with the lively 1X ball, he considered implementing rules about how the ball should bounce and how it should be stored. "I see no reason," he said, "why we can't come up with accurate measurements on how a ball should behave." Kuhn's statement inspired several independent studies, which revealed that the amount of moisture absorbed by the wool in the core could affect the ball's performance by 10 percent. It was known then—in the summer of 1969—that the dryer a ball becomes, the farther it travels.

Fast-forward to 1993. Major League Baseball expanded from 26 to 28 teams and awarded franchises to Florida (where it's very humid) and Colorado (where it's particularly dry). The Marlins finished the season dead last in home runs; everyone blamed the team's lack of talent and its sizable stadium. Two years later the Rockies moved to Coors Field and led the National League in homers; everyone blamed the mile-high elevation and the thin air. The Rockies led the league in home runs again in 1996. And again in 1997. Scientists proved that because the air was 15 percent less dense one mile above sea level, the ball traveled 9 percent farther; what would've been a lazy, 370-foot fly-out in most other stadiums was a 403-foot home run at Coors Field. In 1999 baseball in Denver officially became a joke. Not only did the Rockies lead the league in long balls, but they and their opponents combined to hit 303 homers at the stadium—a single-season record for one venue. Free-agent pitchers were reluctant to sign with the Rockies. The team couldn't compete. The franchise was losing money and fans. Something *had* to be done—but no one could think of a solution and the trend continued. In 2001 there were 268 home runs hit at Coors, the most at any ballpark that year.

Eventually, finally, thankfully, during the winter before the 2002 season, a happy coincidence involving a Rockies employee changed everything. Tony Cowell, a member of the team's engineering department, was getting ready to go elk hunting when he discovered that his leather boots had dried up and shriveled over the summer—and it occurred to him that the same thing might've been happening to the cowhide covers on baseballs. The Rockies investigated his hunch and learned that some of their balls weighed as little as 4.6 ounces and measured just 8.5 inches in circumference—way below specifications. By Opening Day the team had begun to store its balls in a room-sized humidor—and it worked!

Sort of.

Coors Field remained hitter-friendly because of the thin air—curveballs still had 25 percent less bite, and hitters were still able to whip their bats through the strike zone quicker—but offense did subside.[1] That's because the balls were successfully deadened, the covers were no longer slick, pitchers regained their command, and teams stopped trying to outslug each other. Denver had real baseball at last. The Rockies could compete, and in 2007 they charged into the playoffs and reached the World Series for the first time in franchise history.

"I just don't think it's the home run park that it used to be," said Rockies first baseman Todd Helton during the Series. "The ball just doesn't jump out of there like it used to. The humidor obviously played a huge part in that."

Measuring nine feet by nine feet, the humidor resembles a walk-in refrigerator except for the balmy conditions: 70 degrees with 50 percent humidity. Some people have referred to it as a "glorified beer cooler," but technically it's called an "environmental chamber." There's an insulated door at one end, an aisle that runs down the middle, and metal shelves from floor to ceiling on either side. These

---

[1] In the first seven seasons at Coors Field (1995–2001), the Rockies and their opponents combined to score 13.8 runs per game. In the first seven seasons after the humidor was installed (2002–2008), that number dropped to 11.4.

A peek inside the Rockies' humidor

shelves can hold up to 500 dozen baseballs, which are dated and rotated so that the older ones get used first.

In February 2007 the folks at the commissioner's office realized that teams in other cities might also be affected by humidity—so they sent out a leaguewide memo, instructing all 30 teams to start storing their baseballs under uniform conditions.

"We're not going to have humidors everyplace," said Joe Garagiola Jr., the senior vice president of Major League Baseball, "but every place will be temperature-controlled, and so I think there will be a very high degree of uniformity."

Yeah, so much for that.

Three years later, in a crucial late-season game at Coors

Field, Giants ace Tim Lincecum was caught on camera mouthing an expletive along with the words "juiced ball." Never mind what may or may not have been taking place at the other 29 stadiums; rumor had it that the Rockies were secretly using two sets of game balls—one set that had been stored in the humidor and (in order to jump-start their own offense) another that hadn't. The Giants complained to the commissioner's office, prompting numerous denials from the Rockies.

"The integrity of the manager and coaching staff would prevent that," said Kevin Kahn, the team's vice president of ballpark operations.

"I don't know a thing about it. I can't even tell you where the hell the humidor room really is," claimed Rockies manager Jim Tracy. "Since I was asked to manage this club nobody's asked me to approve any baseballs, nobody's asked me to rub any of them up, nobody's asked me if these have been in the humidor. It's absolutely none of my business."

Major League Baseball responded by making it the umpires' business. The following day, the umps were instructed to monitor the process through which the Rockies stored their balls and delivered them to the dugout. Crew chief John Hirschbeck didn't see anything amiss—and that was the end of it.

LENA BLACKBURNE RUBBING MUD

It looks like chocolate pudding, sells for $33 a pound, and gets rubbed on every single game-used ball throughout the major and minor leagues. We're talking about baseball's "magic mud," specifically a brand called Lena Blackburne

Rubbing Mud, which is such a big part of the sport that it was permanently enshrined in the Hall of Fame in 1969. And yet despite all its fanfare, the story behind the mud is a mystery to most fans.

Brand-new baseballs, of course, aren't fit for game use. The covers are too slick and too white, presenting not enough grip for the pitchers and too much glare for the batters. It wasn't a problem in the old days when one ball would last an entire game, but following Ray Chapman's death in 1920 and the subsequent effort to keep new balls in play, everyone looked for a solution. Players and umpires spent the next 18 years rubbing everything on the balls from tobacco juice (too sticky) to shoe polish (too greasy) to a combination of infield dirt and water (too scratchy). In 1938 an ump complained to Athletics third base coach Russell Aubrey "Lena" Blackburne about the condition of the balls.[2] Blackburne, a former utility infielder, decided to do something about it and later discovered that the mud along a tributary of the Delaware River near his home in Palmyra, New Jersey, was the remedy. The stuff worked so well that the Athletics started using it, and by the following season he was supplying it to every team in the American League. Blackburne, having spent most of his playing days with the White Sox, was such a big fan of the American League that he refused to sell his mud to the National League until the mid-1950s. What kept him in business, other than the fact that his mud effectively removed the sheen without scuffing the horsehide or making the ball too dark, was that no one else

---

[2] "Lena" is a derivative of "Lean," Blackburne's original nickname because he weighed just 160 pounds.

When the baseballs got too slick, Lena Blackburne took matters (and mud) into his own hands.

knew where to find it or how to replicate it. The exact location where he dug it up was top secret, as were the ingredients that he added to it.

Blackburne died in 1968 and left the business to a boyhood friend named John Haas. Haas then passed it along to his son-in-law, Burns Bintliff, who turned it over to his own son Jim in 2001. It's not a huge business—Jim makes less than $25,000 a year from it and works nights at a printing press to support his family—yet the secret location is still fiercely guarded. The younger Bintliff claims he was married and had two kids before he revealed it to his wife.

Bintliff used to go by boat to collect the mud. Now he takes his truck through the woods to the secret spot, and when the tide is low, he's able to trudge out into the mucky marshland, skim off the top layer of mud with a shovel, and dump it into five-gallon buckets. Although Bintliff takes the mud from public land that's governed by the Delaware River Basin Commission, he's never gotten into any kind of legal trouble.

"If anybody happens to catch me in the act of harvesting mud," he said, "I come up with a story to give them a reason I'm putting mud in a bucket. I've told people I use it

Lena Blackburne originally shipped the mud in old coffee cans; Jim Bintliff now packs it in plastic containers.

in my garden, I use it for my rosebushes, I use it for bee stings and poison ivy and any kind of story."

Bintliff gathers 1,000 pounds of mud every summer and pours it though a sifter in his backyard. Then he adds the secret ingredients, stores the finished product in 40-gallon trash cans over the winter, and ships two 32-ounce containers to each team the following season. That's it. The stuff is used sparingly and lasts awhile.

According to geological studies (including one by Princeton University and another by the Army Corps of Engineers), 90 percent of the mud is made of finely ground quartz, probably pulverized by the glacier that covered New Jersey more than 10,000 years ago. As for the other 10 percent? Don't ask. Only a handful of people know exactly what's in it, and Bintliff has no intention of selling out the business.

"I just love being part of the sport," he said. "I sit down to watch a game, and it's nice to know that it's my mud on those baseballs."

EQUIPMENT MANAGERS

On May 26, 2004, *Boston Herald* writer Steve Buckley tracked every baseball during the Red Sox game at Fenway

Park. Of the 94 balls that were used, one lasted as long as 11 pitches, 26 were gone after just one pitch, and two (which were thrown in the dirt by pitchers warming up) never even saw game action. Twenty-two balls were tossed into the crowd by players and coaches; 27 were given away by batboys and ballgirls. The final ball lasted one pitch and earned a save for Boston's Keith Foulke, who kept the ball and later said he planned to give it away.

Using 94 balls in one game might seem excessive, especially when compared to the mere handful of balls that lasted for an entire game 100 years earlier, but nowadays it's typical. Do you know who's responsible for rubbing mud onto all these baseballs? Major league umpires used to handle the task until the mid-1980s, but the job now belongs to teams' equipment managers or other clubhouse personnel.

Dan O'Rourke, the equipment manager for the Phillies, rubs up four "cases" of balls for every three games that the team plays at home. How many balls are in a case? Six dozen . . . which means . . . let's do some math here . . . 6 dozen times 4 equals 24 dozen . . . divided by 3 equals 8 dozen balls per game. That's 96 balls—right in line with what the *Boston Herald* reported—and O'Rourke will rub even more if the weather's crappy or if a game goes into extra innings. More math: 96 balls multiplied by 81 home games equals 7,776 balls. That's a lot of rubbing, and wait, there's more. Every team plays at least 15 home games during Spring Training—add 1,440 more balls that need to be rubbed up—and don't forget about the postseason, which can add an extra 1,000 for teams that last deep into October. Playoffs aside, the average team needs at least 9,000 balls per season to be rubbed up; multiply that by 30 teams and we're talking about 270,000 game balls per season throughout the Major Leagues. Last bit of math: 64 ounces of mud divided by 9,000 balls per team equals—get ready for it—$\frac{7}{1000}$ of an ounce of mud per ball. In other words, imagine a U.S. penny cut into 10 pieces. Take one of those pieces. *That's* how much mud we're dealing with.

Even with that small amount, there's still room for controversy. Pitchers prefer darker baseballs; the more mud that gets used, the harder it becomes for batters to pick up the seams—to differentiate between the cowhide and the red stitching. Hitters, on the other hand, like it when the balls are lighter (but not too light!) because the seams help them to detect the spin. Equipment managers, therefore, have to use just the right amount of mud in order to keep everyone happy, including the umpires.

When O'Rourke first began rubbing in 1990, he was working for the Astros and got schooled by a legendary ump whose nickname was "God." Doug Harvey, working his 29th year in the National League, didn't think O'Rourke's baseballs were dark enough, so he dumped an entire bag of them onto the Astrodome floor and, with the help of some tobacco juice, showed him how to do it. O'Rourke took Harvey's advice and made the balls much darker the next day when Jerry Crawford, another long-tenured ump, was working the plate. O'Rourke said:

We were playin' the Reds at the time, and Crawford tells me later how it happened. Barry Larkin's the first hitter. After the first pitch, he turns around and says, "Jerry, I can't see that ball. It's too dark," so Jerry goes into his pocket and pulls the balls out and says, "Barry, they're all dark, stay in the box today." After the game, he said, "Listen, I know what Doug told you—make the balls darker—but honestly, they were a little bit too dark." So then I just tried to find a happy medium, and it's not easy.

O'Rourke eventually learned that the feel of the ball—the texture of the cowhide and particularly the height of the seams—is even more important than the color. The ultimate proof? Several years ago, a starting pitcher on the Phillies (O'Rourke won't say who) examined hundreds of brand-new balls and picked out the ones that he wanted rubbed up for his next start. (As it turned out, the pitcher got shelled and never messed with the balls again, but still, it was a cool idea.)

Actual rubbing techniques vary, but every equipment manager agrees on one thing: the mud is so thick that it needs to be diluted. Some guys spit into their hands and rub saliva into the cowhide along with the mud, but O'Rourke uses something a bit more sanitary. He starts by dabbing several fingertips into the mud, then dips his fingers into a cup of water, and smears the wet mixture all over the palms of his hands. This gives him enough mud for three baseballs, and he rubs each one for approximately 10 seconds, sometimes so vigorously that he takes off part of the logo.[3] Those 10 seconds are often split up; he rubs each of the first two balls for a couple seconds in order to distribute the mud evenly. Then he rubs the third ball from start to finish and returns to the first two. When he's done, if there's still a decent amount of mud on his hands, he'll simply add a little water and squeeze a fourth ball out of it. Basically, his entire process consists of trans-

---

[3] If you've ever caught a game-used ball on the fly and wondered how the *hell* the stamping was already messed up . . . now you know. And by the way, as soon as the rubbed baseballs dry out, there's a fine, powdery residue all over them; you'll never see it or feel it when you snag a ball in the stands because it'll come off long before it gets there.

ferring mud and water from his hands to the balls and mixing and matching as he sees fit. Here's some more math (because you were going to calculate this on your own anyway): one ball every 10 seconds multiplied by 96 balls per game equals 16 minutes of rubbing per game . . . multiplied by 81 home games equals 1,296 minutes over the course of the regular season. That's 21.6 hours of rubbing, and if you add Spring Training and the postseason . . . yeah. Luckily for O'Rourke, he gets to watch the Phillies' road games on TV while he does it.

Does O'Rourke ever mess up and rub too much mud on a ball? Yes, occasionally, but he doesn't worry about it; he'll toss it in the ball bag and let the ump deal with it. Where do game balls end up when they get scuffed and tossed out of play? Major League Baseball saves lots of balls for its authentication program; the rest get used during batting practice. What happens to batting practice balls that get worn out? The Phillies send them to the underground batting cages; then, after another round of abuse, the balls head to the minor leagues. Do teams have to bring their own baseballs with them on the road? Not really. The home team provides two cases of balls every day—a standard allotment throughout the Major Leagues—but visitors still bring some of their own. How many balls does each team use per season? O'Rourke orders 2,000 dozen balls in mid-January (more than half of which are for Spring Training) and 1,500 dozen in June. Then he gauges the supply by sight and, if necessary, places additional orders late in the season. (Math: 2,000 dozen plus 1,500 dozen equals 42,000 balls . . . multiplied by 30 teams equals 1.26 million baseballs per season throughout the Major Leagues.) How much do these balls cost? The exact amount is a trade secret, but as recently as 2009, Rawlings charged $81.50 per dozen.[4] That's $6.79 per ball, and for teams (like the Phillies) that don't use practice or training balls, it's $285,250 per season. Given this cost, does ownership limit the number of balls that players are allowed to give away to the fans? "Not at all," said O'Rourke. "I mean, they're spending forty dollars for a ticket and six dollars for a beer and ten dollars for parking. If that's what it takes to bring them back to a game, so be it."

---

[4] Including shipping and handling.

PART THREE

HOW TO SNAG MAJOR LEAGUE BASEBALLS

Luck is the residue of design.
—Branch Rickey

INTRODUCTION

This part of the book gets its own introduction. It's where we shift gears. Up until this point, you've been reading about the cultural and historical awesomeness of baseballs; now you're about to learn how to walk (or run) inside a major league stadium and catch one (or ten) for yourself. It's also the place where I, Zack Hample, the author, reappear to serve as your personal baseball-snagging guru, so don't be alarmed when I talk about myself. I'm here to help. We can do this.

Now, as I mentioned earlier, I've snagged a lot of baseballs—thousands and thousands of baseballs. Some people think this qualifies as a sickness, and at times it's been hard to argue. I was at Dwight Gooden's no-hitter at Yankee Stadium in 1996, and I'm ashamed to admit that I didn't fully appreciate it. Why? Because I was brooding over the fact that I'd only caught one ball that day during batting practice. On the other hand, being a ballhawk means that an ordinary game between two last-place teams can easily turn into something special for me. That was certainly the case on June 18, 2009, when I set a personal record by snagging 32 balls at an otherwise forgettable Diamondbacks-Royals game in Kansas City. Okay, fine, so

I only got one ball that day during the actual game itself. Forgive me. Most of my balls have come from pregame warm-ups, but I've made some big catches too. In addition to the 125 foul balls I've snagged during games, I caught Barry Bonds's 724th career home run, 2 of the last 10 homers ever hit at the old Yankee Stadium, and the last Mets homer ever hit at Shea. Beyond the obvious questions that this raises—*How do you catch so many balls? Where do you keep them all? Do you even have a job?*—people always want to know why. Why did I start collecting? Why do I keep doing it? Why is it still fun for me after all these years?

Because beating the odds never gets old.

Whether I'm convincing a scrubby middle reliever to toss me an old ball during BP or making a leaping catch on a game-winning home run, I feel like I'm getting my hands on something special. But it's not just the physical memento that I'm after. Chasing baseballs quenches my competitive drive, makes me feel connected to the sport I dreamed about playing as a kid, and sure as hell beats going to the gym. I'll often spend an entire game on my feet, running back and forth from one side of the stadium to the other, depending on who's at bat. Power-hitting righty? I'll race out to the standing-room-only section in left field and hope that he goes yard. Slap-hitting lefty? I'll sprint over to the seats behind the plate and camp out in a tunnel in case he swings late and fouls one back.

For me it's all about creating my own game within the game—one that's far more complicated than simply playing lefty-righty matchups. What if there's no standing-room-only section? What if the ushers kick me out of the tunnel? What if the game is sold out and there aren't any empty seats? What if the weather sucks and the teams don't take batting practice? Every stadium is different. Every season is different. That's the beauty of it. There are always new challenges, and I almost always find a solution; the last time I went to a game and left empty-handed was September 2, 1993. We're talking more than 650 consecutive games—perhaps many more by the time you read this—but enough about my ballhawking stats. It's time to help you compile some of your own.

CHAPTER 9

BEFORE YOU ENTER THE STADIUM

LUCK VERSUS SKILL

When Barry Bonds hit his 714th home run to tie Babe Ruth's career total, the ball was gloved by Tyler Snyder, a 19-year-old junior college student who had snagged hundreds of batting practice homers over the previous decade. Eight days later, when Bonds connected on number 715, the ball bounced out of the bleachers and into the bare hands of Andrew Morbitzer, a 38-year-old marketing director who happened to be standing in line at a concession stand for beer and peanuts.

Luck is a funny thing.

Snyder had essentially attended the game for the sole purpose of catching Bonds's historic blast. Morbitzer, on the other hand, wasn't even aware that Bonds was due to bat when he left his seat in the middle of the fourth inning. And yet Snyder may have been just as lucky. Sure, I could argue that the young ballhawk skillfully chose his spot in the right-center-field bleachers, but what if Bonds had swung ¼ of an inch higher or ¹⁄₁₀ of a second sooner? What if the ball had hit a bird, or if a freakishly tall fan had been sitting directly in front of Snyder? What if the wind had been blowing in that day instead of straight out to center field? What if Brad Halsey, the opposing pitcher, had thrown an off-speed pitch instead of a 90-mile-per-hour fastball? What if that pitch had missed the strike zone, or if Bonds hadn't swung at all?

When you consider all the factors that have to fall into place, and when you hear lifelong season-ticket holders complain about never having even come close to a ball, it might feel like the odds of catching one are nearly impossible. While it's unlikely for any fan—seasoned ballhawk or otherwise—to walk away with a milestone home run ball, there are dozens of other ball-snagging opportunities at every game that have nothing to do with odds or luck. In many cases, if you show up prepared and use a little common sense, you're pretty much guaranteed to go home with at least one ball.

CHOOSING A GAME

Big crowds suck. Tickets are hard to get, parking is a nightmare, stadium security is insane, bathroom lines are endless, and there's lots of competition for foul balls. But don't worry. As long as you live near a stadium that isn't always sold out, you can beat a good chunk of the competition simply by avoiding it. All you need to do is choose your game wisely.

Weekend games, for example, are more crowded than those played during the week. Attendance also increases during the summer (when kids are out of school) and on days with popular promotions (like fireworks or free T-shirts). If possible, resist the urge to see visiting teams with huge fan bases, such as the Yankees, Red Sox, and Cubs; even if you attend a weeknight game in September when it's 39 degrees and the home team is 20 games under .500, there will still be a large crowd.[1] Read the box scores. Look for the attendance. It's always listed at the bottom.

Another thing to consider when choosing your game: batting practice. Teams don't take BP on the field when it rains, and they often skip it on day games following night games (so their fragile superstars can sleep late). This makes it much harder to get balls. Same deal with double-headers. It doesn't matter if they're single or separate admission. There probably won't be BP. I'm not saying you should pass up a chance to see 18 innings of baseball in one day. Just don't expect to see the batting cage or any of the screens set up when you head inside.

STADIUM SECURITY

Imagine going to a baseball game and being allowed to sit anywhere you want. It happened to me in 2009 at Camden Yards when, after two long rain delays chased all but a few dozen fans away, Orioles management flashed a message on the JumboTron and invited everyone to "have a seat in the lower level." If only stadium security could be that laid-back every day, but let's face it, that's never gonna

---

[1] Whenever the Yankees play in Baltimore, there are so many New Yorkers in attendance that Camden Yards has become known as "Yankee Stadium South."

happen. Attending a game should be relaxing, but in the post-9/11 era, some stadiums have become so heavily guarded that they feel like border crossings.

Chicago's U.S. Cellular Field has the strictest policy when it comes to limiting access: if you don't have a field-level ticket, you can't enter the field-level seats. Period. Not even during batting practice. At Yankee Stadium, if you don't have a field-level ticket, the guards will send you back to your seat when the visiting team starts taking BP, and at Citi Field you can't get down into the seats behind the dugouts unless you have a ticket there—not even two and a half hours before game time, when there are 11 other fans in the entire stadium.

Every stadium has its own rules, some much stricter than others, and in some places it seems as if the ushers and security guards change them at will. I could tell you how to break them all—outsmarting stadium personnel is its own game within the game—but I don't want the commissioner to sue me, or worse, for teams to wise up and crack down.[2] The key to snagging lots of baseballs is stay-

---

[2] I can't get in trouble for encouraging criminal behavior in a footnote, right? Because . . . who even reads footnotes? Anyway, just to give you a quick idea of how to handle stadium security, if there's an usher who's being militant about checking tickets in one section, try the guy at the next staircase. Maybe he'll turn his back for a moment and you can walk past him. Maybe, if you're carrying a heaping box of food, he'll feel guilty about making you pull out your ticket and he'll wave you along. If the game hasn't yet started, tell him you're from out of town and you're just hoping to take a few quick photos for your blog. If it's late in the game, hang out in the concourse and ask the fans who are leaving if they can spare a ticket stub. (Don't do this in front of the usher whose section you plan to sneak into. I learned this lesson the hard way.) Be creative and don't worry about getting caught. You won't get fined or ejected or banned from the stadium. The worst thing

ing mobile, and in order to do that you need to have access to as many different seating areas as possible. For the rest of this book, whenever I tell you where to go and when to be there, I'm going to assume that (a) you have a ticket for that section or (b) you happen to be in a stadium where security doesn't mind if you run all over the place.

BUYING TICKETS

I'm not going to tell you how or where to buy tickets. Common sense dictates that it's safer to buy them directly from the team than from some random dude on craigslist, but that's your choice. If you want to take chances in order to save a few bucks, be my guest. But hear this: no matter where you get your tickets, you need to make sure that you'll actually have them in your possession before the stadium opens. Why all the fuss? Because on rare occasions you might be forced to pick them up at a will-call window that doesn't open until the gates open. Imagine how frustrated you'd feel if you were stuck in line, waiting to pick up tickets you'd already paid for, while hundreds of fans were streaming into the stadium to chase home run balls. (This was a bigger issue in the old days, back when tickets didn't have bar codes and America Online hadn't yet been invented. If you waited until the last second, you couldn't get your tickets emailed to you. You had to pick them up in person.)

As for which tickets to buy, you'll get a better sense of that in the next few chapters, but basically, beyond the

that can happen is that the usher will tell you to take a hike. You're at a baseball game. Have fun.

obvious issue of field-level access, there are three main things to consider:

- **Your budget**—If money isn't a concern, you might as well buy seats right behind the visiting team's dugout. You'll have ball-snagging opportunities throughout the day, and when you're ready to check out a different section, the ushers probably won't stop you.

- **Your goals**—If you're only interested in home runs, buy tickets in the outfield. In fact, if you're at a stadium with an outfield standing-room-only area, you can buy the cheapest tickets and just hang out there.

- **Early access**—Some teams allow season-ticket holders to enter extra early; if you can get your hands on season tickets (this is when craigslist might actually be the best option), you'll be on your way to ball-snagging heaven.[3]

WHAT TO BRING

Bring a glove. Bring a glove. Are you paying attention? Bring a glove. Don't make me say it again. It doesn't matter if you're the most athletic person on the planet. I don't care how old you are or how strong your hands might be. Major league baseball players are capable of hitting line drives in excess of 120 miles per hour. Trying to catch one barehanded doesn't make you tough; it simply means you're an idiot. But beyond the safety factor, a glove serves two big purposes. First, when you're lunging or jumping

---

[3] Print-at-home tickets are never season tickets. It doesn't matter where you get them. They won't get you in the stadium extra early.

for a ball, it'll provide a few extra inches of reach, and second, when you're trying to get a player to throw you a ball, it'll help convince him to give it to you instead of the gloveless fans who will also be shouting his name.

Of course, if you don't know the player's name, you won't be able to ask him for a ball in the first place, so before you leave for the stadium, print the rosters of both teams that you'll be seeing. They're easy to find, and you can get them for free. Go to any team's official website. Hover your cursor over the "Roster" link near the top. Several options will appear. Print both the "40-Man Roster" (in case some players on the disabled list are working out with the team) and the "Coaches" (because anyone on the field might give you a ball—even the bullpen catcher or the strength and conditioning coach). Then, if you have some extra free time, pull up the roster on a different site like espn.com or sports.yahoo.com and click each player's name to see his head shot. (MLB.com no longer has head shots.) Copy and paste these images onto one page—make a collage out of them—and label each photo with the guy's name and number. Players often wear nameless, numberless warm-up shirts over their jerseys during batting practice; having a sheet of paper with all their faces will help you recognize them, especially when they're a bunch of cookie-cutter white guys who belong in Triple-A.[4]

Look, don't get overwhelmed by all this stuff. You don't have to print faces or rosters if you don't want to. You

---

[4] These photos get taken during Spring Training; a player who has a goatee in late February might be clean-shaven by the time you see him during the regular season, so don't rely solely on facial hair as a recognizable feature. If you're going to the third game of a series, watch the first two on TV. You'll start to recognize the players and coaches, and you'll also get a sense of the stadium.

Blue Jays pitchers wearing shirts over their jerseys at the new Yankee Stadium

don't even need to attend batting practice. I'm just show-ing you every possible strategy. Take the ones you want and ignore the rest. That said, if you do plan on taking most of my advice, you should definitely bring a backpack; you're going to end up snagging so many baseballs that you'll need it to carry them all.

WHEN TO ARRIVE

Every major league stadium opens at least 90 minutes early, and as long as you have a ticket, you're allowed to head inside and start snagging baseballs. I'd list all the opening times for you, but they sometimes change from one season to the next, and anyway, it's easy to find this info on the teams' websites. Look for the link that contains the stadium name and hover your cursor over it. Then select the "A-to-Z Guide" and scroll down to the "Gate" section. Not only will you find out when the stadium itself opens, but you'll learn if certain gates open earlier than others.

Don't show up *when* the stadium is about to open; get to the gate at least half an hour early so you can be first in line. There've been games at which I've snagged three or four balls within the first few minutes of batting practice—and nothing else for the rest of the day. Being the first fan to enter the stadium is huge. I can't stress this enough. It's one of the most important things you can do to increase your chances, and here's why:

- *Easter eggs*—When balls land in the seats before a stadium opens, ushers are supposed to retrieve them and toss them back onto the field. This doesn't always happen. Some ushers are lazy, and others aren't good at finding them. (To be fair, balls do sometimes hide in weird places.) If you're the first fan to enter, you might find one of these balls, aka "Easter eggs."

- *Empty seats*—Since you'll have the stadium to yourself, a home run that lands anywhere near you will be all yours. If the ball lands three sections over, you'll be able to walk through the seats and pick it up.

- *Thrown balls*—Players toss lots of balls into the crowd, but some guys might only give away one ball all day—and they often give it to the first fan that asks.

- *Corner spot*—At some stadiums, there's a "corner spot" where it's much easier to snag batted and thrown balls—that is, a seat in the front row at the end of a section where you'll be more visible to the players and have a better chance of reaching anything that flies your way. If you don't get there first, the spot will be taken by the fan who does.

When you arrive at the stadium, don't be too shy to ask for help. Although you might know which gate to go to, there might be a certain part of it that opens first, or a whole row of turnstiles that won't get used until game time. Almost every stadium has see-through gates, so when the ticket takers are setting up on the other side, ask them if you're standing in the right spot. Never trust the crowd—everyone else might be lined up in the wrong place—and when the gates do open, make sure you know which end of your ticket to stick inside the scanner. Every seconds counts. If there's a giveaway, don't even stop to get it. (It's probably something lame anyway.) Just forget it and run in—but not too fast or you might get stopped by security.

CHAPTER 10

BATTING PRACTICE

THE FIRST 60 SECONDS

The home team usually starts hitting two and a half to three hours before game time. For some stupid reason, most stadiums don't open that early, so when you first run inside, there's a good chance that batting practice will already be under way. Every stadium is different, so strategies will vary a bit, but basically, you should head toward the seats in straightaway left or right field. Look for Easter eggs along the way, and don't stop searching if you find one. I once found seven in a single day at Progressive Field, so anything's possible. Scour every row—baseballs can hide anywhere—but keep an eye on the batters. They'll be hitting ball after ball, and if you're not paying attention, you might miss your chance to catch one, or worse, possibly get drilled. I've seen some gruesome injuries over the years, and they almost always happen when fans aren't looking at the field.

Toward the end of batting practice, as the stands get crowded, most home runs are either caught on the fly or

An Easter egg in the upper deck at the old Yankee Stadium

snatched as soon as they land in the seats. But early on, when there aren't many other fans, long balls often land in empty sections. Most fans cut through the row where they see the ball land, and by the time they get there it will have trickled down the steps. Be smart. Don't forget about gravity. Head several rows below the landing spot, and if the ball hasn't rolled anywhere, climb over the seats until you see it.

One great thing about being inside a stadium so early is that you'll get to see stuff that most fans aren't aware of—and yes, I know you'll be in full snagging mode, but try to appreciate it. A corner outfielder might be taking fungoes off the wall to practice fielding the caroms. The fastest guy on the team might be rolling balls down one of the base lines to gauge the slope of the field and determine if his bunts will stay fair. Listen to the crack of the bat as it echoes through the empty stadium. Smell the freshly cut grass and watch the groundskeepers doing their thing. There's something magical about having the stadium to yourself. Be sure to take full advantage.

GENERAL ADVICE ON POSITIONING

Left or right field? Fair or foul territory? Bullpens or dugouts? Power alleys? Straightaway? Front row? Tenth row? Field level? Second deck? Don't get overwhelmed by all the options. We'll get to them in a bit. But first, here are some basic strategies on where to position yourself in the stands:

- *Avoid your weaknesses*—If you're bad at judging fly balls, don't stay in the outfield. Grab a spot down one of the foul lines and try to scoop up grounders—or just focus on getting the players to throw balls to you.

- *Consider who's batting*—If there's a small lefty taking cuts, it won't do you any good to stand in deep left field. And if there's a whole group of lefties taking turns in the batting cage, you probably shouldn't be in left field at all.

- *Beware of the batting cage*—The cage is designed to prevent foul balls from flying straight back into the stands, but because of the way it encloses the home plate area, it also prevents foul balls from shooting into the crowd near first and third base. Therefore, if you're trying to catch a batted ball in foul territory, stay in the outfield and remain close to the foul line.

- *Consider the competition*—Don't stand near fans who are much taller than you, especially if they're wearing gloves and bragging to their friends about how they're gonna do whatever it takes to catch the next ball. If you have to stand near anyone, pick out people who are more interested in their food than the action on the field. They'll probably need the protection anyway.

- ***Don't get trapped***—Never ever, under any circumstances, sit or stand in the middle of a long row of fans. Even a short row of fans. Even a short row that's empty. Don't do it. Balls usually won't come right to you, so you need to have room to run. If possible, find a spot where you can move in all four directions: up and down a staircase and left and right through an empty row or aisle. (This strategy applies to BP and the game itself, and it's very very very important.)

- ***Avoid the front row***—It's tempting to stand close to the field and lean over the wall and shout at the players—but it's the dumbest place to wait for the action to unfold. You can't move forward, it's too crowded to run left or right, and if a ball happens to be hit right to you, 10 other people will reach in front of your face for it. You're better off staying several rows back and moving to the front only when a specific opportunity presents itself.

- ***Stay mobile***—There are opportunities everywhere, and you have to keep moving. This can mean running from one side of the stadium to the other, or simply shading each hitter differently within one section. For example, if the cleanup hitter steps into the cage, move back a few rows. (The farther back you go, the emptier it'll be.) Then, if he starts pulling lots of sharp grounders down the third-base line, move from straightaway left field toward the foul pole in case he gets under one and jerks it into the seats.

It's all about anticipation. You need to recognize the players' tendencies and make educated guesses about where the balls are likely to be hit. Every manager does it when he positions the defense. There's no reason why you can't too, but it takes time. You really have to know and love and understand the game. Even if you memorize every word in this book, you shouldn't expect to catch 10 balls the next time you attend batting practice. There are days when I only get one or two—when I make horrendously stupid mistakes and the snagging gods are clearly out to get me. The same thing will happen to you. Just roll with it and know that you'll have many more chances.

LEFT FIELD VERSUS RIGHT FIELD

Generally speaking, left field is the place to be. Think about it. There are more right-handed batters, and since most home runs get pulled, there are more batted balls that land in the left-field seats. But it's not always that simple. Some teams have more lefties, while others have a bunch of switch-hitters who will end up batting left-handed if the opposing pitcher is a righty. (Don't forget that managers try to stack their lineups with batters who hit from the opposite side of the plate from which the pitcher throws.) Since you'll already have rosters with you, count the number of righties and lefties on both teams.[1] Then, for example, if you discover that there are more of the latter, you should go to right field—unless that side of the stadium is an architectural nightmare from a home

---

[1] Every roster has a "B/T" category, which stands for "Bats/Throws." If it says "L/L" next to a particular player's name, that means he bats and throws left-handed. If it says "S/R," that means he's a switch-hitter who throws right-handed.

run–catching standpoint. How can you tell? Easy. Just consider the following factors:

- *Bullpen placement*—Most home runs are hit straightaway or to the power alleys. If there's a bullpen in one of those places, it'll swallow a frustratingly large number of baseballs and cost you lots of opportunities. Example: left field at Comerica Park.

- *Outfield dimensions*—How deep is it to the power alley? If it's close to 400 feet, that's good for the pitchers, but bad for you as as a ballhawk. Example: right field at PETCO Park.

- *Number of rows*—You don't want the batter to have to hit the ball 400 feet, but in case he does, you want to be able to run up the steps and chase it. (Or, if you know that the guy is going to hit bombs, you want to be able to position yourself there in advance.) If the section only has 10 rows of seats, or if the second deck is low enough (and close enough to the field) for lots of balls to land there, that's bad. Example: everywhere at Rogers Centre.

- *Height of the walls*—If the outfield wall is too high, you'll never be able to catch a ground-rule double. Watch out for any wall that exceeds 10 feet. Example: right field at Nationals Park.

- *Steepness of the stands*—It's harder to maneuver and run around for balls when the steps are steep. Example: right field at Great American Ball Park.

Right field at Citi Field is such a disaster that I could've used it for each of the examples listed above. Therefore, whenever I go to that stadium, I don't bother counting the righties and lefties. I simply stay in left field unless a group of three or four lefties starts hitting. Then I run over to the right-field side and focus on getting balls thrown to me.

*The right-field stands at Great American Ball Park
are tough to navigate.*

Thankfully, Citi Field and other new ballparks have been designed with concourses that wrap all the way around the outfield—great news if you have a fear of commitment. It means you don't have to choose one side of the stadium and stick with it throughout batting practice; you can run back and forth and position yourself differently whenever you want. The only problem is that it takes at least a minute in most stadiums to run from right field to left, so it might not be worthwhile to do it for each hitter.

Keep in mind that when a batter steps into the cage to begin his first round of swings, he lays down a couple bunts and then works on hitting the ball to the opposite field. He probably won't go yard during this round, but there's a decent chance that he'll slice at least one ball into foul territory. At some stadiums, you'll be able to take a direct route to the foul line by cutting through an empty row of seats. In other places, where the stands are segmented, you'll have to race up the steps, run 100 feet through the concourse, and then hurry back down toward your new spot. Whatever the case, make sure you're wearing comfortable shoes and a generous amount of deodorant.

Stadium design and right-handedness aside, there's one key factor that makes left field better in most venues: it's usually the visiting team's side. The visitors often throw more balls into the crowd than the home team, and in the next chapter you'll learn how to snag them.

HOME RUN BALLS

Catching home runs in the stands is much harder than catching fly balls on the field. When a fly ball starts to descend, the outfielder almost always catches it on the move. Have you ever noticed that? Because he's standing on a flat, wide-open piece of land, he has the luxury of drifting with the ball right up until the last second—but you won't. You'll be blocked by seats and railings, and there might be 50 other fans getting in your way. In order to beat the competition, you need to try to predict where the ball will land and then get there as quickly as possible. When you guess right, it'll feel great (especially if your route involves running up or down some steps). When you guess wrong, don't beat yourself up too much. Remember, you'll be trying to do something that's extremely challenging.

If you know you won't be able to catch a ball on the fly, you should still keep running toward it. Anything can happen. It might ricochet wildly off a metal armrest or get bobbled and kicked around for a few seconds by a group of clumsy fans. It doesn't matter if the ball is going to land two sections away. You have nothing to lose by moving in that direction, so don't be lazy. You might even be able to snag a ball that lands all the way across the stadium. If you notice that a home run gets launched into an empty section in the second or third deck, keep your eye on it. Those seats might stay empty for a while, if not all day. Count the number of staircases from that spot to the foul pole so you'll remember where to look for the ball later on. Continue to snag as you normally would, but keep watching the section to make sure that no one wanders up there. Don't tell anyone about the ball—not even your mother—and then go looking for it after BP.

At any given moment during BP, there could be half a dozen balls in use. It's impossible to keep your eye on them all, so if you sense that the people around you are jockeying for position, it's probably a sign that there's a ball nearby, either sitting on the field or flying your way. Use your intuition. Be aware of your surroundings. Be prepared for balls to bounce into the stands. It seems that no one else ever is. And take off your backpack. Leave it on a seat (but don't stray too far from it). Wearing it will only slow you down and limit your reach. You need to think of every little detail that will give you an edge.

GROUND BALLS

There's no such thing as fan interference during batting practice. You won't get in trouble (like you would during a game) for reaching out of the stands and catching a ball, so don't hold back. Three of the four oldest major league

Fenway Park has a great spot to scoop up grounders during batting practice.

stadiums—Fenway Park, Dodger Stadium, and Angel Stadium—have sections in fair territory with very low walls, but if you plan to snag grounders anywhere else, you'll have to settle for a spot in foul territory.

Watch out for the protective screen in front of first base. It blocks lots of balls from rolling down the foul line, so you're better off avoiding the right side completely. Make sure that wherever you go, there's not a screen directly between yourself and the batter.

If the stadium has a corner spot—Fenway has a great one down the left-field line—you must claim it. Even if you're the first fan to enter the stadium, someone at another gate might beat you to it, so you really have to run fast.

When a ball starts rolling toward you, don't wait until the last second, and don't simply lean over the railing. That's what most other fans do, and it limits their reach. Instead, crouch down and pounce over the railing as if you're an infielder who's diving headfirst for a ball in the hole. As long as some part of your body remains in the stands, you won't get in trouble, so here's what to do: hook your feet over the top of the railing and use your hands to walk yourself out onto the warning track in a push-up position. This move is not for everyone. It requires lots of upper body strength and might leave you somewhat bruised and scraped, but if you can pull it off, you'll be able to reach balls as far as eight feet out from the wall—balls rolling well into fair territory that other fans wouldn't even think of catching.

THE GLOVE TRICK (AND OTHER DEVICES)

When I was eight years old, I saw something on TV that left quite an impression. A baseball fan was using a fishing pole to lower a small metal can over a ball that was sitting beyond his reach on the field below. The can descended slowly onto the ball, and when the guy lifted it back up, the ball was gone. I never figured out how that contraption worked, but it didn't matter because I invented my own device years later—and best of all, mine didn't require any clunky materials. All I needed was my glove, some string, a large rubber band, and a Magic Marker.

The "glove trick" (as it came to be known) was ideal in the outfield corners at the old Yankee Stadium, where the height of the wall varied from eight to ten feet. Anytime a ball rolled onto the warning track, I was all over it, and as I began traveling to games across North America, I discovered that the trick was just as useful in other ballparks. Wrigley Field and Kauffman Stadium? The high walls along the foul lines were not a problem. Turner Field and Miller Park? The gaps behind the outfield walls became prime real estate. And then there were the bullpens. God bless the bullpens. All the home run balls that landed there were potentially within reach.

Even now, all these years later, whenever I lower my glove, the crowd grows silent, or at least mostly silent. There are always a few hecklers who insist that the trick won't work. Then, when I raise the glove with the ball tucked snugly inside, I usually receive a thunderous ovation and a dozen high-fives, followed by a barrage of questions about how the dang thing works. It always amuses me when the hecklers ask. I never tell them. I just shrug and walk away. But I'm gonna tell you. Because you're nice.

Start by tying a long piece of string around the wrist of your glove (figure 1; next page). Then stretch the rubber band over the fingertips in order to create a space that's slightly smaller than the ball—and wedge the Magic Marker inside the pocket to prop it open (figure 2). That's pretty much it. When you dangle the glove by the string (figure 3) and lower it onto the ball, its weight will force the rubber band to stretch to the side (figure 4) and allow the ball to slip in (figure 5). Then, when you lift it back up (figure 6—view from below), the band will hold the ball in place.[2]

Make sure that the string is tied really tight. Wrap it around several times and tie multiple knots to be safe. I've seen people lose their gloves when the knots come undone.

---

[2] Ta-daa!!!

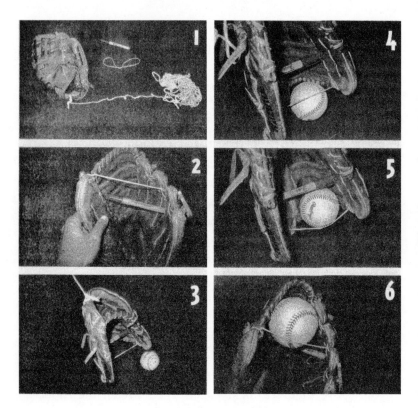

Behold the glove trick!

Also, keep in mind that if the rubber band is too tight, it won't stretch to let the ball in, and if it's too loose, the lack of tension will allow the ball to slip out. Practice using the glove trick at home before you bring it to a game for the first time. Stand on a chair or a balcony or a fourth-floor fire escape. The higher up you go, the easier it'll be when you're using it at a stadium.

Here are some other glove trick strategies:

- ***Extra supplies***—Bring extra string, rubber bands, and Magic Markers. You never know what might happen. (For the record, size 117 rubber bands work best for me. They're 7 inches long, ⅛ of an inch wide, and ¹⁄₁₆ of an inch thick.)

- *Mind the gap*—Just as you should search for Easter eggs in the seats, you should look for balls in the bullpens and in the gaps behind the outfield walls. Even if you don't have a device, you might be able to get a player or coach (or a random stadium employee) to toss the ball to you.

- *String storage*—After each use, coil the string and tuck it neatly inside the palm of your glove. It might be a bit uncomfortable at first, but you'll get used to it. Don't bunch up the string and jam it in or it'll get tangled.

- *Study your surroundings*—Think about every surface and stadium feature that might make it tough to use the glove trick. The back walls in most bullpens, for example, are made of concrete; when home runs land there, they often ricochet back toward the field and end up beyond your reach. Or, if you're at a ballpark that has a rubberized warning track, most balls that roll toward you will bounce off the outfield wall and trickle back toward the edge of the grass—once again, beyond your reach. The point is, don't rely on the glove trick in these places.

- *Knock it closer*—If there's a ball sitting several feet out from the wall, don't give up on it. Let out some string, fling the glove onto the field, and tug it back to knock the ball closer. Don't do this with the marker in the glove. It'll probably fall out. After moving the ball, you'll need to raise the glove and set up the trick before swooping back down for the kill.

- *Wedgie warning*—Whether you're pulling a ball closer or lowering the glove straight down, be careful not to wedge the ball under the padding of the outfield wall or knock it anyplace where it might get trapped.

- ***The Dangle Method*** — Some fans who rely exclusively on ball-retrieving devices like to lower their contraptions as soon as they reach the front row of the outfield stands—even if there's no ball in sight. This creates two advantages. First, if a ball rolls to them, they'll be able to snag it in an instant, and second, it might entice a curious player to place a ball on the warning track for them. Sounds good, right? Well, there's one glaring disadvantage that the danglers face: if a ball rolls 20 feet to either side, or if a home run starts flying toward their section, they're screwed because they have to reel in the device before they can run anywhere. Since mobility is crucial, I prefer to wait until a ball rolls to the wall before making my move. Sometimes I get there too late, but I'm able to cover much more ground.

Another popular ball-retrieving device is the "cup trick." In order to make one, you'll need a sturdy plastic cup and some type of weight to help push it down over the ball. The opening of the cup (assuming it slants in and isn't perfectly cylindrical) should be three inches in diameter. You can line the inner rim with duct tape to help the ball stick inside, but this isn't necessary if you find the perfect fit. Just play around with it. Experiment with different cups and methods for weighing them down. It's all about trial and error, so be creative and see what you can come up with. I once saw a fan snag a ball with an actual roll of duct tape; the center hole was just the right size, and he skillfully wedged the ball inside. Any object with a hole that's slightly smaller than a ball can work, especially if there's a little bit of stretchiness or stickiness involved.

No matter what type of device you use, you're going to receive a mixed reaction from the players. Over the years, dozens of guys have (jokingly) tried to sabotage me by firing balls at my glove, while others have walked over for a closer look and congratulated me when I was done.

"Let me see how you did that," they'll say.

"Put another ball down there for me, and I'll show you," I'll reply.

It feels pretty special to do something that impresses a major league baseball player, and it feels even better to have a player on my side. At Great American Ball Park in 2005, Giants reliever Scott Eyre moved a ball closer to the wall for me during BP, then argued with an usher who stopped me from using the glove trick, and finally picked up the ball and tossed it to me.

This raises one final issue: stadium security. The use of ball-retrieving devices is against the rules at some stadiums, so be careful and proceed at your own risk. At worst, your glove or cup could get confiscated, but that's unlikely. Security will usually give you a warning, but you still need to use common sense. Don't start flinging your glove onto the field if there's a guard standing nearby—or at least ask for permission first. It's hard to predict how any particular stadium employee will react, but as you attend more and more games, your instincts will guide you.

CHAPTER 11

HOW TO GET A PLAYER TO THROW YOU A BALL

DRESS FOR SUCCESS

One of the easiest ways to snag a ball is to get a player (or coach) to throw one to you during batting practice. In fact, some old-school ballhawks think it's so easy that they don't even bother trying. But it's only easy if you know all the tricks. Players tend to be selective. They prefer to toss balls to (a) little kids or (b) young, attractive women. Assuming you don't fall into either of those categories, you need to give the players a reason to throw balls to you—but if you're not careful, you'll end up giving them a reason not to.

Early in the 1992 season, when I first started attending lots of games, I made the mistake of asking Braves right fielder David Justice for a ball while decked out in Mets gear. It happened during BP. Shea Stadium had just opened. I pretty much had the place to myself, so you can imagine how stupid I felt when he turned and shouted, "I'm not gonna throw you a ball if you're wearin' a Mets jacket!"

The next day I took off the jacket (as well as the cap I'd been wearing) before calling out to him from the right-field stands. I had no idea what to expect. I thought he might recognize me and start talking trash, but instead he threw the ball my way. That was the last time I ever wore my Mets jacket to Shea, and I soon began leaving my cap at home too. Dressing neutrally made a big difference; the Mets still assumed I was a fan, and visiting teams were more willing to show me some love.

A month later, during BP at Yankee Stadium, Angels coach Ken Macha offered a ball to the first fan with an Angels cap. That inspired me to take my clothing strategy a step further—a step some people might not take. I started wearing caps of the visiting teams, and the baseballs started pouring in. I remember getting seven balls tossed to me by the Expos during a four-game series. Several players practically went out of their way to hook me up, presumably for being such a big "fan" and traveling all the way from Montreal to see them.

How important is team loyalty? I can't answer that for you. I realize that it's a way of life for most baseball fans, but for me, personally, I just enjoy the game no matter who's playing. Although I'll always have a soft spot for the Mets, I root more for individual players and simply consider myself a fan of the sport, so I don't feel guilty about switching caps. My advice to you is as follows: look in the mirror, take a deep breath, and ask yourself if you're willing to dress up like the enemy in order to snag an obscene amount of baseballs. And if the answer is yes, consider investing in T-shirts of the visiting teams to go with the caps. You'll look like such a big fan that the players will feel guilty about not taking care of you.

The visiting team's gear will be more effective if the color differs from that of the home team. For example, if you wear a Reds cap to Busch Stadium, you might go unnoticed in the sea of Cardinal fans, but if you have a bright yellow Pirates shirt at Coors Field, you'll definitely stand out amid the purple and black. If you don't have any gear of the visiting team, you should still try to color-coordinate your outfit. Going to see the Royals on the road? Throw on a generic blue shirt. It won't command as much attention as a retro Mark Gubicza jersey, but it certainly won't hurt.

One last clothing-related piece of advice: don't wear the same stuff day after day. The players will recognize you (especially if you stand in the same spot and shout the same requests), and when you're trying to get them to throw you baseballs, that's usually a bad thing. I can't count the number of times that I've asked for balls and gotten rejections ranging from "Didn't I throw you one yesterday?" to "How many balls do you need?!" In the late 1990s, Mets pitcher Rick Reed not only refused to throw me balls but prevented me from snagging them on my own; whenever he saw me during BP at Shea Stadium, he moved near the foul line and scooped up foul grounders before they reached me. Over the years, however, there've been a few players who continued throwing me balls even after learning about my collection. Heath Bell, the friendliest of them all, saved a couple balls for me from the 2009 World Baseball Classic and All-Star Game—and texted me to let me know he'd bring them to Citizens Bank Park on a certain date. That's the beauty of asking for baseballs. It's not just the balls themselves that are special; it's the chance to interact with the players and actually feel special. And when you get flat-out dissed, you can at least tell your friends that you were dissed by a major leaguer.

A MISHMASH OF STRATEGIES

Regardless of what you're wearing, you need to get the players' attention and ask them properly. Since you can't run out onto the field and tap them on the shoulder,

Heath Bell makes dreams come true.

you need to use your voice and be assertive. Don't be shy. It's not rude to ask. Fans do it all the time. It's not even rude to shout as long as you're polite. Always say "please"—some players won't acknowledge you unless they hear the magic word—and remember that baseballs aren't cheap. When you ask for one, the player might not be allowed to give it away. Some teams limit the number of balls that get tossed into the crowd, so if you call out to a guy and he ignores you, don't take it personally. He might have already given away his one ball for the day, and if you're the first fan to enter the stadium and you still get rejected, he might be waiting to see if you catch a batted ball on your own—or he might have already promised a ball to someone else. I once bumped into Trevor Hoffman as he was getting off the number 7 train at Shea Stadium;

rather than harassing him for an autograph, I asked if he'd toss me a ball during BP—and he did. Hoffman was always generous with baseballs. He probably tossed a dozen into the crowd that day, but it still felt great to have sniffed out an unusual opportunity and taken advantage.

Here are some ways to create more opportunities for yourself:

- *Separate and elevate*—The front row is the easiest place to be seen, but if that row is packed and you're dressed like everyone else, you won't stand out. Separate yourself from the masses. Move back a few rows, and if you have good balance, climb on a seat to elevate above the crowd. Jump up and down and wave your arms. Some players might make fun of you by waving back sarcastically, but others will pick you out and toss balls right to you over everyone else's heads.

- *Audio-visual*—When you call out for a ball and get a player to turn around, he might not have seen you. To make sure that he ends up throwing it to you and not some random fan in your section, shout a few more words (so he recognizes your voice) and add some type of physical gesture to catch his eye. Tip your cap. Flap your glove. Start doing yoga. It doesn't matter. Just make sure he hears and sees you.

- *Foreign languages*—Although many foreign players do speak English, it'll impress them if you ask for balls in their native languages. To ask in Spanish, all you have to say is "Dame la bola, por favor." It's not particularly fancy or polite—it simply means "Give me the ball, please"—but it'll do the job. Japanese, the second-most common foreign language in the majors, is much harder because of the inflections. Ask a Japanese friend to teach you the phrase or watch my YouTube videos. I've said it in lots of interviews.

- **A woman's touch**—If you find yourself in the company of a woman (and you're not a woman yourself), get her to ask for baseballs on your behalf. The players will be excited to hear a melodious voice coming from the stands—and they'll suddenly become much more, shall we say, accommodating.

- **A personal touch**—If you have something in common with a particular player, mention it when you ask for a ball. The more random it is, the better. I once got Chad Bradford, who shares a birthday with me, to toss one by saying, "How about a ball for a fellow September 14 guy?" Another time I got a ball from Zack Segovia by shouting, "My name is Zack too, and I have ID to prove it." I even convinced Ty Wigginton to throw me one by removing my cap and showing that I, like he, had a shaved head. Anything can work. Mention the guy's hometown or high school baseball coach, but don't be creepy or stalker-ish about it. There are enough ways to snag baseballs that you don't need to memorize random tidbits of info about the players.

- **Asking for help**—If you don't know a player's name, ask the fans around you to help identify him. Warning: if the other fans are trying to get a ball from him too, they might not tell you.

- **Hide your balls**—Don't celebrate after catching balls during BP. If any player sees you with a ball, he definitely won't give you another. Along these lines, if you've already snagged three balls, don't let the ushers hear you begging for a fourth (unless they see you giving balls to kids, which is always a nice thing to do).

- **Fan interference**—When you're about to catch a ball, don't stand back passively and wait for it to come to you. Lean forward and reach all the way out for it in order to prevent other fans from snatching it.

- ***Airmail*** —When two guys are playing catch perpendicular to the stands, position yourself directly behind them in case there's an overthrow. If you happen to catch one, they might ask you to toss it back so they can finish throwing. Do it. They won't forget about you, and in the meantime it'll feel great to watch major league players using *your* ball.

- ***Second chances*** —Balls that get thrown into the crowd don't always stay in the crowd. If half a dozen fans reach for a ball and collectively bobble it back onto the warning track, the player who tossed it will probably give them another chance. Run over there and get in on the action. (Always get as close to the balls as possible. If you're standing in straightaway left field and a ball rolls to the wall in left-center, move near it. Sometimes that's all it takes—not being the youngest or prettiest or biggest fan, but simply standing in the right spot.)

Don't worry if your hand-eye coordination isn't great. Players are perceptive about these things. They'll gauge your athleticism and throw the ball accordingly. They might toss it gently from a short distance or roll it in your direction if you're standing in a spot where the railing is low, or they might even walk over and place the ball in your glove.

DON'T BE ANNOYING

A funny thing happened at Minute Maid Park in 2005. It was ten minutes before game time, Astros shortstop Adam Everett was playing catch along the right-field foul line, and in addition to me, there was only one other fan with a glove—a middle-aged man with tight jeans and a mustache who screamed for the ball every time Everett caught it. Meanwhile, I politely asked Everett if I could have it when he was done. That's all it took. Everett appreciated that I understood that he was actually using the ball (what a concept!) and threw it to me before jogging off the field. "Oh, *man*!!!" shouted the other fan as if he were the unluckiest guy in the world.

The moral of the story? Don't be annoying.

Baseball can't be played without balls—the players have to keep some for themselves—so be patient and strategic. If the third baseman is fielding fungoes, don't ask him for a ball every time he catches one. Wait until the batter hits an extra grounder his way, and then ask. If several pitchers are shagging balls in the outfield, wait until a ball rolls nearby before calling out to them. And if you're going to ask while two players are throwing, you better request the ball when they're done.

No matter when you ask for a ball, there's no need to use the word "Mister" in your request. Players, for the most part, prefer to interact with the fans on an informal basis, so call them by their first names or their nicknames. Don't whistle at them or call out their uniform numbers or shout their last names. It won't work. Don't bother telling them that it's your first game, or that they're on your fantasy team, or that your mother is in the hospital with some incurable disease. That won't work either, even if it's true.

TAILOR YOUR REQUEST TO THE SITUATION

When you first enter the stadium, you probably won't need to be too creative when asking for a ball. You might not even need to say anything. In some cases, simply pounding your glove and holding it up (as if you're giving a target) will do the trick. But when it's crowded and noisy, or if you're dealing with a player who's ignoring everyone, you'll need to find some way, however silly or offbeat, to get inside his head.

In the mid-1990s, it was nearly impossible to get a ball from the Astros. For whatever reason, the entire team was unbelievably stingy, so one day, when all the pitchers headed toward left field to play catch, I called out to reliever Todd Jones and asked, "Is there *any* possible way to get a ball from you guys? What would it *possibly* take to make that happen?"

"I've never been asked like that before," he said. "You know what? Just for that, I'm gonna get you one."

Years later, I found myself trying unsuccessfully to convince the Dodgers' equipment manager to spare one of the hundred or so balls that he was slowly transferring to a zippered bag after BP. I figured that because of his relatively low rank with the team, he probably wasn't supposed to give balls away, and because of his job description, he was hyperaware of their condition—so I came up with a request that covered everything.

"There's gotta be a really dirty ball in there," I finally said. "I don't want a new one. I want the ugliest ball you got. I want the ugliest ball you've ever seen. There's gotta be a ball so ugly that it's a disgrace to the entire Los Angeles Dodgers organization, and it would be my pleasure to take it off your hands."

The guy fought back a smile and eventually flipped a ball to me—proof that anyone can be cracked.

Here are some other ways to tailor your request to the situation:

- ***Shhhhh!!!***—Ask more politely when it's quiet. Begin by saying, "Excuse me," and follow it with a question like, "Is there any chance that you could throw me the ball, please?" If the player doesn't look up, don't repeat your entire request. Wait a few moments and then just say his name.

- ***Keep talking***—If it's crowded and the player is standing nearby, don't yell his name and wait for him to look up. Everyone will be shouting at him for different reasons. The autograph collectors will want him to sign. People with cameras will want him to pose. Someone might even be trying to get his phone number, so be loud and make your entire request at once.[1] He'll hear you.

- ***Long distance***—When a player is standing far away from you, try yelling, "Let's see the gun!" or simply, "Reach me!" (Remember to personalize your request by using his first name.)

- ***Age factor***—If you're with a kid, make sure the players know it. Shout, "How 'bout a ball for this young man right here?" or, "This little girl would really love to have a baseball." If you're old enough to be a parent, but you're at the game by yourself, ask

---

[1] If you get really lucky, you might snag a baseball and a phone number at the same time. That's what happened to a fan named Molly Ray at Safeco Field in May 2009. Mariners bullpen catcher Jason Phillips spotted her in the stands, wrote his phone number on a ball, got her attention, and tossed it to her. Thirteen months later, the two got married. In similar fashion, A's ballboy Kevin Fennell attempted to make a love connection of his own in August 2010. He spotted a young woman in the stands named Jacki Lynch—and wooed her with a bouquet of baseballs. The 21-year-old Fennell, stationed along the left-field foul line, handed her four foul balls over the course of the game. Other fans grumbled about it, but the move paid off as the two made plans to meet for drinks the following week.

the players if they can "spare a ball for a big kid." (If you can't hide your age by crouching down and raising your voice, you might as well embrace it.)

- **Be a fan**—If you're dying to get a ball from a particular player, tell him how much it would mean to you. Say that you love how he plays the game. Wear his jersey. Make a sign with his name on it and hold it up during BP.

When you ask for balls and the players say no, you might be able to get them to change their minds if you're persistent and friendly. At a game at Camden Yards in 2006, I ran to the right-field seats as soon as the gates opened and asked Orioles pitcher Kurt Birkins for the first ball he fielded.

"They'll hit plenty of 'em your way," he said as he fired it back toward the infield. "Don't worry."

"Yeah, but within a few minutes this place is gonna be overrun by munchkins."

"Ya gotta overpower 'em!" he shouted. "You're big! You can do it!"

"C'mon, Kurt," I said, "hook me up before this place gets crazy."

A minute later, the batter hit a deep fly ball that one-hopped the wall in front of me. Birkins jogged over, scooped it up, and tossed it to me.

Don't forget that baseball players are human beings. They can get bored too, especially during BP when they're standing around shagging balls for the 12th day in a row. Engage them in conversation. Ask them if they want to play catch. Ask them to show you their changeup or knuckleball. Tell them you're "going deep" and then run up the steps like a wide receiver waiting for a pass. When it's crowded and the players are being bombarded with generic requests, you need to stand out. Offer to get them something to eat or drink. Seriously, you never know. I once saw a fan at the old Yankee Stadium trade two gigantic cannoli (from a famous bakery) to a player on the visiting team for two baseballs.

WHERE TO GO AND WHEN TO BE THERE

It's pretty simple. If you want to get baseballs from the players, you need to be near them—not just when they're standing around in the outfield during batting practice but at all times. Any one of them can give you a ball, and if they don't have one, they can get one. It doesn't matter if they're signing autographs near the photographers' box, eating sunflower seeds in the bullpen, or walking slowly off the field. Be there. Follow them. No exceptions.

The home team always takes BP first, but before they start hitting, they stretch and run and play catch in the outfield on their side of the stadium—most likely the right-field side. If the gates open at least two and a half hours early and BP hasn't yet started, find a spot in the seats along the foul line. Meanwhile, the coaches (who are just as likely to toss balls into the crowd) might also play catch in front of the dugout. If that happens, go wherever it's less crowded.

Approximately 90 minutes before game time, the home team clears the field. Make sure you're already in the front row behind their dugout. With so many players and coaches heading your way, you might get two or three balls

The Red Sox playing catch at Camden Yards.

in a 30-second span, but don't waste time admiring them. The visiting team will already be playing catch in the outfield—most likely along the left-field foul line. Hurry out there and get the players' attention before they finish. If you don't, they might end up chucking the balls toward the bucket in shallow center field.

When two guys play catch, they always start close together, then move farther apart (to stretch out their arms by long-tossing) before bringing it back in. Study their body language to determine when they're going to finish. If one of them holds up three fingers, that means he'll be making three more throws; a flick of the wrist means he's about to make his final throw. If the players start throwing knuckleballs or any other goofy pitches, it's a sign that they'll soon be wrapping it up.

Batting practice usually ends 40 to 50 minutes before game time, and when it does, you need to be in the front row behind the visiting team's dugout. Don't wait to run over there until you see the players jogging off the field. You won't make it in time. Head to the dugout with a few minutes to spare; you'll know BP is about to end when the groundskeepers are standing near home plate. (They'll be waiting to break down the cage and prepare the field for the game.) Always ask the coaches for baseballs, even if it appears that they have none. One of them could have a ball hidden in his back pocket.

When I first started attending games, the players regularly took infield/outfield practice after BP, followed occasionally by a quick round of pepper down the foul line. It was great. The snagging opportunities kept on coming. Nowadays, unfortunately, once the last BP pitch crosses the plate, that's it—but don't be too quick to bolt for the concourse. Look for baseballs that might be hiding somewhere. If you see one tangled in the L-screen, get one of the groundskeepers to free it for you. If you discover one wedged behind the rolled-up tarp, ask an on-field security guard for some help. Check all the nooks and crannies—the flower beds near the bullpens, the gaps behind the outfield walls, and the area in front of the batter's eye. If you manage to point out a ball that someone on the field doesn't see, there's a great chance he'll give it to you.

Once your scavenger hunt concludes, you'll have about 20 minutes of free time before the players come back out. Use it wisely. Get your eating and peeing out of the way first. Take some photos for your blog, chat up the ushers, look for ticket stubs, wander all over the place, familiarize yourself with the stadium, and make your way back to the seats behind the visiting team's dugout. (There are just as many snagging opportunities on the home team's side, but it's more crowded.) When the players start throwing, try to predict which one of them will end up with the ball—usually it's the guy with more major league experience—and then move toward his end of the dugout. The first baseman, as a general rule, won't toss you his ball because he'll soon need it to warm up the infielders, but it doesn't hurt to ask.

The dugout is not your only pregame option, so don't worry if you can't make it down into that section. Several guys usually play catch (and then sign autographs) along the foul line in shallow left field, and the starting pitcher always throws near the bullpen. He won't give away his ball until after he finishes warming up in the pen, and even then he might hang on to it. He might tuck it in his glove when he starts walking back across the field, and when he returns to the dugout, he might toss it into the crowd, so keep your eye on him. You should always pay attention. Any ball you see can potentially end up in your hands.

IF IT RAINS

Players are more likely to reward you with a baseball for standing out in the rain like a putz. That's the good news. The bad news is that there won't be batting practice, but don't stay home just because it's wet outside. The stadium will still open early, and as long as it's not pouring, the players will still come out and throw. Tell them you were hoping to get a ball during BP and then ask for one as a consolation prize. They'll hear you. There won't be nearly as many fans (or security guards), so the stadium will be quiet and laid-back. After the players finish throwing, they won't have much to do. Some of them might stick around and talk to the fans and sign autographs. Later on, if there's a delay during the game, you'll get a bonus snagging opportunity when the players come back out to warm up all over again. Don't use an umbrella. It'll slow you down. Just load up on vitamin C and wear a raincoat, and you'll be fine.

CHAPTER 12

THE GAME ITSELF

WHAT ARE THE ODDS?

It's much harder to snag a ball during a game than during batting practice, but it's probably not as hard as you think. Let's say the paid attendance is 30,000. And let's say 30 foul balls reach the seats. What does that mean? That your odds of catching one are 1 in 1,000?

Uh, no.

Your odds are way better than that. Think about all the fans who won't be competing with you. For starters, there'll be thousands of people sitting well beyond foul ball range; at many stadiums, balls never reach the upper deck, so you can forget about anyone who sits there. Then there will be thousands more who don't even bring their gloves, so you can pretty much forget about them too. Of course, most fans who do bring gloves are too young to judge the trajectory of foul balls or too uncoordinated to catch them. And finally, at any given moment, there will be hundreds (if not thousands) of fans who aren't in their seats. They might be standing in line at a concession stand or browsing for souvenirs in the team store or testing their arms at the Speed Pitch booth or making their way toward the bathroom or fighting rush-hour traffic. Naturally, you don't need to worry about these people either. Don't worry about anything. Think happy thoughts. The odds are not insane. And when you start planning strategically (and factor in all the game-used balls that get tossed into the crowd), they'll become even better.

FOUL BALL THEORY

Have you ever seen a batter hit back-to-back foul balls to totally different sections? You know what I'm talking about, right? He'll bloop one into the seats behind the first-base dugout, then jerk the next pitch 430 feet into the second deck down the left-field line—and leave every fan in between thinking, "WTF!!!"

Foul balls appear to be random and unpredictable. They tend to fly all over the place. It's why everyone assumes they're so hard to catch—and can you blame them? How the hell are you supposed to position yourself in the right spot when luck seems to be the guiding factor?

I'll tell you how, but you're gonna have to pay extra-close attention. It's a complicated three-part process, but I promise it'll be worth it. It's the crux of Foul Ball Theory— 20 years' worth of my expertise—boiled down to 237 words. Here we go. . . .

- *Step 1*—Draw an imaginary line from the left fielder through home plate and back into the stands. Although foul balls can land anywhere, right-handed batters hit lots of them in this particular direction. Balls hardly ever fly straight back; they

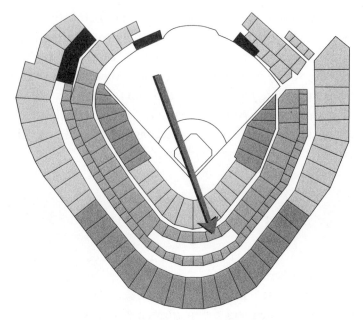

Right-handed batters often hit foul balls in this direction.

deflect off the bat at an angle, so you should never sit directly behind home plate. To find the best angle for lefties, draw the line through the plate from the right fielder.

- **Step 2**—This is the trickiest part. You have to pick the optimal level of seating, and in order to do that, you'll need to make a judgment call. Basically, you don't want to be so high up that balls won't reach you, or so far down that the protective screen behind the plate will be in your way. At Rogers Centre, for example, the screen is so short that foul balls often shoot back into the last few rows of the field-level seats.[1] Wrigley Field, on

---

[1] At many stadiums (including Rogers Centre), the field level is known as the "100 Level," the second deck is called the "200 Level," and so on.

the other hand, has a tall screen and a low upper deck, so your best bet in that ballpark is to head upstairs.

- ***Step 3***—Find the spot that gives you the most range. Sit at the end of a row so you can drift up and down the steps, or better yet, if the stadium has a cross-aisle, stay near it so you can run left and right. Remember, lateral mobility is key.

Once you're in the perfect seat (or as close to it as you can get), it's quite possible that a foul ball will come right to you. If that happens, great. Stick your glove up and think of me when you catch it—but it's more likely that balls will fly in your general vicinity. Here are three things you can do to increase your chances of snagging them:

- ***Deflections***—Foul balls behind the plate sometimes shoot back so fast that they bounce off people's bare hands and deflect deeper into the crowd. Therefore, if a ball appears to be falling several rows short, don't give up on it. Try to get directly in line with it and be ready to pounce.

- ***Rebounds***—Don't give up on balls that fly well over your head. They might bounce off something (like the facade of the press box) and ricochet back toward you. In fact, you should try to sit where it's possible to snag a ball on the rebound because it'll double your chances. Protip: when you first get to the section, take a look around and consider how balls will bounce off various surfaces. For example, if a ball hits a concrete wall, it'll shoot back toward the field, but if it strikes a Plexiglas window, it'll probably drop straight down.

- ***Stand up***—If you can get away with standing somewhere, do it. You'll get a quicker jump on the ball, and you'll be able to cover much more ground. Be advised: you won't be able to

stand unless the section has a tunnel or a cross-aisle, and even
then, the ushers might tell you to take a seat—but it's worth
a try.

Do you remember the strategy from chapter 10 ("Batting Practice") about positioning yourself differently for
right- and left-handed batters? Well, depending on the
architectural layout of the stadium, you might be able to
move back and forth behind home plate during the game.
That's the *real* way to double your chances—to be in the
best possible section no matter who's at bat.

Don't worry if you can't get into the seats behind the
plate. There are several other solid options, starting with
the areas that are marked with an "X" in the diagram on
the right. The best thing about these spots is that anyone
can hit a ball there. Let's say you're sitting near the "X"
down the right-field line. Not only will right-handed batters slice balls in your direction, but lefties will be able to
pull them toward you as well. See the arrows in the diagram? Even though foul balls can go anywhere when
they're hit to the opposite field, a reasonably high percentage of them travel in these general directions. This isn't a
strict rule. It's just a guide, so don't get too hung up on
finding the perfect spot. Just make sure you stay at least 20
or 30 rows back—these balls tend to fly deep into the
stands—and leave yourself some room to run.

Another great way to catch foul balls is to scoop them
up when they roll into foul territory—that is, if you're able
to grab a front-row seat where the wall is low enough.
Whatever you do, don't reach out of the stands and touch
a ball that's in play. Doing so will result in an automatic
ejection, and you could really mess up the game. Try not to

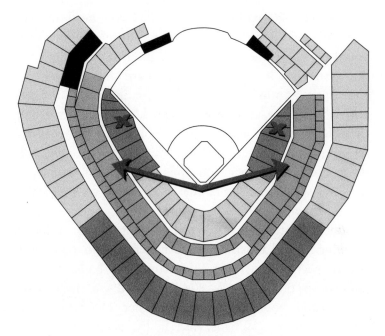

Read the middle paragraph on page 248 to make sense of this diagram.

sit too close to the ballboys or ballgirls; they catch everything near them and hand the balls to little kids. (Of course, if you are a little kid—or if you're with one—you should try to get as close to them as possible.)

When security is lax and the stadium is half-empty, you might be tempted to stay on the move—but don't overdo it. Running all over the place often backfires. If you're not careful (or if you're just unlucky), you'll end up maneuvering yourself out of position. An effective strategy, therefore, is to stick with one spot and play the law of averages. If you sit in the same seat all day, all week, all month, all season, all decade, someone will eventually hit a ball there.

It should go without saying that you need to pay attention—as soon as you look down to read a text from your best friend, the batter will inevitably hit a ball in your direction—but if you focus extra hard and analyze the game, you'll know when foul balls are likely to be hit and you'll be able to pounce much quicker. Why does a ball shoot back into the seats behind the plate? Because the batter swings too late and too low. Which batters are likely to do that? Power hitters who uppercut, pitchers who have slow bat speed, and left-handed slap hitters who typically aim for the opposite field.

When a batter has a two-strike count, he's more likely to swing late on a fastball because he has to guard against an off-speed pitch. The result? More foul balls. When a pitcher tops out in the mid-90s, his fastballs reach the plate quicker and cross the plate a bit higher. The result? You guessed it, more foul balls. And finally, when the manager calls for the hit-and-run play, the batter tries to swing late and poke a ground ball to the opposite field. The result? You get the point. Study the game. Learn the strategies. Consider the physics. Think like a manager. When you sense that a foul ball might be coming, scoot up onto the edge of your seat. Lean forward. Shift your weight to the balls of your feet. It really makes a difference.

You know how a hot hitter will sometimes talk about the game appearing to slow down, almost as if everything is moving in slow-motion while he's able to operate at full speed? If you attend enough games and keep all these strategies in mind, that's how it'll feel when a foul ball starts flying your way. From the instant that the ball leaves the bat, you'll know it's yours. It'll feel like other fans are frozen in place, paralyzed by slow reflexes, as you glide into position and prepare for the catch.

GAME HOME RUNS

Snagging any type of game-used ball is exciting, but catching a home run is monumental. In addition to the intense adrenaline rush that you'll experience, there's the guarantee of being seen on TV, the chance of walking away with an incredibly valuable collector's item, and the satisfaction that comes with owning a piece of baseball history. For the rest of your life, whenever you see the name of the batter who hit it, you'll be able to take pride in having caught a ball that contributed to his statistics—not just his home run total, but also his at-bats, runs scored, RBIs, hits, batting average, slugging percentage, and so on.

The toughest thing about catching home runs is that there aren't many of them. Of course, when you see your favorite team getting pounded on TV, it'll feel like there's a homer plague, but when you're sitting in the bleachers day after day, you'll realize how rare they are. That said, there are times when the batter is prone to go deep, and if you look for all the clues, you'll be prepared. Is he a power hitter? Is he ahead in the count and sitting on a fastball? Is the wind blowing out? Is the ballpark smaller than average? Does the pitcher belong in Triple A? Try to keep these things in mind, but don't let them drive you crazy.

The most important factor is your location in the stands, and guess what? You already know most of the strategies. Everything you read about home runs in chapter 10 applies to the game itself. The main difference is that the stadium will be much more crowded, so in order to run left and right you'll probably have to take advantage of the cross-aisles and standing-room-only sections. Camden Yards has a huge standing-room-only section down the right-field line, and Progressive Field has one in left. If you're at either of those ballparks, those are the places to be, but there are less obvious areas in other stadiums that'll give you room to maneuver. Wrigley Field? Hang out on the walkway behind the bleachers down the right-field line. Dodger Stadium? Although you never see it on TV, there's lots of room to run behind the outfield walls. Safeco Field? Try to get a ticket for the party deck (officially known as the "Budweiser Landing") in left-center. Busch Stadium? There's a sliver of standing room at the back of the cross-aisle behind the right-field bullpen. The list goes on and on. PETCO Park, PNC Park, AT&T Park, and Kauffman Stadium all have great places to stand, and you'll read about them in chapter 13. In the meantime, here are three more things to consider when deciding where to position yourself for game home runs:

- *Competition versus probability*—Is it better to sit in a crowded section where home runs are plentiful or an empty section that only sees occasional action? It's a matter of personal preference. My rule is: if a crowded section has a cross-aisle, I'll be there. I don't care how much competition there is as long as I can get up out of my seat and move. But if you're not good at catching fly balls, then you'll do better with empty seats all around you.

- *The cutoff line*—At most stadiums, when the attendance is below capacity, fans aren't allowed to sit beyond a certain point in the stands. That point is called the "cutoff line," and it's usually enforced in remote sections where you wouldn't want to sit anyway. Every now and then, however, when the attendance is abnormally low, the cutoff line will take effect on the field level—and when that happens, you need to be there. As soon as a ball lands in the empty seats, the race is on.

- ***Hit Tracker***—There's a website you need to know about called Hit Tracker (www.hittrackeronline.com). Go there immediately. The site charts all the home runs in the majors. It shows you exactly where they landed. It tells you how far they traveled. Just click on the name of any player or stadium and you'll see what I'm talking about.

The best place to catch home run balls at some stadiums might actually be outside the stadium. We've all seen highlights of balls sailing onto Waveland Avenue and splashing into McCovey Cove, and you know that homers often fly completely over the Green Monster, right? Those are the three best options in the majors, but it's possible to snag baseballs outside several other stadiums. Do you remember all those balls that bounced into the Allegheny River during the 2006 Home Run Derby at PNC Park? Did you know that Adam Dunn once hit a 473-foot bomb that flew completely out of Miller Park?[2] It's even possible to get balls outside of Progressive and Target Fields, where homers that land in the standing-room-only sections down the lines often bounce all the way back to the gates.

No matter where you are or how slim the odds might seem, you need to pick the right seat and plan your route to the ball. Take a look at the diagram on the top of the next page—an aerial view of the outfield stands—and I'll show you what I mean.

See the dark square? Let's say that represents your ticketed seat, located in the middle of the second row. Should you actually sit there? Hell no, you'll never be able to

---

[2] It happened on July 28, 2009. Nationals versus Brewers. Top of the fourth inning. No outs. 1-1 pitch from Carlos Villanueva. Go look for the footage on MLB.com.

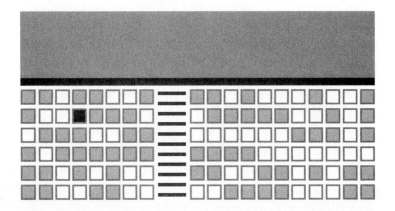

move, so here's what to do. Look around at all the empty seats—those are the white squares—and move to the one that'll give you the most room to run. It's marked with a circle in the following diagram:

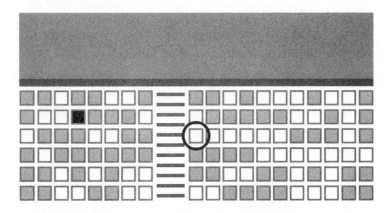

Your new, unofficial seat is great for two reasons. First, it's at the end of the row, so you'll be able to move up and down the steps, and second, if a ball gets hit to your right, you'll be able to do this:

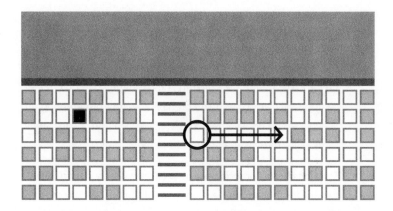

But wait, that's not it. If you really study the section, you'll be able to cover even more ground. Check it out:

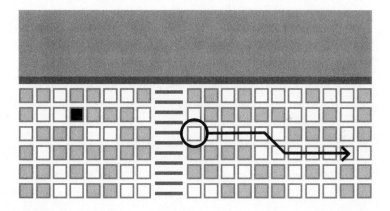

Yes, it's possible to climb over a row of seats (while the ball is in midair) and continue running. You need to be agile, and it helps to be tall, but the key factor is preparedness. As soon as the batter makes contact, you need to start moving.

Everything becomes much more intense when a player is on the verge of a major milestone. The chance to catch a million-dollar baseball brings out the worst in people.

That's the only way to describe it, but there are some specific things you can do to survive the chaos:

- *Buy the right ticket*—If the milestone is truly significant (and if the people who run the stadium know what they're doing), security will clamp down and prohibit anyone from entering the bleachers who doesn't belong there—so don't be cheap. Spend a little extra money and buy a seat in the outfield.

- *Practice during practice*—Use your time wisely during BP to prepare for the big moment. Instead of running all over the place and trying to get the players to throw balls to you, stay in the outfield and focus on catching homers. Take extra care not to get hurt. Watch out for aggressive fans and don't attempt any circus catches. You need to save yourself for the game.

- *Look both ways*—This is something you should always do, but it's even more important when trying to catch a milestone home run: look around before every pitch to make sure your path is clear. If you're sitting at the end of a row, turn around and make sure there's not a vendor crouching behind you on the steps. If you're sitting near a cross-aisle, glance left and right in case the ushers are standing nearby.

- *Raise your hand*—If you're trapped with lots of other fans in a standing-room-only section, don't keep your arms at your sides. You won't be able to lift them if you get pinned against people in the crowd. Cross your arms in front of your chest and rest your glove on your shoulder. That way, no matter how packed it gets, you'll at least be able to reach for the ball.

- *Think positively*—Don't assume that you're not going to get the ball. The odds might seem impossible, but you need to stay focused and truly believe that you're going to catch it. I'm not talking about fate. I'm just telling you to jump up instinctively and start moving toward the ball as if the whole thing were scripted.

- ***Move with urgency***—As soon as the batter makes contact, other fans are going to jump out of their seats in anticipation, even on a pop-up to the shortstop or a foul ball behind the plate. Everyone's gonna be so geeked up that they'll be flinching at the first sign of action—so you can imagine how they'll react once they realize that the ball is actually flying in their direction. Other than running at full speed, the best thing you can do is to take nothing for granted. Fans will be closing in on the ball from all sides; even if it looks like you have a clear path, someone might appear out of nowhere and try to cut you off.

- ***Prepare for impact***—As you're getting ready to make the catch, expect other fans to be physical. Don't wear a floppy glove. The ball might get knocked loose. Brace yourself and try to make the catch with both hands, but don't reach up too soon or your arm might get yanked down.

When you catch a milestone home run ball, don't hold it up and celebrate because it might get ripped out of your hand. Keep the ball in your glove, squeeze it shut, pull it tight against your chest, and wrap your bare hand around it. Don't let anyone else hold it or touch it. Other fans will ask. They'll want to take pics. They'll be persistent. Tell them no. Be rude if you have to. Keep your death-grip on the ball until you're surrounded by stadium security.

NICE CATCH! NOW WHAT?

On average, roughly one of every 15 home runs is so important that the player or team will try to get the ball back. There's not an official stat for this. It just seems to work out that way, and the ball might be meaningful for any number of reasons. It might be the batter's first major league homer, or the 100th, 200th, or 250th of his career. It could be his first long ball with a new team or in a new league or in a new stadium. It might represent his 500th career hit or his 1,000th lifetime RBI. It could be the team's 10th grand slam of the season or the 10,000th home run in franchise history. You never know—and sometimes the significance is totally personal. When Brewers second baseman Rickie Weeks hit a seemingly ordinary homer on April 15, 2009, he sent a team representative into the stands to retrieve it. Why? Because Weeks is African American, and Major League Baseball was celebrating Jackie Robinson Day.

If you catch a significant baseball, the first thing you should know is that MLB does not have an official policy for getting it back from you. That task is left to the individual teams, and some handle it better than others. In most cases, the representative will start by offering you another piece of memorabilia for it—usually a ball signed by the player. If you think that's fair (as many fans do), then go ahead and make the trade. The player will appreciate it, and you'll have a special item to add to your collection. If, however, you feel that your home run ball is worth more—emotionally or financially—than what's being offered in exchange, you have every right to ask for something else or to simply say no. That's what happened with the Weeks homer. The rep made a lousy offer, and the fan decided to keep it. That's how these things work. Nobody owes anybody anything, so go with your gut.

What's the "right thing" to do? It depends on who you ask, and sometimes there's just not an answer. When Mark

McGwire hit his 62nd home run in 1998 to break Roger Maris's single-season record, the ball was grabbed by Tim Forneris, a Cardinals groundskeeper, who returned it. No questions asked. Just like that. One week later, when McGwire connected on number 63, a fan named John Grass made the catch and requested the following: three signed bats, three signed caps, three signed gloves, three signed balls, three signed photographs, five signed jerseys (including two from Stan Musial), two signed jackets, four season tickets, four round-trip plane tickets to the Cardinals' Spring Training home in Jupiter, Florida, along with hotel accommodations for a week, the honor of throwing out a ceremonial first pitch with his son at Busch Stadium, and an additional signed ball and bat for every member of his family.

Did the Cardinals actually give Grass all this stuff?

No. And he kept the ball.

Did he have a right to ask for all that in the first place?

Absolutely. And he got skewered by the media for being greedy.

But was he really out of line? When you consider that the items on his wish list probably would've cost the team less than $5,000 and that he later received a $200,000 offer for the ball, Grass could have been praised for giving the Cardinals a hometown discount.[3]

---

[3] The $200,000 offer came from Todd McFarlane—the same collector who ended up paying $3.005 million for McGwire's 70th home run ball of the season. Grass, unfortunately, turned it down and sent the ball to auction, where it sold for $50,000. As for homer number 70, do you want to guess what the Cardinals offered to Phil Ozersky, the fan who snagged it? C'mon, think big. We're talking about the most valuable baseball in history. Ready? The team offered him a signed bat, a

And what about Forneris? Was he really such a hero? At least one member of the media didn't think so.

"Returning a pricey baseball to an athlete is not refreshing. It's sickening," wrote *Boston Globe* reporter Michael Holley. "It's the American phenomenon of doing for the famous what you might not do for your next-door neighbor. It's the puzzling action of restaurateurs and clothiers who invite millionaires to their businesses and let them eat for free."

See what I mean? There's not an answer, but I'd say Jameson Sutton had the right idea after snagging Barry Bonds's final home run in 2007. He decided to send the ball to auction, and when a reporter asked him at the press conference how he'd feel if the Giants slugger were interested, he replied, "Mister Bonds is welcome to come bid on it."

Players never seem to buy back their milestone balls, but fans occasionally hold them for ransom anyway. The most outrageous example took place in 2005 when the guy who snagged Jorge Posada's 1,000th career hit—a ground-rule double at U.S. Cellular Field—demanded $20,000 for it. The incident was so absurd that the media barely covered it, yet die-hard fans who hold out for memorabilia are often portrayed as villains. In 2009 a well-known ball-hawk named Nick Yohanek got blasted by the media and received hate mail from people all over the country. His crime? Catching Marlins outfielder Chris Coghlan's first major league homer and requesting too many goodies in return—two signed bats and a signed ball, to be specific—

---

signed ball, and a signed jersey. Yeah, thanks. (Naturally, there were people who criticized Ozersky for selling the ball.) Deni Allen, the fan who snagged McGwire's 60th long ball of the season, returned it for a signed ball, two signed bats, two season tickets, and the chance to take BP with the team.

from a franchise that Forbes.com had recently valued at $244 million. But there was more to it than that. The Marlins had initially promised Yohanek the bats, then reneged and accused him of pawning off a phony ball despite the fact that he'd been the first one to suggest having it authenticated.[4] Ultimately, Yohanek gave Coghlan the real ball in exchange for just one bat; the Marlins promised him tickets to an upcoming series, but never delivered.

What do we learn from all of this? That if the ball isn't *that* valuable, and if a team arbitrarily decides that you're a jerk, things can get messy. If you want to play it safe, ask for a signed bat from the player who hit it. That's a common and reasonable request, but if you're not into lumber, ask for a pair of batting gloves. Or a cap. Or hell, even a jockstrap, if that's your thing. At the very least, you should be allowed to meet the player and hand the ball to him, so make sure that's part of the deal. You might get escorted to the clubhouse or to some other secret part of the stadium during or after the game, but you know what? It doesn't matter where the transaction takes place. If the player won't give you a minute of his time, then the ball obviously isn't that important to him.

———————

[4] If you ever snag an important ball, you should immediately ask for an authenticator. There are at least two at every game, but they work so covertly that some ushers and security guards won't know what you're talking about. If that happens, keep asking. Tell them to call their supervisor. Then tell the supervisor to call *his* supervisor. You might get weird looks—these people might not realize that a baseball is worth all the fuss—but don't give up. If you leave without getting the ball authenticated, you'll never be able to prove that it's *the* ball. When a player is on the verge of hitting an ultra-valuable home run, the balls get marked with serial numbers. Then they get put into play sequentially by the home plate umpire and tracked by MLB representatives, so no one can make a phony claim about snagging one.

If the ball isn't that important to you, or rather, if it's less important than your team loyalty, there's something else you can do with it: throw it back onto the field. In the summer of 1969, a Cubs fan named Ron Grousl—one of Wrigley Field's original "bleacher bums"—did exactly that after catching a Hank Aaron homer. The crowd went wild. His gesture was seen as the ultimate sign of disrespect to the visiting Braves, and a tradition was born. Limited to Chicago at first, the practice eventually spread to other cities, and it's now such a common occurrence that some teams have written policies explaining the procedure. The Diamondbacks' website states that "guests are allowed to return a visitor's home run ball to the field; however, it must be done immediately and in such a way that it does not endanger any player." In other words, don't wait half an inning and then try to peg the guy who hit it.

The first time I ever caught a game home run on the fly, I happened to be at the old Yankee Stadium, and it happened to be hit by a player on the visiting team. I knew what was coming next. More than 25,000 fans started chanting, "*Throw it back!! Throw it back!!*" and when I sat back down with the ball, they all began chanting a certain seven-letter word that isn't fit for print.

Peer pressure is rough. Even die-hard Cubs fans have their way around it. Some of them keep an extra ball handy, just in case they catch a visiting team's homer that they secretly want to keep. Then they'll make a quick switch and throw back the dummy ball—sometimes with a message written on it like, "Don't throw that pitch again," or, "Cardinals suck." Then again, some fans are so loyal (or perhaps just clueless) that they'll hurl the real ball regardless of its value. The first home run in Marlins history (hit by Benito Santiago in San Francisco), as well as

A-Rod's 40/40 ball (hit in Anaheim) and Ivan Rodriguez's 300th career dinger (hit at Wrigley), were all tossed back.

Depending on the city, you might not be allowed to participate in the tradition. The Oakland Coliseum "A-to-Z Guide," for example, warns that "guests entering unauthorized areas of the stadium to retrieve home runs and throwing balls back on the field are subject to ejection and/or arrest for trespassing." So in other words, watch yourself.

Finally, there's one more thing you can do after catching a valuable home run: donate it to the Hall of Fame. Not only will the act of giving back to the baseball world leave you feeling warm and fuzzy, but the Hall will acknowledge you as the donor and give you a lifetime pass for free admission.

THIRD-OUT BALLS AND OTHER TOSSES

The easiest way to snag a foul ball is to get one thrown (or handed) to you. Ballboys, ballgirls, first- and third-base coaches, on-deck batters, and corner outfielders all give them away with some degree of regularity. And that's just the start. Balls that roll into the dugout often get flipped into the seats. Balls that land in the photographers' boxes usually get handed to young fans. Balls that fly into the press box almost always get tossed into the crowd below. And remember, stadium employees are not supposed to keep balls, so when a vendor, usher, security guard, or mascot nabs one, they usually hand it to the nearest kid. Even the first- and third-base umpires occasionally scoop up grounders that ricochet off the walls in foul territory. If you're sitting near one of the umps, don't get discouraged if he grabs a ball and sticks it in his back pocket; he might be waiting until the third out to pick a worthy recipient.

THE THIRD OUT.

Those three words are so important that they deserve to be capitalized on their own line. Nearly every half-inning, the fielder who records the third out ends up tossing the ball into the crowd. Sometimes, when an outfielder catches it, he'll fire it into the bleachers or flip it to a fan sitting along the foul line as he jogs in, but the third-out ball usually gets tossed over the dugout. *This* is the easiest way to snag a game-used ball, and these are the strategies:

- ***Pick an end***—After the third out, the catcher will head toward the home plate end of the dugout, while his teammates hustle toward the outfield end. Therefore, it helps to predict which player will bring the ball back or, in other words, how the third out will be recorded. How can you tell? Check out the pitcher's stats. If he averages a strikeout per inning, there's a good chance that the catcher will end up with several third-out balls. (Of course, if the pitcher is striking out that many batters, it probably means that he throws hard, in which case there'll be lots of foul balls shooting back into the seats, and you might want to rethink your entire strategy.)

- ***Race to the front***—The ball often gets tossed to a fan in the front row. Assuming you're not already sitting there, you need to get there as quickly as possible. During the first few innings, there won't be much competition; most other fans won't be aware of the incredible snagging opportunities, but they'll soon catch on and start streaming down the steps when each inning ends. The way to beat them is to anticipate the third out and start moving as soon as the ball is put in play. That way you'll already be in the front row by the time the out is recorded.

- *Keep your eye on it*—The player who catches the ball for the third out might not be the one who ends up tossing it into the crowd. Guys sometimes throw the ball around as they head back to the dugout, so never take your eye off it.

- *First baseman comes first*—Pay extra-close attention to the first baseman. He'll be the fielder providing most of the action, so you should try to learn his tendencies. Does he generally lob the ball into the front row behind the middle of the dugout, or does he have a habit of chucking balls to fans near the back of the section? Are those fans kids? Are they wearing gear with his team's logo? Are they doing anything special to get his attention, or is he picking his targets randomly? Look for all the clues.

- *Hold your ground*—Whether or not you've ever given any serious thought to snagging baseballs, you may have noticed that the first baseman catches a ball every inning as he jogs off the field. That ball gets thrown from the dugout by the first-base coach. It's the infield warm-up ball. There's no real reason why it gets thrown. The coach could just as easily hand it to him, but whatever, that's how it's done—and it seems to confuse people. Fans mistakenly think that *that's* their chance at getting a ball, so when the first baseman (predictably) ignores them, they'll turn around and head back up the steps. Don't follow the crowd. Stay in the front row and wait for the other fielders to come in. One of them should have the ball, and if you've been keeping your eye on it, you'll know who it is.

There are other ways to get balls thrown to you during the game. When each new half-inning is about to start, the first baseman will lob the infield warm-up ball back toward the dugout, where one of the coaches may give it away. In rare cases, that lob will accidentally land on the warning track and bounce into the seats, so stay alert. Meanwhile, outfield warm-up balls also end up as souvenirs, especially late in games, though some players throw them into the stands every inning. Game-used balls can get thrown into the crowd unintentionally; there are 55-footers that occasionally deflect off the catcher and wild throws across the diamond that elude the first baseman. Finally, home run balls often bounce out of the stands and then get tossed back in—so it's not always that tough to snag a piece of baseball history.[5]

AFTER THE FINAL OUT

Don't bolt for the exit. There's all kinds of snagging potential after the game, and it starts with the home plate umpire.

Yes, the umpire.

When the game ends, the ump will have a few extra baseballs in his pouches—and if he has any respect for humanity, he'll give at least one of them away. In order to take advantage of this lesser-known opportunity, you'll

---

[5] You never know when a valuable ball will land in your lap. In 2007, after Rockies shortstop Troy Tulowitzki turned the 13th unassisted triple play in major league history, his teammate Todd Helton absent-mindedly tossed the ball into the crowd. The following season, Indians second baseman Asdrubal Cabrera turned a triple play of his own and made the same mistake. And let's not forget Phillies second baseman Mickey Morandini, the pioneer of triple-play brain-farts. When he turned one in 1992, he dropped the ball on the mound as he jogged off the field—and no one noticed. "That was stupid on my part," he later told the Associated Press. "It was probably hit as a foul ball to some fan."

need to find out two things ahead of time. The first is the exact location where the ump will walk off the field, and the second is his name. Fortunately, you can get this info right before the game starts. Just pay close attention when the umps are announced. You'll hear their names and see them walk onto the field. That's all there is to it. Wherever they enter—perhaps from the outfield end of the third-base dugout or through a tunnel directly behind the plate—that's where they'll exit.[6]

As soon as the game goes final, you'll have approximately 10 to 30 seconds before the umpires make it off the field. Fight your way (not literally) past all the fans who are walking up the steps and hurry down to the front row. Then, when the home plate ump approaches, shout the word "Mister" followed by his last name. Although it hasn't been scientifically proven, last names work better in these situations because the umpires tend to be a bit older and don't usually get any respect—but don't be too polite. It's going to be loud, and the umps will be walking fast, so if you waste even one second by shouting, "Excuse me," you might miss your chance.

Next up: the winning team's dugout.

After every game, the winning team gathers near the mound to exchange some combination of fist-bumps, high-fives, handshakes, hugs, and pats on the buttocks—but the lovefest won't last long. By the time the umpires are gone,

---

[6] I know I've mentioned lots of stuff that you should bring to the game, but there's one more item that could come in handy: Major League Baseball's official umpire roster. Keep a copy with you at all times—you can find it online by searching for "MLB Umpire Roster"—and you'll be able to identify the home plate ump if you miss his name when it's announced. In case you never noticed, umpires have uniform numbers too.

the first few players might already be walking off the field. More specifically, they'll be heading toward the home plate end of their dugout, so if possible, get over there as fast as you can. Any player or coach can potentially toss you a ball—guys sometimes take balls from the dugout just to give them away—but the pitcher is your best bet. The game-ending ball will probably get handed to him, and if it wasn't used to record a milestone, he'll have no reason to keep it. (In the event of a walk-off win, there's no telling where the final ball will wind up.)

If the umpires' exit is nowhere near the winning team's dugout, you'll have to pick one spot over the other. Whenever I'm forced to choose, I usually go for the dugout when the visiting team wins; it's too noisy and crowded otherwise. The advantage of choosing the dugout is that the opportunities keep on coming. After the initial horde of players and coaches clears the field, the unused relief pitchers (along with the bullpen coach and bullpen catcher) will be walking in from the bullpen. Move to the outfield end of the dugout—that's where they'll enter—and if one of them has a ball, try to be the first fan to ask for it. Shout his name before he crosses the foul line. Make him decide as early as possible that he should throw it to you. (If you happen to be in the bleachers when the game ends, try to get the relievers to toss you a ball before they make the trek toward the dugout. I've gotten several balls like this. It's a solid option.)

Once all the players and coaches are gone, the ushers will probably tell you that it's time to go home. Humor them. Make it look like you're leaving. Head for the concourse. Move toward the exit if they happen to be watching you, but don't leave the stadium until security kicks you out.[7] In the meantime, consider every possible place where a ball could be hiding. There might be a BP home run ball in the bushes in front of the batter's eye or a scuffed warm-up ball tucked underneath the bench in one of the bullpens. Go investigate, and if you're lucky enough to spot one, stay calm. Try to snag it with your glove trick or get one of the groundskeepers to retrieve it for you. I said it before, and I'll say it again: anything's possible.

---

[7] In most cities, that'll take half an hour; in New York, it's like two minutes.

CHAPTER 13

TOP 10 LISTS AND OTHER THINGS OF INTEREST

TOP 10 BALLHAWKS OF ALL TIME

Most dictionaries define "ballhawk" as an athlete who plays good defense and handles the ball well. There's no telling when this word was first used to describe ball-snagging baseball fans, but one thing is certain: the mere mention of it makes some people uneasy. Given that a hawk is a predatory animal, and that maniacs in the stands occasionally trample little kids, it's not really surprising. But the fact is, experienced ballhawks are much more likely to hand your kid a baseball than to steal one from him. And when it comes to the most accomplished ballhawks of all time, you're often dealing with the most knowledgeable and well-respected fans in the stadium—guys who've been going to games for decades, who hang out with the players, who know the clubhouse attendants, who serve as the watchdogs of the bleachers and the unofficial historians of the sport. And yet, despite all their TV appearances, they remain largely unknown. Here, then, for the first time ever, is a collection of interviews with the top 10 ballhawks of all time:

NAME: MOE MULLINS (aka "Mr. Inside")

Moe Mullins

Born: October 11, 1950, in Lima, OH

Occupation: Truck driver

Regular at: Wrigley Field

Total Balls Snagged: 5,441 (including 1,500 to 2,000 at Spring Training)

Game Home Runs: 241 (all from major league games)

Notable Balls: Sammy Sosa's 62nd home run in 1998, plus five grand slams

Greatest Feat: Snagging four game home runs in one game

Did you really snag number 62? "I know I had the ball. I had it for a long time at the bottom of the pile with both hands cupped around it, and everybody was just pullin' and pushin' and reachin' in there, and I'm bein' jumped on, and you know pretty soon I had 15, 20 people on top of me. I couldn't breathe anymore. My knuckles and hands were all swollen from bein' dragged on the concrete—they were all bloodied up and everything—and I actually believe that I passed out for a couple seconds from lack of oxygen, and I was tellin' myself, 'Moe, give up the ball, it ain't worth dyin' for,' but I was thinkin' that sooner or later people are gonna start pullin' these people off of me.

Well, finally, the guy I took to court, Cunningham, got ahold of my thumb and he pulled it all the way back—I had torn ligaments in it for three years—and I'm already expended. I had no more energy. He just took it out of my hand, and he ran and everybody ran after him. He ended up going a block down and then got into a squad car because the people were chasing him. We thought that ball was worth a million dollars."

What does your wife think about all of this? "I think she's very appreciative of what I do. She knows that it's like the last grasp of my youth, and it keeps me young and in shape, and although I have had some skirmishes with the law doing this, believe it or not, usually it's unwarranted."

Is ballhawking ever a burden? "Sometimes I can't fall asleep, knowin' what the wind and the weather is gonna be the next day. You know, you're layin' in bed thinkin' about it, and I'm countin' balls instead of sheep, tryin' to fall asleep. Yes, it can be a burden at times."

First Ball: "I was in third grade. I was comin' home from lunch, just walkin' down the street, and a ball came out right by the alley, and I picked it up and a bunch of guys—people that I didn't know at the time, these old ballhawk guys—were all chasing towards me, and they said, 'Hey, good grab, kid.' I didn't know that I could actually catch baseballs out there, and there was a reward for it. You could actually give the ball back and get into the park or you could sell it, and I sold balls for as little as 50 cents back then and go buy a hamburger at O'Henry's, and hamburgers were 24 cents. I got two hamburgers for catching a ball."

Media Highlight: Featured in several books and movies, including a documentary called *Wrigley Field: Beyond the Ivy*

NAME: RICH BUHRKE (aka "Mr. Outside")

Born: June 22, 1946, in Chicago, IL

Occupation: Security guard

Regular at: Wrigley Field, Old Comiskey Park

Total Balls Snagged: 3,476 (including 1,059 from Spring Training and 95 from the Minor Leagues)

Game Home Runs: 179 (including 4 from Spring Training)

Notable Balls: Jay Johnstone's 100th career home run, Bill Melton's 100th, Ron Santo's 300th, and five grand slams

Rich Buhrke

Have you ever been accused of knocking a kid over? "Oh yeah, we've all been accused of that, but I can honestly say that I never ran down anybody in my life, and I never will. To me, that's not what it's all about. I've hurt myself banging into seats trying to avoid people rather than running into them."

How have you been able to attend so many games? "My son was born in '69, and when he was just old enough to go to the ballpark, I used to take him with me. I was Mr. Mom. My wife and I exchanged roles for 10 years, and I also went to college at the time and got my degree—two degrees, actually."

Have you given any balls away? "I supplied baseballs for Little Leagues that my son played in for years, so they'd use 'em as practice balls. Sometimes they'd use them as game balls if they were good, but I never give away my last ball. You never know in life when that *is* gonna be your last. I don't care if I got 3,000, I'm not givin' that last one away."

Have you sold any balls? "I sold home runs for my 30th wedding anniversary, and it paid for an entire trip to Jamaica. They were game home runs—some of them signed, some of them not—and then for our 35th anniversary I paid for our whole vacation to Florida, which included the airfare, the hotel, and the car rental. Do I wish sometimes I had some of those back? Yeah, I do, but not when I consider what it was all about. It was an anniversary situation. If I had it to do all over again, I'd do it again."

How many balls are still in your possession? "I have two full-sized black garbage cans—you know, the huge cans that you have outside—filled to the top and into the lid. I have all that and home runs. I couldn't tell you exactly how many of those I have left."

Do you have any superstitions? "I used to try and wear the same shirt out if I had a really good day, but that was way back."

Did you wash the shirt between games? "Nope."

Media Highlight: Featured in a *Sports Illustrated* article in 1977, interviewed by Oprah Winfrey in 1984, and featured in the documentary *Ballhawks*

NAME: JAY DIDION

Born: April 2, 1959, in Tucson, AZ

Occupation: Building contractor

Regular at: Oakland Coliseum, 1981–1995

Total Balls Snagged: 3,500–4,000

Game Home Runs: 112

Notable Balls: Six Rickey Henderson leadoff homers, six Mark McGwire homers, and three World Series homers

Greatest Feat: Caught three home runs on the fly during Game 3 of the 1988 American League Championship Series

Ballhawking—is it luck or skill? "I think it depends on the stadium. The Coliseum was conducive to what I did . . . it was devastating for me for the stadium to be remodeled. It upset my life incredibly. I went to no more games."

Any temptation to come out of retirement? "If the Coliseum was configured correctly, I'd be so happy to go out there and compete with any of these kids."

How was the Coliseum configured before the renovation? "It had a set of steps similar to Dodger Stadium, where you could walk down behind the fence. I developed the technique of sliding down the rail on my hands so that I didn't have to touch the stairs. That would give me time to get down below and be able to catch the ball on the fly."

Can you describe this technique? "I basically dove down the rail on my hands . . . headfirst, straight down. My feet would be in the air and I would be sliding on my hands. The rail was about 15 steps long. My left hand was my lead hand."

Best Player Interaction: "Mark McGwire came up into the bleachers [during BP] and sat down with me for five minutes until too many people came around. He was like, 'So, when you catch my balls, where are you?' He was just trying to get an idea of how it worked."

What is the most unusual way you've ever gotten a game home run ball? "They had a temporary ticket booth underneath the bleachers in left field. There was no roof on this booth, and it was filled with debris from the game—hot dog wrappers and sodas—and the ball went right in there, and everybody was inside that thing—probably three, four, five of us were throwing that debris around and trying to get that ball. It was like mayhem, and the longer it took, more people kept getting into this thing, and we were on our hands and knees digging through a foot of garbage. Finally I felt it inside of a malt cup, and I picked it up and said, 'Got it!' "

Media Highlight: "I never did interviews. . . . I was too cool for school. It was one of those times in my life, you know? I knew I was the best out there, and I didn't need to talk to the media to make myself the best."

NAME: ARTIE LAURAIN
(aka "The Original Mayor of Right Field")

Born: February 28, 1939, in New York, NY

Occupation: Retired Teamster

Regular at: Yankee Stadium

Total Balls Snagged: 4,002 (plus one in Oakland that he doesn't count because he didn't catch it at Yankee Stadium)

Game Home Runs: 44

Notable Balls: Roger Maris's 8th home run in 1961 and Rickey Henderson's 35th career leadoff home run (which tied Bobby Bonds's record)

Artie Laurain

First Ball: Tossed by Yankees catcher Bill Dickey in 1946

How did you get into ballhawking? "Bein' poor. When we got to the game, we saw we could catch 'em. We saved 'em 'cause we loved to play hardball in Central Park or along the East River Drive."

What motivates you to keep ballhawking? "The thrill of it. That feeling. It's better than fishin', better than skydivin', it's better than anything . . . better than sex. Just get there as soon as the gates open and run in and go."

What would your wife say if she heard you say that catching a ball was better than sex? "I don't think she'd be too happy."

Best Player Interaction: "Babe Ruth lived at 76th Street. I lived at 77th Street. So when he rode around the block, I went on his running board. I was holdin' right onto his mirror, and he said, 'Okay, son,' and patted me on the head. 'Gotta get off of there now because you're gonna get hurt.' Mister Ruth's running boards—he was a very nice man."

Worst Injury: "Carl Yastrzemski hit a home run, and a kid put his glove in front of my face, and the ball hit me in the face. I had two black eyes. I'm lucky I didn't break anything."

Biggest Life Sacrifice Because of Ballhawking: "Being away from my family. Missing a lot of dinners 'cause of extra innings, and most of them were Sunday dinners, which were big years ago."

What do you miss about the old days? "There were doubleheaders every other week, and the ballplayers were very friendly."

How have balls changed over the years? "They go a lot farther now. They're really juiced. Years ago the ball felt heavier when you caught it. It felt like it had more cork in it, more twine. They didn't make it as firm."

Media Highlight: Featured in a *New York Times* article in 1996

NAME: JOHN WITT
(aka "Half-Witt," "Nit-Witt," "Dim-Witt")

Born: August 25, 1969, in Melrose Park, IL

Occupation: "Professional ballhawk"

Regular at: Angel Stadium, Dodger Stadium, Wrigley Field, Old Comiskey Park

Total Balls Snagged: 5,071 (including 2,093 from the Minor Leagues, Spring Training, and the World Baseball Classic)

John Witt

Game Home Runs: 101 (not including any from the Minor Leagues or Spring Training)

Notable Balls: Dante Bichette's first career home run, Bob Boone's 100th, Dave Winfield's 450th, Mike Schmidt's 523rd, and Sammy Sosa's 61st in 1998

Most Money Received for a Ball: $7,500 for the Sammy Sosa homer

Are you really a professional ballhawk? "I'm seriously contemplating going back to chasing baseballs full-time, because I know that I can probably make enough money just doing that. It's like, do I want to enjoy myself or do I want to work for a living?"

Worst Injury: "There've been so many. In the mid-'80s, I was in the upper deck at Old Comiskey and went over some seats backwards and messed up my back, and so I actually have a herniated disc, which causes sciatica."

Have you ever met women as a result of ballhawking?
"Definitely. At Angel Stadium, there were a couple times where I'd get baseballs and girls would be askin' for the balls, and I'd be like, 'No, I'm not gonna just give one away,' and then I'd put my name and number on the ball and give it to the usher, and they'd give it to the girl, and a few times I got phone calls."

What's the most annoying thing that other fans do? "The ones that don't have a glove on—you know they're not gonna catch the ball, and they still stick their hands up in your face."

What type of glove do you use? "Right now I'm using an $11 Walmart special."

Greatest Moment: "I got the last rooftop home run at Old Comiskey Park. That was mainly because it was hit by Ron Kittle. He was a friend of my dad's, and my dad had passed away about five years prior to that."

Biggest Regret: "Not going to games and then seeing balls hit. Gary Carter hit his 300th at Wrigley, and I should've been there but wasn't and I have no idea why."

How important is baseball to you? "If baseball didn't exist, I probably wouldn't exist. . . . I'd probably be an indigent living on the streets because I gambled all my money away. Baseball for me is sanity."

Media Highlight: Featured in a Levi's commercial in 1990 called "501 Home Run Kings"

NAME: TRACY COLLINS (aka "T.C.")

Born: December 28, 1967, in San Diego, CA

Occupation: Newspaper subscription salesman

Regular at: Jack Murphy Stadium, PETCO Park, Angel Stadium

Total Balls Snagged: Approximately 3,500 (including 500 or so from Spring Training)

Tracy Collins

First Ball: Doesn't remember

Game Home Runs: 204 (including 50 or so from Spring Training)

Notable Balls: Chad Curtis's first career home run, Terry Pendleton's 100th, Adam Dunn's 250th, and Bip Roberts's walk-off grand slam on May 20, 1995

Greatest Feat: Catching two Ken Caminiti homers on the fly in one game, hit from both sides of the plate

Biggest Regret: "I dropped [Mike] Piazza's 400th career. I jumped for it, and it hit off the top of my glove. That pissed me off. The guys above me got it."

Worst Injury: "Water on the knee. I had that one time. They had to drain the water with a needle. I bumped into a seat during batting practice. Swelled up."

What are your strengths as a ballhawk? "When I was a door-to-door salesman, we used to go up stairs all the time. It builds up your leg muscles good. I'm a firm believer in that. That's what got me so good. I did door-to-door sales for like 20 years. That was like 10 years before I even started ballhawking, but it got me all ready for it."

Any weaknesses? "I can't scramble good, like when [the ball] bounces away, I'm not good at that. I always leave those for other people. I guess I'm too tall. I can't bend down fast."

What is the farthest you've thrown a visiting team's home run ball back onto the field? "All the way back to the shortstop."

Ballhawking—is it luck or skill? "Probably skill. You learn how the balls fly after a while. A lot of people say, 'How did you know where that was gonna land?' You learn the arc of the ball."

What would make you enjoy baseball even more? "Six-out innings. There's too many commercials. Instead of nine innings, I guess it'd be four or five innings or something."

Media Highlight: Acknowledged in 1998 by Chris Berman on ESPN's *Baseball Tonight* after making a nice catch at Jack Murphy Stadium

NAME: ALEX PATINO
(aka "Little Capone" as a kid)

Born: July 24, 1967, in San
Francisco, CA

Occupation: "Trade show installer
and hustler"

Regular at: Candlestick Park, AT&T
Park, Oakland Coliseum

Total Balls Snagged: Thousands

Game Home Runs: 91 (approximately
30 on the fly)

Alex Patino

Notable Balls: Chris Iannetta's first
career home run, Jeff Kent's home run in Game 5 of the 2002 World
Series, and Barry Bonds's 671st, 680th, and 700th career home runs

So, you count number 700 in your collection? "Yeah, I count it
because I got the court document. It says, 'This document hereby
certifies that Alex Patino participated in all aspects of the litigation
and lawsuit related to Barry Bonds's 700th home run ball.' They wrote
it on the piece of paper and they framed that. So that *is* the ball—and
plus they gave me some money too."

How much money? "Just say 'undisclosed amount' because the
judge said, 'Don't say the money.' "

Worst Injury: "I got taken out by a big fat usher lady. We call her
Helga. She checked me, like, I ran into her stomach. She's about

six-three, but to me she's like six-a-hundred, and I ran into her panza. I went down, bro. I didn't even move. My knee twisted, and I didn't want to show it, but I was [in serious pain]. And she knew she did it too. You've seen those boxing videos where they get knocked out and the guy's just looking down at you 'cause you got knocked out? That's what it looked like."

What motivates you to keep ballhawking? "For me it's not just baseball. It's collecting things wherever I go. If we go to Marine World, I'm gonna get something that was a part of something out there. No matter where I'm at—you know the garter belt at weddings? I've got like nine of those. It's not just the baseballs—the baseballs just happen to be a bigger deal."

Do you have any superstitions? "In batting practice, I never look at the guy that's pitching the ball. I'm definitely not a superstition person, but for some reason it just overwhelms me. I feel that if I watch him, the ball's not gonna go where the guy can knock it out. I feel like I'm jinxing him."

Best Player Interaction: "I met Willie Mays, and I told him I'm Mexican, and he told me he played overseas in some Latin games. He said a lot of Latin players are pretty good baseball players. He had a lot of pride—he was proud of playing Latin players. When I heard that, I felt happy that he acknowledged not just Mexicans but Latin people in general. That was kinda neat."

Media Highlight: Featured on ESPN numerous times for home run catches; covered by local news crews showing up at his house during the controversy surrounding Bonds's 700th home run

NAME: LEE WILSON (aka "Doc")

Born: August 18, 1949, in
Hayward, CA

Occupation: Electrician

Regular at: Candlestick Park, Oakland
Coliseum, AT&T Park

Total Balls Snagged: 2,000–3,000

Game Home Runs: "About 60."

Lee Wilson

Notable Balls: Nomar Garciaparra's
first major league hit (which was a
home run) and Barry Bonds's 64th homer in 2001

First Ball: Batting practice home run hit by Willie Mays, caught on
the fly at Candlestick Park in 1964

How did you get into ballhawking? "Having one thing or another
not go quite right . . . it would be something to do in the absence of
being married or having a lot of other good things going on."

What did your mother think of your ballhawking? "She
encouraged me to go more than I should've. She was always saying,
'Go,' and dug the [bleep] out of it when she saw me on TV."

**What is the most annoying thing that people ask you about
being a ballhawk?** " 'What do you *do* with all those balls?' That's
kinda gettin' out of the realm of what they should be concerned
with."

What* do *you do with all the balls? "I get a lot of them signed. I give some away. Some I label because it was a memorable catch for some reason."

How many balls have you given away? "I'd say about maybe a quarter of what I've gotten. There've been a fair number of instances where I've seen adults go diving and grab a ball away from a kid or knock a kid down to get the ball, and I go ahead and give 'em another ball. Sometimes when I get carried away and jump and get one and realize somebody was in position for it, I'll turn around and hand it to 'em. I just try to say that's the normal course of things. I would rather get into a mode of coexisting with a crowd."

What is the best thing about being a ballhawk? "It rounds out the experience. The game is fine, you know, the experience of watchin' the game is fine. Call me spoiled, but I need to get the buzz of participating a little bit."

Do you try to get players to throw balls to you? "No. Having been a failed player, I'm more concerned with makin' plays. I go for the fun of catches more than sheer numbers."

Media Highlight: Included in *SportsCenter*'s top 10 fan catches of all time and in the documentary *Baseball: The Tenth Inning* for his acrobatic play on the Bonds homer in 2001; featured again on *SportsCenter* nine years later after making another impressive grab on a Carlos Pena long ball (ESPN mentioned Wilson by name and showed both catches side by side in a split-screen)

NAME: DAN SAUVAGEAU
(aka "Mister Ticket Mister")

Born: May 13, 1973, in
Bozeman, MT

Occupation: Financial services
professional

Regular at: Coors Field

Total Balls Snagged: Approximately
2,500

Game Home Runs: 77 (including 43
on the fly)

Emily and Dan Sauvageau

Notable Balls: Roberto Alomar's 200th career home run, Sammy
Sosa's 299th, and Alfonso Soriano's 46th in 2006 (which broke the
Expos/Nationals single-season record)

Greatest Feat: Catching two home runs on the fly in one half-inning

Biggest Regret: "I've missed 73 home games in 12 years, and I was
not at the game that Bonds hit 762, and that ball landed 30 feet to my
left. Who knows what would've happened?"

Worst Injury: "I cut my leg open on one of those seats and got a
three-inch scar. I had a couple guys look at it a couple days later, and
they said I should've had stitches. I would've had to miss the rest of
batting practice, so I just sat there and bled."

First Game Home Run on the Fly: "Ellis Burks was my first one, and I went home and I turned on the VCR and my wife looked at me like I was a seven-year-old kid, thinkin' I'm crazy. She didn't understand. You know, they don't understand. This was the first time I ever caught a real home run during a game, and I go home just excited as heck to record it so I have proof."

What does your daughter think of your ballhawking? "Emily loves it. She's actually the one who gives 'em away when I catch 'em during batting practice. She will find the kids to give 'em away to, and she'll always be about three steps ahead of me. She'll come up and say, 'Dad, you gotta catch one. I already told a little boy up there in the blue shirt that I'm gonna give him one.' She has a blast, so it's pretty cool."

Best Player Interaction: "I got to play catch with Mike Maddux from my seat. They didn't have batting practice, and Mike walks out, and he was looking for somebody to bring a ball out and play catch, and I said, 'I'll play catch with ya,' and he said, 'I don't have a ball.' Well, I had one, so we stood there and played catch for probably 20 minutes before the other guy came out, and then once the other guy came out—I don't even remember who it was—we played three-way catch for the next 10, 15 minutes."

Media Highlight: "When I caught the two in an inning, I had *Good Morning America* and the *Today* show call me and want to interview me, but I was headin' out of town the next day to go on a golf trip, so I passed up goin' on both of those 'cause I had a plan forever. I couldn't tell my dad, 'I'm not goin' on the golf trip because I have to be on the *Today* show.' " (*Note:* Sauvageau was later featured on FOX's *You Gotta See This.*)

NAME: GREG DRYDEN (aka "Waldo")

Born: October 13, 1961, in
Minneapolis, MN

Occupation: "I work on cars, do
landscaping, do some mowing,
wintertime I shovel—just a laborer."

Regular at: The Metrodome, Target
Field

Total Balls Snagged: Approximately
2,500

Greg Dryden

Game Home Runs: "At least 50"
(plus a few dozen ground-rule doubles)

Notable Balls: Jim Thome's 299th career home run, Rocco Baldelli's
first career grand slam, and a Todd Sears walk-off homer

How did you get into ballhawking? "I was trying to get my kid
away from wanting to collect Pokemon cards and trying to make
baseball exciting for him. Next thing you know, instead of going to
five or six games a year, I started going to 20 or 30, and then I was
like, 'I wanna try a perfect season.' Do you know how hard it is to go
to 81 games a year? That's a lot of work—stayin' healthy. You come
sick or you got a bad tooth or whatever, you know? I was still there,
cheerin' for the Twins."

How many consecutive games did you attend? "Five years and
68 games. I missed game 13 in '04 and then never missed another
game at the Dome, countin' playoff games too."

What do you do with all the balls? "If I've kept any baseball, it's got an autograph on it. I'll carry baseballs around with me wherever I go. . . . Everybody always freaks out—'You want me to sign a major league ball?' Marie Osmond? Holy cow. She came out of her limo, and I asked her if she could sign, and I handed her a baseball, and I said, 'But I need you to sign the sweet spot.' She goes, 'I've heard about that. What *is* the sweet spot?' So I got to rub elbows with her, and I hooked her up with one. I said, 'Here's a batting practice ball from the Metrodome.' She goes, 'Really?! This is my first baseball!' and I says, 'See? Baseballs are fun.' She blew everybody off and sat and BS'd with me for about five minutes."

Best Player Interaction: "When Torii Hunter came out every game, right before the first pitch, I would stand up and go, 'Heeeeeey, Hunter!' and then everybody around me would start clappin' and Torii would turn around, give me a chest pump, and point right to me."

Worst Player Interaction: "There were players that would reach up and try to catch a ball hangin' off the wall kinda like what Hunter would do, you know, robbin' people, and I'd be hangin' the other way. Jose Cruz Jr. came up and smacked me in the nuts with his glove 'cause he thought I was gonna steal it from him. He climbed up the wall and gave me a low blow."

Media Highlight: Got his nickname from Twins TV announcer Bert Blyleven, who kept spotting him catching baseballs in the stands and started referring to him on-air as "Waldo" after seeing him catch a Rocco Baldelli grand slam

TOP 10 MEMORABLE BALLHAWKING MOMENTS

It doesn't always take a lifetime of ballhawking to grab headlines. Sometimes all it takes is a single game or even a single moment. Here are 10 lesser-known fans who achieved ballhawking immortality:

DANNY VINIK In October 2007, Danny Vinik was celebrated as the "anti-Bartman" for catching a foul ball at Fenway Park that helped the Red Sox. With one out in the bottom of the fifth inning of Game 2 of the ALCS, Manny Ramirez lifted a foul pop-up that drifted toward the stands near Boston's on-deck circle. As Angels catcher Jeff Mathis raced over and lunged into the front row, the 17-year-old Vinik reached straight up above his seat and robbed Mathis with a bare-handed catch. Ramirez ended up drawing a walk, Mike Lowell followed with a game-tying sacrifice fly, and the Red Sox went on to win the game and eventually the World Series. As for Vinik, there was a song written about him by the Boston Baseball Band (which you can buy on Amazon for 99 cents).

SHAUN DEAN Astros fan Shaun Dean caught two home runs at Game 4 of the 2005 NLDS between the Braves and Astros—the longest game in postseason history. Seated in the second row in left field, Dean caught Lance Berkman's grand slam in the bottom of the eighth inning and later snagged Chris Burke's solo homer in the bottom of the 18th—a walk-off shot that sent Houston to the next round of the playoffs. "All my life," wrote Dean in an article on MLB.com, "I had always dreamed of catching a ball, any ball, at an Astros game. . . . It was special to be a part of

Astros history and to have something to pass down to [my] son."

LARRY QUESENBERRY Lots of fans, believe it or not, have caught two home runs in one game, but on June 10, 2009, at a Royals-Indians contest at Progressive Field, Larry Quesenberry became one of the few to catch two in one inning. With no outs in the top of the fourth, the 59-year-old retired autoworker made a fairly routine two-handed catch on a homer by Jose Guillen. Four batters later—with two outs and a runner on second—Quesenberry used every inch of his glove to make a leaping one-handed grab on a towering blast by Miguel Olivo. His accomplishment was featured on *Baseball Tonight,* where the hosts jokingly analyzed his catches and discussed his solid fundamentals.

LARRY ELLISON When Barry Bonds blasted his 660th career home run to tie his godfather Willie Mays for third place on the all-time list, the ball was fished out of McCovey Cove by a 53-year-old kayaker named Larry Ellison. It was a *big* deal. Mays was at the game. He and Bonds wore "660" T-shirts at the postgame press conference. They both wanted the ball, and Ellison generously returned it. (Karma, anyone?) The next day, when Bonds connected on number 661, Ellison was back in the water and grabbed that one too. He decided to keep it and eventually sold it for $17,000.

DOUG ROHRKASTE On June 22, 2005, longtime Pirates fan Doug Rohrkaste snagged three foul balls at PNC Park within a 15-minute span. He bare-handed a Jason Bay foul ball in the bottom of the first, then snatched two consecutive Jack Wilson fouls that landed near his club-level seat one inning later. Rohrkaste told the *Pittsburgh Post-Gazette* that in the 30 years he'd been going to games, he never came close to catching a foul ball. "It was one of the most amazing things that ever happened to me," he said. "I never had to move more than an arm's length for any of them."

C. J. RAMSEY Snagging two foul balls in one game? Pretty cool, but not necessarily newsworthy. Catching two foul balls on the fly during one at-bat at the age of 12? Now we're talking. That's what C. J. Ramsey did at Rangers Ballpark on August 16, 2009. With one out in the bottom of the fifth, Josh Hamilton fouled the first pitch toward Ramsey's seat on the third-base side, and less than a minute later he sliced another ball in the same direction. Ramsey, who was wearing a glove, reached high over his head for the first ball and elicited a standing ovation with a backhanded catch on the second. "I was, like, wow," Ramsey told Channel 33 *News* the next day. "The chance of me getting one was almost impossible, and two is, like, *not* gonna happen, but it happened."

NICK YOHANEK Unlike the other fans on this list, Nick Yohanek was already well known as a ballhawk; his notoriety, however, reached a whole new level after he made one dazzling catch during Spring Training.[1] It was April 1, 2009. The Brewers were hosting the Diamondbacks at Maryvale Baseball Park in Phoenix, Arizona. Yohanek was standing on the grassy berm beyond the wall in straightaway left field, and in the bottom of the fourth inning Corey Hart jacked one his way. Yohanek sprinted 50 feet to his left, reached the spot where he predicted the ball would land, and looked skyward at the last second to prepare for what should have been an easy play. It just so hap-

---

[1] Yes, Spring Training. It was *that* awesome. And by the way, this is the same Nick Yohanek that you read about in chapter 12.

pened that a bikini-clad sunbather was sprawled out on a bright pink blanket in front of him—a young and very attractive sunbather who not only blocked him as he began to drift forward but was in danger of being struck by the ball. The quick-thinking Yohanek sidestepped her and caught the ball right in front of her face as he tumbled forward into a headfirst dive. The play became an instant highlight-reel classic, but it wasn't the first time that Yohanek, a 30-year-old police officer from Milwaukee, had been featured on TV.[2]

SHANE GIFT In a brilliant display of parenting and athleticism, Shane Gift, a high school baseball coach from Gilbert, Arizona, caught a foul ball with his left hand while holding his three-year-old son with his right arm. But this didn't take place at a high school game, and it wasn't an easy catch. The ball was hit by Phillies catcher Carlos Ruiz at Chase Field on July 28, 2009, and Gift made a barehanded grab, high above his head with full extension. "That's some concentration right there," remarked Phillies TV announcer Tom McCarthy. Gift's son also displayed some skills on the play; the little guy got ever so slightly

---

[2] Yohanek caught two home runs at County Stadium on May 29, 1999, and as you might expect, he celebrated in a rather exuberant manner. When the cameras zoomed in on him, Brewers TV analyst Bill Schroeder said, "There's a ball for a happy youngster." The following off-season, Yohanek met Schroeder's broadcast partner, Matt Vasgersian, who remembered the catches and encouraged him to make a HAPPY YOUNGSTER T-shirt. Yohanek took the suggestion and later told Vasgersian that he planned to wear the shirt on May 16, 2000. Yohanek ended up catching two homers that day, a stunning achievement that sparked a national media frenzy. Now known as "the Happy Youngster," his career totals include 58 game home runs (from major league stadiums) and more than 1,000 balls overall.

jostled, but managed to hang on to his gigantic souvenir soda cup.

STEVE MONFORTO It wasn't the catch itself that turned Steve Monforto into a famous father; it was his good-natured reaction after losing the ball moments later. Monforto, a Phillies season-ticket holder who had never snagged a ball, was at Citizens Bank Park with his three-year-old daughter Emily on September 15, 2009. With two outs in the bottom of the fifth, Jayson Werth hit a foul pop-up toward their seats in the front row of the club level. Monforto leaned over the railing, made a spiffy bare-handed catch, and received some congratulatory fist-bumps from his fellow fans. Then he handed the ball to his toddler, who immediately chucked it over the railing and down into the seats below. Monforto's jaw dropped as he threw his arms up in disbelief, but instead of getting mad, he smiled and gave his little girl a hug. "I didn't want her to think she did anything wrong," he said in a local radio interview—the day before he and his family shared their feel-good story on the *Today* show. (And for the record, the Phillies gave them two replacement baseballs and a set of personalized jerseys.)

ROB MARCHESE This one falls into the "epic fail" category. Rob Marchese, a 41-year-old businessman from Queens, New York, dropped two home runs balls in one game on July 7, 2005, at the old Yankee Stadium. Sitting in the front row of the short porch in right field, he booted an Alex Rodriguez homer in the bottom of the first, then bobbled a shot hit by Jason Giambi one inning later. (The second ball bounced back onto the field. Indians right fielder Casey Blake retrieved it and flipped it into the crowd—right over Marchese's head.) Was Marchese wearing a glove? Of course not. "My son is going to kill me," he told the Associated Press, "because I'm always telling him to keep his eye on the ball."

TOP 10 STADIUMS FOR BALLHAWKING

There are lots of factors to consider when judging stadiums: ticket prices, sight lines, the food, wheelchair accessibility—you name it. It's all up for debate, and yet there's one major element that often gets overlooked. I'm talking about ballhawking, of course. Here are the top 10 snag-friendly stadiums:

CAMDEN YARDS, BALTIMORE This place was built for ballhawks. There's a cross-aisle that extends nearly all the way around the field-level seats, a mammoth standing-room-only section down the right-field line, and a gap behind the wall in right-center. If your goal is to snag a foul ball, stand in a tunnel behind home plate, use the aisle to move laterally, and don't give up when balls fly high above you. They'll often ricochet off the broadcast booths and bounce back. If you're hoping to catch a home run, head to the standing-room-only area (aka "the Flag Court") and stay near the back. Unfortunately, right-handed batters won't hit balls there, and even worse, you won't be able to see the batters in the first place, but it's totally worth it. That spot is usually empty—most fans crowd the front—and there's a ridiculous amount of room to run. Left field is also great for homers. It's only 364 feet to the power alley, making the front rows an easy target for both righties and lefties, and because there are so many rows, you'll have the option of playing deep. You basically can't go wrong at this stadium.

The Flag Court at Camden Yards

KAUFFMAN STADIUM, KANSAS CITY Just like Camden, there's a cross-aisle that wraps around the field level, but forget about chasing foul balls. This stadium was made for snagging homers. In left field, there's a cross-aisle (roughly 400 feet from home plate) that runs behind the seats. In right field, there's a two-tiered deck (aka "the Pepsi Party Porch") with a long stretch of standing room. Both of these spots are outstanding, and as if that's not good enough, there's a walkway directly behind the batter's eye that connects them. In other words, it's easy to run back and forth for righties and lefties. And it gets even better. On both sides of the outfield—directly behind the aisle and the party deck—are fountains with long, narrow pools at the bottom. Yes, balls frequently land in the water. No, you're not allowed to jump in after them. But you can scoop them out with a good waterproof contrap-

The cross-aisle and fountain at Kauffman Stadium

tion.[3] Just make sure you move fast. Balls only float for 30 to 60 seconds.

AT&T PARK, SAN FRANCISCO The most annoying thing about AT&T Park (other than its name and the handful of aggressive ballhawks) is the weather. Because San Francisco rarely gets hot or humid, fly balls don't carry—a real shame considering the stadium's dreamlike configuration. The huge bleacher section in left field has a cross-aisle at the front, as does the smaller section in deep right-center. Meanwhile, there's a long strip of standing room just behind the seats in right field. There's room to run almost

---

[3] I recommend a stainless steel, collapsible vegetable steamer. That's what I used when I visited The K in 2009, and it worked great.

The concession area below the batter's eye at AT&T Park

everywhere, even behind home plate on both the field and club levels, but let's go back to the outfield. At most stadiums, the batter's eye is completely off limits; any home run hit to dead center is literally gone. At AT&T Park, however, there's an open-air concession area below the batter's eye where long balls sometimes end up. It's not a great spot because it's tucked out of view and sits 425 feet from the plate, but at least it's possible to snag there.[4] Another great thing about this stadium is that it's fan-friendly. Giants management allows people to bring in all sorts of ball-retrieving devices—even lightbulb changers (long poles

---

[4] This is where Andrew Morbitzer grabbed Barry Bonds's 715th career home run—a ball, you may recall, that bounced out of the bleachers and later sold for $220,100.

with grabbers on the end). Finally, there's the opportunity to snag baseballs outside the stadium. If you're willing to get wet, rent a kayak and paddle into McCovey Cove. Otherwise, hang out on the promenade (aka "the Portwalk") between the stadium and the water. In addition to snagging homers that fly or bounce out of the park, you'll also be able to get the players to throw balls to you; there's an alcove near the foul pole where passersby can peek inside. Give a good yell during BP and a fielder might arc one your way.

RANGERS BALLPARK, ARLINGTON Rangers Ballpark, perhaps the most underrated stadium in every sense, is like a playground for ballhawks. Want to use your glove trick? Not only are devices permitted, but there are gaps in front of every outfield section. Want to chase foul balls? Not

Fans spilling onto the berm for a BP ball at Rangers Ballpark

only is there a cross-aisle behind the plate in the second deck, but the protective screen is so low that balls shoot back into the field level. Want to catch a game home run? Get ready for an opportunity unlike any other. The batter's eye (aka "Green's Hill") is a grassy berm with bleachers on both sides; whenever a ball lands there, fans are allowed to jump over the side railings and race for it. During BP, opposing players sometimes find it amusing to throw balls onto the hill just to see the wild scrum that ensues. If you'd rather play it safe (and avoid the inevitable grass stains), stand behind the seats in straightaway left field. There's a wide cross-aisle roughly 400 feet from the plate, and because of the extreme heat and humidity, it won't be tough for right-handed batters to reach you.

PROGRESSIVE FIELD, CLEVELAND Before the stadium opens, you might be able to snag a ball or two outside gate A. It's located behind the standing-room-only area (aka "the Home Run Porch") down the left-field line; homers and deep foul balls will smack the pavement and shoot back in your direction. The inside of the stadium has several great spots. In addition to the standing room, there's a cross-aisle at the front of the bleachers in straight-away left field and a huge patch of seats in right. I mean really huge. You can play shallow and hug the foul line or stay 25 rows back in right-center—and when the batter launches a ball to dead center, you might be able to snag that one too. Race over to the Indians' Hall of Fame (aka "Heritage Park") and head down to the lower level. There's a slatted wall at the front and a row of trees on the other side. The wall has a narrow space at the bottom. Crouch down and peek through. If a ball lands in the trees, you might be able to see it, and if it's sitting within arm's length, you can reach through and grab it. Finally, the

The Home Run Porch at Progressive Field

cross-aisle behind home plate makes it easy to catch foul balls, and the extra-wide front row behind the dugouts is ideal for snagging third-out balls and other toss-ups.

TURNER FIELD, ATLANTA Aesthetically, there's nothing remarkable about Turner Field. It's cavernous and nondescript, and its near-symmetry is painfully dull, but the stadium is a ballhawking paradise. Never mind the fact that it opens two and a half hours early. What makes the stadium so great is the massive expanse of seats in left field and the five-foot-wide gap in front of it. Home run balls, glove trick balls, and even ground-rule doubles—the opportunities are endless. When the left-field stands start to fill up (or when a bunch of lefties are due to bat), you can run over to the section in right-center, but beware of the deep dimen-

The gap behind the outfield wall at Turner Field

sions. The batters have to hit the ball 400 feet just to reach the seats, and because the front row is always crowded, we're talking 410 to 420 in order for them to reach a spot where you'll have some room to run. Fortunately, there's a gap in front of that section too. There's also a cross-aisle that runs through the entire field level, so it's easy to move left and right for foul balls. The only problem is that the protective screen is rather tall, so balls have to loop back over it at just the right trajectory. That won't happen often, but on the plus side, the press level is positioned just right to provide a fairly steady supply of ricochets.

MILLER PARK, MILWAUKEE Two words: early access. Miller Park doesn't officially open for the start of BP, but there's a (legal) way to beat the system and get inside. When you first arrive, walk around the outside of the stadium and head to the left-field gate. Then, when you find the Friday's restaurant, go inside and ask for a table on the terrace. The host will lead you to an area of seating that overlooks the outfield—and voilà! Let the snagging begin. The best thing about the terrace is the gap right below it (so come prepared with a device); the worst thing is the one-hour time limit on game days (so don't show up too early). During the regular portion of BP, catching home runs can be tricky because the most expansive outfield sections are in the second deck. What this means is that you'll have more room to roam upstairs, but lots of balls will fall short. It's pretty frustrating, but Miller Park makes up for it by providing the best in-game foul ball opportunity in the majors. The place to be is the second deck (aka "the 200 Level") between the seats and the press box. There's a

The cross-aisle in front of the press box at Miller Park

The Beach at PETCO Park

wide cross-aisle that was custom-built for snagging. It's the perfect height and distance from the plate, but since the ushers probably won't let you stand there, try to buy a ticket in that area. Go for row 10—the back row—in section 217 for right-handed batters and section 220 for lefties. (You're welcome.)

PETCO PARK, SAN DIEGO For the average fan who arrives at game time and doesn't bring a glove, PETCO Park is simply gorgeous. For the serious ballhawk who relies on mobility, the stadium is a giant obstacle course. Aisles end unpredictably. Staircases lead to railings. Concourses are strangely disjointed. Getting from point A to point B can be a real pain, yet the stadium is still great for snagging baseballs. It all begins with the Padres team store, located within the Western Metal Supply Co. Building.

Don't tell anyone about this—it's a well-kept secret—but if you enter the store early in the day and walk to the very back, you'll find a set of glass doors that open up into a small alcove near the left-field foul pole. (Cheers to early access.) Now, in case you haven't noticed, the dimensions are deep to most parts of the outfield. Don't let that discourage you. There's lots of room to run in the stands. In left field, there's a cross-aisle in the second deck, which gets a decent amount of action. In right field, there's an aisle with standing room at the back. In right-center, there's a gigantic sandbox-like thing (aka "the Beach") with lots of open space. And if you want to catch a foul ball, the entire field level has an aisle as well. Not too shabby for a pitcher's park.

CHASE FIELD, PHOENIX Thank God for Friday's. The restaurant chain has a location inside Chase Field, and you don't even need to order anything. Find the entrance marked FRIDAY'S FRONT ROW SPORTS GRILL, take the elevator to the second floor, and make your way out to the terrace in deep left field. Home runs hardly ever land there—you'll be in the second deck more than 400 feet from home plate—but players often toss balls up. Once the rest of the stadium opens, you'll have ample room to maneuver in both the left- and right-field bleachers. Just be careful around the ends of the benches; the sharp metal corners are so hazardous that you should consider wearing long pants, even if it's 127 degrees. For long home runs, you can stand in the concourse on either side of the batter's eye. For shorter blasts (and a unique vantage point), buy a ticket in the narrow area (aka "the Home Run Patio") directly behind the wall in right field. If you have $5,500 to spare, you and 34 of your closest friends can spend the day

The Home Run Patio at Chase Field

chasing home run balls around the swimming pool in right-center. And if you want to snag a foul ball, there's a cross-aisle on the field level behind the plate and dugouts.

PNC PARK, PITTSBURGH It's not quite McCovey Cove, but baseballs do occasionally fly (or bounce) out of the stadium and into the Allegheny River. At its closest point, the water is 443 feet from home plate, and like AT&T Park, there's a promenade (aka "the River Walk") along the edge. Inside the stadium, there are two good standing-room-only areas for home runs. The first is in straightaway left field, just in front of the staircases that lead to the second deck. The second is in right-center on the open-air concourse. There's also a cross-aisle from foul pole to foul pole, but best of all, the paltry attendance means little

The left-field bleachers at PNC Park

competition for you as a ballhawk.[5] It kind of makes up for the retina-searing glare from the late-afternoon sun; PNC Park is one of several stadiums where you might want to bring a pair of shades.

SPRING TRAINING, HOME RUN DERBY, AND THE POSTSEASON

Snagging baseballs during Spring Training is easy. Really really easy. Almost embarrassingly easy. The crowds are

---

[5] This, of course, is a dreadfully selfish way of looking at it, but the way I see it, if a team can't compete and the stadium is empty as a result, you might as well enjoy it.

smaller, there's much more room to run, and the atmosphere is super-laid-back—but don't let that stop you from going. That's what makes it fun. Most of the snagging strategies in this book apply to Spring Training, but here are some extra things you should know:

- *Florida versus Arizona*—Because it hardly ever rains in Arizona, there's usually batting practice, but the ballparks in Florida tend to open earlier. Also, because the Cactus League facilities are all located fairly close to each other, the road teams often take BP at their own stadiums before busing over. Finally, Arizona ballparks generally have better berms (prime home run–catching areas) and provide better access; at some venues, you'll need an actual berm ticket in order to get out there.

- *Size matters*—Spring Training stadiums are so small that balls regularly fly completely out. Whether you're hoping to snag a BP homer or a game foul ball, the best place to stand might be outside.

- *Coming and going*—At some ballparks, fans are allowed to go in and out, but at other places they're not. Make sure you learn about the reentry policy before bolting through an exit and chasing after a ball.

- *Numbers game*—Bring full rosters that list every single player and coach—even minor leaguers and special assistants. Simply knowing some scrubby guy's name could result in an easy toss-up.

- *Backfield in motion*—Many teams hold morning practices on backfields; at some complexes, you might have access to those areas, so do some research ahead of time to find out where you can and can't go. Arizona is usually better in this regard, but Florida provides some opportunities as well. (In Arizona, the dry terrain surrounding certain fields camouflages baseballs. You can save yourself a long walk and scour the ground for balls if you bring binoculars.)

The Home Run Derby is insane. Forget about finding Easter eggs or using a retrieval device; the stadium is packed by the time batting practice starts, and security is incredibly tight. If you're even allowed to enter the bleachers during BP (you might need a ticket for that area), try to claim a corner spot or at least grab some space in the front row. You'll be in the perfect place to get balls tossed to you by the players' kids—not the most exciting way to snag, but it's worth it because many balls will have the commemorative Home Run Derby logo. Two minutes after regular BP ends, there's a brief bonus round for the eight guys who are about to participate in the Derby. Most fans won't realize it, and they'll head back to their seats. Don't be fooled by the mass exodus. During the Derby itself, balls don't get tossed into the crowd, so you'll have to catch one directly off the bat. Don't get trapped in a sea of aggressive fans; you'll be better off standing in the front row of the upper deck 480 feet from home plate than in the 10th row of the lower deck where it's only 380. Guys will be hitting bombs. They'll reach you. Ideally, though, you should try to find a cross-aisle or any other open area where you can run.

The postseason is much simpler. Batting practice is crowded (but not *that* crowded), security is strict (but not *that* strict), and you won't see commemorative World Series balls until the games get under way. On the East Coast, some games start so late that you'll get to experience the strange phenomenon of nighttime BP, but other than that, things are fairly routine. Players still toss third-out balls into the crowd, and the "fans" will leave early if the home team is losing.

BALLHAWKING ETIQUETTE

If you catch two baseballs during batting practice, should you give one away? If a ball is sitting near the bullpen mound, should you feel guilty about snagging it with your glove trick? Is it ever okay, under any circumstances, to reach in front of a kid? The answers are not that simple, so here, once and for all, to help ensure civility in the stands, are the definitive rules of ballhawking etiquette:

- *Sharing the wealth*—No matter how many baseballs you've snagged, it's okay to run around and try to catch another. Once you get a ball, you can do anything you want with it. You can keep it, play with it, sell it, or cut off the stitches and unravel it. You can, of course, also give balls away, and while I certainly encourage that and give away plenty of my own, there's no rule that you have to.

- *To reach or not to reach*—When a player points to another fan before throwing a ball, that's the one time when you shouldn't reach for it, but when a ball is batted or tossed randomly into the crowd, you have every right to go for it. That said, you should still use good judgment. If you see a kid camped underneath a home run ball, consider backing off and letting him catch it—unless he's not paying attention and doesn't see it coming. In that case, you'd actually be a hero for reaching in front of him, even more so if you then hand over the ball.

- *No fighting, no biting*—Do not use physical force against other fans. Don't push or shove, don't yank people's arms down if they're reaching for balls, and don't ever knock anyone over. (Think of it this way: if it would be a foul in a basketball game, then you shouldn't do it in the stands at a baseball game.) If you're racing someone else for a ball, you might accidentally bump into each other. You might slip, get boxed out, or simply lose. It happens. Deal with it and move on.

- *Down in front!*—This applies to all fans, but it's even more important for ballhawks: when moving around during the game, make sure you're not blocking anyone's view or standing in anyone's way. If, for example, the pitcher starts his windup while you're walking down the steps, crouch down and hold still until the action is done—or if you're standing in a tunnel, stay toward one side so that fans and vendors can get past you. Look around. Be courteous.

- *Laws of possession*—If you're scrambling for a ball and someone else grabs it, don't try to knock it out of his hands. If, however, someone pins the ball against the ground by sitting or stepping on it, it's fair game. (This happens more often than you'd think.) Finally, if a fan snags a ball with his cap, net, umbrella, or glove trick, that constitutes possession—even if he hasn't yet grabbed the ball with his bare hand, so let him have it.

- *Glove trick guilt*—Some ballhawks swear by retrieval devices, while others insist that the use of such objects is nothing more than theft. The bigger issue is how the team feels about it. If you're allowed to use a device, go for it, and if you're not, then don't—but there's no need to feel guilty. Even small-market teams are worth hundreds of millions of dollars; they can afford to spare a few extra baseballs.

- *Fan interference*—If the ball is in play, don't reach out of the stands for it. It doesn't matter how valuable or historic it might

be. Respect the game. As I mentioned before, you'll be ejected
if you break this rule, and the ball might get confiscated
anyway (and even worse, you might end up like Steve
Bartman), so there's really nothing to gain.

- ***Sportsmanship***—If another fan plays by the rules and beats
you out for a ball, give him a high-five. Tell him, "Nice catch."
Share the love.

If you're serious about ballhawking, you need a level of
focus and determination that borders on obsession. It also
helps to be strategic and athletic (and to have a job with
flexible hours), but most important, you have to be careful
and respectful. That can be a pretty big challenge, so if you
find yourself struggling with it, just remember—there are
plenty of baseballs to go around.

DOCUMENTING YOUR COLLECTION

Let's say you're sitting in the front row behind the third-
base dugout, and the batter hits a squibber to the third-
base coach, who picks up the ball and tosses it to you.
Pretty simple, right? You're gonna high-five everyone
around you, then call your parents to ask if they saw you
on TV, and eventually brag to all your friends. But what
exactly are you going to tell them? That you caught a foul
ball? Would that really be an accurate way to describe it?

Let's take it a step further.

Suppose the ball gets tossed to another fan, who catches
it and hands it to you. How would that ball count in your
collection? Should it even count in the first place, since you
didn't snag it yourself? What if a stadium employee gets a

ball and gives it to you? Employees aren't allowed to keep balls, so would that be any different? And what about Spring Training balls? Can you count those, or do they belong in a separate category? What about minor league balls? What if you happen to snag a minor league ball at a major league stadium? What if you catch a ball and give it away? Can you still count it even though you no longer own it?

The answer to that last question is yes, at least for me, but here's what it all comes down to: there's not an official scorekeeper for ballhawks. There's no rules committee—no national association or governing body[6]—so ultimately you'll have to make these decisions for yourself.

But hold on. Before you start worrying about how to tally your ballhawking stats, you need to record the details for each ball you snag. Let's go back to that hypothetical toss-up from the third-base coach. If you've only caught a handful of baseballs in your life (which, by the way, is a handful more than most people ever get), you'll probably remember the name of the coach who gave it to you. You'll also remember which stadium you were at, but if you don't jot down a few notes on a piece of scrap paper, you might forget the date. You also might forget who hit the ball and who pitched it. And what about the inning, the outs, and the number of balls and strikes?

When I snagged the first two balls of my life on June 20, 1990, I had no idea how much I'd eventually care about

---

[6] *Guinness World Records* doesn't care. Isn't that sad? I mean, the book features the man who can squirt milk from his eye the farthest. It lists records for the youngest cider pourer, the fastest stamp licker, and the largest collection of airplane sick bags—but there's no love for ballhawks.

these details. Luckily, I happened to save my ticket stub, so I remembered the date—but that's all I remember. I can't recall the names of the Mets players who threw the balls to me, and unfortunately, by the time I got home that day from Shea Stadium, I wasn't sure which ball was which.

This brings up another issue: identifying the balls after you snag them. If you don't have a huge collection, you can keep each ball on a separate shelf or in a different drawer. You can buy plastic cubes for them or simply tell them apart by their markings. One ball might be scuffed. Another might have a smudged logo or a grass stain or a practice stamp or a bat imprint or an extra-dark coating of mud. You can also try to get the balls autographed by the players who hit and threw them, but what if a grounds-keeper pulls a muddy ball out from under the tarp and hands it to you? Are you going to have *him* autograph it? What if you find a ball in the seats or use your glove trick to snag one from a gap behind the outfield wall? Who's going to sign it then? What if you catch a BP homer, but you're not sure who hit it? (It's not easy to identify batters from 400 feet away, especially when they're wearing warm-up shirts over their jerseys.) What if you know who hit it, but the guy refuses to sign it? Will you be able to sleep at night if your autograph collection is incomplete? What if you end up snagging thousands of balls? Are you willing to spend more time going for autographs than for the balls themselves? Can you afford to buy thousands of ball cubes? Would you even have enough space to display them, and given the fact that sunlight darkens baseballs over time, would you really want to?

I spent years trying to figure out a solution and finally, after snagging my 2,000th ball in 2003, started labeling the balls by writing on them. It pained me at first because it felt like I was defacing them, but I got over it pretty fast and ended up appreciating my collection even more. Anyway, it's not like I was scribbling sloppily all over the balls. As soon as I snagged number 2,001, I wrote a tiny "2001" under the sweet spot and later typed the corresponding details into a file on my laptop: "5/24/03, Olympic Stadium, LF bleachers, BP, thrown by Phillies reliever Rheal Cormier."

Meanwhile, I kept a separate game log that looked like this:

DATE	BALLS	STADIUM	BP	ATTENDANCE
May 24	2	Olympic	yes	33,236
May 25	3	Olympic	no	17,023
June 3	4	Shea	no	rainout
June 4	5	Shea	no	rainout
June 5	6 (1)	Shea	yes	19,048
June 10	4	Yankee	yes	37,602
June 11	17 (2)	Miller	yes	12,419
June 12	4 (1)	Comerica	no	13,644
June 13	3	Comerica	yes	19,212
June 24	10	Shea	yes	22,226

The "BP" column simply indicates whether or not there was batting practice; the numbers in parentheses show how many game balls I snagged.[7]

This is how I document my collection. It's not how you

---

[7] Ballhawks are always debating what should and shouldn't count as a "game ball." Technically, any game-used ball should fall into that category, but I don't count the ones that get tossed into the crowd—not even game home runs. It's an arbitrary decision that I made in 1992. Even then, as a 14-year-old with very little ballhawking experience, thrown balls during games seemed a bit too easy and predictable to be counted separately.

have to document yours. If you don't care about the attendance, then don't worry about it. If you don't want to write on your baseballs, then feel free to skip that part of the process. But you should seriously consider keeping track of every game you attend, along with the number of balls that you snag. (Single-admission doubleheaders should be counted as one "game.") Keep a separate list of the players and coaches who throw balls to you. (If a player throws one too short and it lands on the warning track and a security guard walks over and hands it to you, you're allowed to add the player's name to your list.) Keep track of your personal records or let mygameballs.com do it for you. (Most balls in one game, most balls in one season, most game balls in one season, most balls in one game without batting practice, most consecutive games with at least one ball, etc.) And finally, wear cargo pants whenever possible; if you snag six balls in a 90-second span, you're gonna want to stick each one in a separate pocket until you have a chance to label them.

BALLHAWK GLOSSARY

assist—a statistic awarded to a fan who catches a ball on someone else's behalf

authenticator—a Major League Baseball employee who certifies historically significant memorabilia

balligraphy—the use of baseballs to write a number or word

Bob Feller used "balligraphy" to commemorate his 250th career win on May 23, 1954.

berm—a sloped, grassy area inside a stadium

bleacher bite—a cut or scrape caused by running into the corner of a bench

blem ball—a defective (or "blemished") ball; sold to teams at a discount for use during batting practice

BP—batting practice

caddy—a person who performs snagging-related tasks (such as carrying equipment and labeling balls) so the ballhawk doesn't have to

cheat sheet—a printed roster that helps a ballhawk to identify the players and coaches

clean up—to snag a large amount of balls in one day

commemorative ball—a baseball with a special logo

contraption—a ball-retrieving device

corner spot—an end seat in the front row that's closest to the field or players

cross-aisle—an aisle that runs parallel to the rows of seats and provides lateral movement

cup trick—a popular ball-retrieving device

cutoff line—a boundary established by stadium security to prevent fans from spreading out when there are lots of empty seats

device—a ball-retrieving contraption

double digits—ten or more balls snagged at a single game

double up—to snag two balls back-to-back

dugout access—the ability to enter the seats behind the dugouts

dummy ball—a worthless ball that gets substituted for a more valuable ball

early access—entry to a particular section (or to the stadium itself) before the general public can get there

early BP—a bonus session of batting practice that takes place well before the stadium opens

Easter egg—a ball that's lying in the empty seats when a stadium opens to the public

gamer—a game-used ball

gap—an inaccessible, walled-off space between the field and stands

garbage ball—a snagged ball that isn't caught on the fly

glove love—a high-five with glove-to-glove contact

glove trick—a popular ball-retrieving device

jaked—knocked down (or crashed into) by another fan while attempting to catch a ball; named after an aggressive Bay Area ballhawk named Jake Frazier

jump ball—a ball that two or more people jump for at the same time

Lansdowne Street—the street behind Fenway Park's Green Monster

lifer—a ballhawk who's been attending games at one stadium for as long as anyone can remember

logo—the printed stamp on a baseball

McCovey Cove—the body of water beyond the right-field edge of AT&T Park

milestone ball—a ball that's used to achieve a significant statistic

moat—a walled cross-aisle that prevents the common fan from entering the fancy seats behind the dugouts

negotiation—the act of bargaining for memorabilia before returning an important ball to the player who hit it

on the fly—before it bounces

oppo—to the opposite field

overhang—the portion of the second deck that sticks out above the field-level seats

pearl—a brand-new baseball

poach—to enter another section and catch a ball that would've been snagged by the people sitting there

posterize—to make a fantastic catch that's worthy of having a still photograph blown up to poster-sized proportions and placed in a public area

practice ball—a ball that has the word PRACTICE stamped on it

range—the area that a ballhawk is able to cover

reentry—permission to leave a stadium and get back inside

regular—a ballhawk who attends every game at a particular stadium

retriever—a ball-retrieving device

robbed—deprived of a ball that would have been easy to snag

rubbed up—describes a ball that's been rubbed with mud and was therefore probably used during a game

seesaw—an acrobatic catch during which a ballhawk's feet go up in the air and his upper body lowers over the side of a railing

700 Club—the group of fans who have caught a player's career home run number 700 or greater

Sheffield Avenue—the street beyond the right-field edge of Wrigley Field

shut out—sent home without a single ball

snag—to obtain a ball; not to be confused with "caught," which suggests catching a batted ball on the fly

splash hit—a home run that lands in a body of water

spotter—a fan on the inside of a stadium who helps a fan on the outside by indicating when to get ready and which direction the balls are heading

statue—a ballhawk who stays in one place and waits for the ball to come to him

stonehands—a gloveless fan who lets a ball clank off his hands

sweet spot—the area on the ball opposite the main part of the logo

third-out ball—a ball that is used to record the final out of an inning

toss-up—a ball that gets thrown gently to a fan

training ball—a lesser-quality ball used by some teams during batting practice

trickable—able to be snagged with a glove trick or cup trick

tunnel—a passageway that leads from the seats to the concourse

warm-up ball—a ball used by players before the game or between innings

Waveland Avenue—the street beyond the left-field edge of Wrigley Field

ACKNOWLEDGMENTS

Although he doesn't know it, Barry Bonds indirectly contributed to this book with one swing of the bat, so let me start by saying thanks to him.

August 16, 2006—that's when the magic happened. The Giants were in San Diego, Chan Ho Park was on the mound for the Padres, and in the top of the second inning, Bonds launched his 724th career home run into the right-field stands. I was there. I caught that ball. And when my celebration ended, I frantically started calling everyone I knew to find someone to tape *SportsCenter*. Another fan overheard me. He said he had a friend in San Francisco who was taping the game, and then without warning, he called his friend and handed me the phone. Long story short: the guy from San Francisco is now a great friend of mine. His name is Brad Paterson, and he helped me with this book more than anyone. When the project was in its infancy, he brainstormed with me for hours every night. Whenever I wrote a new section, he listened patiently as I read it, and when the first draft was complete, he looked it over and gave me countless suggestions. Quite simply, this book is much better than it would've been had I never met Brad—so perhaps I should also thank Chan Ho for serving up such a meatball.

Two other friends also edited for me: the lovely Lia Norton and the Cubs-obsessed Kelly McMahon. They both gave me great notes, and I didn't even ask for their help. They offered. That's special.

Jona Jolley is also special. Very very extremely special. (Anyone who's willing to be my girlfriend during four different baseball seasons has to be.) She kept me sane when my writer's block was crippling, when my deadlines were overwhelming, and when life itself was a bit much. All those times she made me watch *Jersey Shore,* all those organic vegan meals she made me eat, and all those afternoons when she made me step away from my laptop and go jogging with her in Riverside Park—even though I might've been bitching about these "interruptions" at the time, I must admit that they really helped.

Like most writers, I endured a bunch of ups and downs over the course of this project. My parents, Stuart and Naomi, were there for all of them. They, too, edited parts of the book, but they mainly helped just by being there for me—by being loving and supportive and embracing my inner nerd.

Big thanks to six folks in particular at the Office of the Commissioner of Major League Baseball. Matt Bourne and Jeff Heckelman fielded my initial questions and invited me to ask them in person. Howard Smith not only answered those questions, but helped set up my trip to the Rawlings baseball factory in Costa Rica. Don Hintze and Megan Pearce granted permission to use dozens of photos, and Ryan Samuelson followed up with me on everything.

Rawlings, as you may have gathered, came through for me in a major way. Mark Kraemer, my main contact there, answered more of my questions than any human being should ever have to deal with. He and his boss, Mike Thompson, traveled to San José (and then to Turrialba) to give me a personal tour of the factory, led by plant manager Alejandro Cotter. (On a personal/cheesy note, I had wanted to visit the factory long before I started working on this book, so these guys really did make a dream come true.)

My debt to the Hall of Fame is enormous. Tim Wiles jump-started my research by sending me a phonebook-sized stack of ball-related articles and clippings. Pat Kelly dug up dozens of obscure photos from the archives. Mary Bellew pulled vintage baseballs from the collection, and Milo Stewart photographed them to perfection.

During the 18 months that I worked on this book, editing advice trickled in from all directions, but Jenny Jackson, my editor at Vintage, gets the official tip of the cap. She helped me figure out exactly what the book would be and gave outstanding suggestions throughout the process. Special thanks are also in order for her assistant, Andrea Robinson, for Nicole Pedersen in production, for Cathy Aison in the design department, and for Dan Ozzi, whose publicity efforts began a year in advance.

Gillian MacKenzie, my literary agent, is flat-out amazing. She believed in this project from the start, helped me tackle various challenges that popped up along the way, and continues to share my hatred for a certain major league team. Her assistant, Allyson Paty, and contract manager, Kirsten Wolff, deserve fist-bumps for all their hard work.

I'd also like to thank Ben Acree, the assistant equipment manager of the Atlanta Braves, for giving me some insights about his job; Dina Wathan, the Media Services Coordinator for the Kansas City Royals, for serving as my liaison with George Brett; Jay Alves, the Vice President of Communications and Public Relations for the Colorado Rockies, for letting me poke my head inside the humidor; George Hocker, the president of Maryland Cork, for explaining the role that his company plays in the baseball manufacturing process; Cowles "Pete" Horton III, the owner of Muscle Shoals Rubber, for describing in great detail how his company used to make the pills; Dan Halperin, a Harvard tax law professor, for explaining the financial implications of snagging milestone home run balls; Mell Lazarus, a famous cartoonist and friend of my father, for putting me in touch with Patti Hart-Pomeroy; Patti Hart-Pomeroy, the business coordinator of John Hart Studios, for allowing me to use her father's cartoon strip; George Amores and Dorkys Ramos, two Spanish-speaking friends, for translating for me when I (unsuccessfully) attempted to interview someone in Costa Rica; Bob Weil, a superstar editor and longtime family friend, for generously taking time away from his own work to have a look at mine; Mike Manese, a longtime member of my writing group, for ordering *It's Garry Shandling's Show* for me from Netflix; Leon Feingold, a great friend and former minor leaguer, for being the voice of reason on all things baseball; Zach Mazefsky, webmaster of bigleaguebaseballs.com, for photographing so many baseballs from his own collection; Rick Gold, a veteran ballhawk from Oakland, for putting me in touch with Jay Didion; Leigh Barratt, a long-tenured ballhawk from San Diego, for being the first person to let me in on a little secret about PETCO Park; Kevin Kruse, the unofficial mayor of AT&T Park, for leading me to Brad Paterson; Greg Barasch, my toughest competition at Citi Field, for spending time with me away from the stadium and giving unbelievably good advice; and Jules Owen, one of my all-time best friends, for being a guiding force even while spending nine months a year in Australia.

The following people helped in less obvious ways: Ronen Barzel, Jerome Buie, Wayne Cimons, Michael Fierman, Andrew Gonsalves, Henry Hample, Joe Hample, Martha Hample, Ben Hill, Erik Jabs, Gary Kowal, Maria Maggenti, Steve Mandl, Mike Miles, Linda Paczkowski, Brian Powell, Ryan Restivo, Mike Roberts, Bob Schaefer, Alan Schuster, Ryan Sloan, Brandon Sloter, Mike Smith, Carla Tayao, and Naturi Thomas.

Finally, let me give a quick shout-out to the 1,169 major league players and coaches who have given me baseballs over the years. They are: David Aardsma, Jim Abbott, Kurt Abbott, Paul Abbott, Reggie Abercrombie, Jeremy Accardo, Jose Acevedo, Juan Acevedo, Alfredo Aceves, Manny Acosta, Manny Acta, Mike Adams, Jeremy Affeldt, Benny Agbayani, Chris Aguila, Matt Albers, Manny Alexander, Antonio Alfonseca, Edgardo Alfonzo, Eliezer Alfonzo, Luis Alicea, Armando Almanza, Edwin Almonte, Sandy Alomar Jr., Sandy Alomar Sr., Moises Alou, Clemente Alvarez, Wilson Alvarez, Alfredo Amezaga, Brian Anderson, Marlon Anderson, Alex Andreopoulos, Brad Andress, Matt Antonelli, Bob Apodaca, Rick Aponte, Kevin Appier, Alex Arias, Tony Armas Jr., Brad Arnsberg, Rene Arocha, Bronson Arroyo, Rafael Arroyo, Pierre Arsenault, Paul Assenmacher, Scott Atchison, Garrett Atkins, Brad Ausmus, Bobby Ayala, Luis Ayala, Manny Aybar, Willy Aybar, Mike Bacsik, Burke Badenhop, Kevin Baez, Andrew Bailey, Cory Bailey, Dusty Baker, Paul Bako, Collin Balester, Grant Balfour, Brian Banks, Brian Bannister, Rod Barajas, Jesse Barfield, Clint Barmes, Michael Barrett, Jeff Barry, Jason Bartlett, Daric Barton, Brian Bass, Kevin Bass, Miguel Batista, Tony Batista, Jose Bautista, Jason Bay, Jonah Bayliss, Don Baylor, Billy Bean, Josh Beckett, Steve Bedrosian, Joe Beimel, Stan Belinda,

David Bell, Derek Bell, Heath Bell, Jay Bell, Rafael Belliard, Ronnie Belliard, Carlos Beltran, Rigo Beltran, Adrian Beltre, Marvin Benard, Bruce Benedict, Andy Benes, Shayne Benett, Armando Benitez, Joaquin Benoit, Kris Benson, Chad Bentz, Jason Berken, Mark Berry, Sean Berry, Steve Bieser, Craig Biggio, Mick Billmeyer, Kurt Birkins, Bud Black, Willie Blair, Casey Blake, Hank Blalock, Henry Blanco, Matt Blank, Joe Blanton, Jeff Blauser, Willie Bloomquist, Geoff Blum, Tim Bogar, Brian Bohanon, Jeremy Bonderman, Ricky Bones, Bobby Bonilla, Eddie Bonine, Boof Bonser, Pedro Borbon, Mike Bordick, Chris Bosio, Thad Bosley, Ricky Bottalico, Michael Bourn, Larry Bowa, Ryan Bowen, Blaine Boyer, Chad Bradford, Darren Bragg, Bill Bray, Craig Brazell, Joe Breeden, Reid Brignac, Rico Brogna, Jeff Bronkey, Scott Brosius, Kevin Brown, Jerry Browne, Jonathan Broxton, Jay Bruce, Brian Bruney, Eric Bruntlett, Damon Buford, Jim Bullinger, Kirk Bullinger, Dave Burba, Jamie Burke, Ellis Burks, A. J. Burnett, Pat Burrell, Sean Burroughs, Mike Busby, Homer Bush, Brian Butterfield, Alan Butts, Marlon Byrd, Paul Byrd, Eric Byrnes, Jolbert Cabrera, Melky Cabrera, Miguel Cabrera, Orlando Cabrera, Matt Cain, Miguel Cairo, Alberto Callaspo, Mike Cameron, Matt Capps, Chris Capuano, Jesse Carlson, Buddy Carlyle, Hector Carrasco, Brett Carroll, Jamey Carroll, Chris Carter,[1] Dave Cash, Vinny Castilla, Alberto Castillo,

---

[1] There are two Chris Carters in Major League Baseball; this is the one who debuted with the Red Sox in 2008. More disambiguation: the Alex Gonzalez on my list is the guy who debuted with the Marlins in 1998; Luis Gonzalez refers to the Rockies' infielder from 2004–07; Jose Reyes is the All-Star shortstop; Francisco Rodriguez is the closer known as K-Rod; Mike Stanton is the reliever who appeared in 1,178

Alberto Castillo, Carlos Castillo, Luis Castillo, Bill Castro, Juan Castro, Ramon Castro, Roger Cedeno, Matt Cepicky, Joba Chamberlain, Norm Charlton, Endy Chavez, Jesse Chavez, Bruce Chen, Randy Choate, Shin-Soo Choo, Ryan Christenson, Jason Christiansen, Vinnie Chulk, Ryan Church, Alex Cintron, Galen Cisco, Chris Clapinski, Dave Clark, Mark Clark, Phil Clark, Tony Clark, Royce Clayton, Bob Cluck, Alan Cockrell, Todd Coffey, David Coggin, Chris Coghlan, Phil Coke, Michael Coleman, Vince Coleman, Dave Collins, Jesus Colome, Roman Colon, Jeff Conine, Guy Conti, Jose Contreras, Aaron Cook, Steve Cooke, Brian Cooper, Alex Cora, Archie Corbin, Marty Cordova, Bryan Corey, Rheal Cormier, Jim Corsi, Tim Cossins, Danny Cox, Jeff Cox, Steve Cox, Jesse Crain, Joe Crawford, Doug Creek, Jack Cressend, Coco Crisp, Deivi Cruz, Jose Cruz Sr., Luis Cruz, Mike Cubbage, Michael Cuddyer, Omar Daal, Johnny Damon, Bill Dancy, John Danks, Vic Darensbourg, Ron Darling, Doug Dascenzo, Darren Daulton, Jim Davenport, Tom Davey, Ben Davis, Chris Davis, Ike Davis, Kane Davis, Rajai Davis, Zach Day, Mark De John, Jorge De La Rosa, Valerio De Los Santos, Mike DeJean, Manny Delcarmen, Jose DeLeon, Wilson Delgado, David Dellucci, Rick Dempsey, Bucky Dent, Mark DeRosa, Jim Deshaies, Delino DeShields, Elmer Dessens, Einar Diaz, Victor Diaz, R. A. Dickey, Chris Dickerson, Jason Dickson, Mike DiFelice, Lenny DiNardo, Jerry DiPoto, John Doherty, Scott Dohmann,

games; Chris Young is the outfielder who debuted with the Diamondbacks in 2006. Finally, Alberto Castillo appears twice because two different players with that name have given me baseballs. The first is the journeyman catcher. The second is the left-handed reliever. (Or maybe it's the other way around.) I'd use middle initials to differentiate the players, but that's not always possible.

Luis Dorante, Octavio Dotel, Rick Down, Scott Downs, Doug Drabek, Darren Dreifort, Rob Ducey, Brandon Duckworth, Zach Duke, Shelley Duncan, Adam Dunn, Alan Dunn, Scott Dunn, Trent Durrington, Lenny Dykstra, Adam Eaton, David Eckstein, Dave Eiland, Joey Eischen, Scott Elarton, Mark Ellis, Juan Encarnacion, Yunel Escobar, Bobby Estalella, Shawn Estes, Johnny Estrada, Marco Estrada, Seth Etherton, Tony Eusebio, Nick Evans, Dana Eveland, Adam Everett, Carl Everett, Scott Eyre, Kyle Farnsworth, Steve Farr, Jeff Fassero, Ryan Feierabend, Jesus Feliciano, Pedro Feliciano, Pedro Feliz, Alex Fernandez, Mike Fetters, Robert Fick, Nelson Figueroa, Jeremy Fikac, Steve Finley, Brad Fischer, John Flaherty, Bryce Florie, Cliff Floyd, Gavin Floyd, Tom Foley, Matt Ford, Brook Fordyce, Bartolome Fortunato, Keith Foulke, Andy Fox, Jeff Francis, Ben Francisco, John Franco, Julio Franco, Ryan Franklin, Jason Frasor, Ryan Freel, Marvin Freeman, Brian Fuentes, Frank Funk, Rafael Furcal, Mike Fyhrie, Matt Galante, Armando Galarraga, Dave Gallagher, Mike Gallego, Ron Gant, Danny Garcia, Karim Garcia, Ron Gardenhire, Ryan Garko, Dillon Gee, Josh Geer, Samuel Gervacio, Chris Getz, Dan Giese, Brian Giles, Bernard Gilkey, Keith Ginter, Matt Ginter, Doug Glanville, Troy Glaus, Tom Glavine, Mike Goff, Jonny Gomes, Alexis Gomez, Carlos Gomez, Chris Gomez, Adrian Gonzalez, Alex Gonzalez, Edgar Gonzalez, Fredi Gonzalez, Luis Gonzalez, Mike Gonzalez, Raul Gonzalez, Andrew Good, Dwight Gooden, Tom Goodwin, Tom Gordon, Tom Gorzelanny, Ruben Gotay, Mauro Gozzo, John Grabow, Curtis Granderson, Danny Graves, Dallas Green, Nick Green, Scarborough Green, Sean Green, Todd Greene, Rusty Greer, Kevin Gregg, Alfredo Griffin, Jason Grilli, Marquis Grissom, Buddy Groom, Gabe Gross,

Eddie Guardado, Sandy Guerrero, Matt Guerrier, Carlos Guillen, Jose Guillen, Eric Gunderson, Jeremy Guthrie, Christian Guzman, Tony Gwynn, Jerry Hairston, John Halama, Roy Halladay, Cole Hamels, Darryl Hamilton, Joey Hamilton, Josh Hamilton, Mike Hampton, Tim Hamulack, Lee Hancock, Marcus Hanel, Ryan Hanigan, Joel Hanrahan, Craig Hansen, Aaron Harang, Mike Harkey, Toby Harrah, Lenny Harris, Shigetoshi Hasegawa, Ron Hassey, Billy Hatcher, LaTroy Hawkins, Von Hayes, Nathan Haynes, Chase Headley, Chris Heintz, Todd Helton, Scott Hemond, Ramon Henderson, Rickey Henderson, George Hendrick, Mark Hendrickson, Tom Henke, Brad Hennessey, Butch Henry, Doug Henry, Clay Hensley, Jeremy Hermida, Anderson Hernandez, Chuck Hernandez, Felix Hernandez, Livan Hernandez, Orlando Hernandez, Roberto Hernandez, Alex Herrera, Orel Hershiser, Bobby Higginson, Aaron Hill, Glenallen Hill, Perry Hill, Eric Hillman, Bruce Hines, Luke Hochevar, Glenn Hoffman, Trevor Hoffman, Matt Holliday, Mike Holtz, Paul Hoover, Vince Horseman, Ryan Howard, Steve Howe, Glenn Hubbard, Mike Hubbard, John Hudek, Rex Hudler, Tim Hudson, David Huff, Phil Hughes, Mike Humphreys, Nick Hundley, Todd Hundley, Brian L. Hunter, Butch Huskey, Ryota Igarashi, Tadahito Iguchi, Omar Infante, Brandon Inge, Jeff Innis, Garth Iorg, Hideki Irabu, Kazuhisa Ishii, Jason Isringhausen, Cesar Izturis, Al Jackson, Damian Jackson, Edwin Jackson, Grant Jackson, Mike Jacobs, Chuck James, Dion James, Dave Jauss, Gregg Jefferies, Jeremy Jeffress, Ryan Jensen, Derek Jeter, Jose Jimenez, Kelvin Jimenez, Ubaldo Jimenez, Ben Johnson, Brian Johnson, Chris Johnson, Howard Johnson, Jason Johnson, Jonathan Johnson, Kelly Johnson, Mark P. Johnson, Nick Johnson, Reed Johnson, Russ Johnson,

John Johnstone, Adam Jones, Andruw Jones, Bobby J. Jones, Bobby M. Jones, Brandon Jones, Chipper Jones, Chris Jones, Todd Jones, Brian Jordan, Kevin Jordan, Wally Joyner, Jorge Julio, David Justice, Matt Karchner, Takashi Kashiwada, Scott Kazmir, Greg Keagle, Austin Kearns, Roberto Kelly, Jason Kendall, Kyle Kendrick, Adam Kennedy, Logan Kensing, Jeff Kent, Jeff Keppinger, Jimmy Key, Darryl Kile, Paul Kilgus, Sun Woo Kim, Craig Kimbrel, Jeff King, Ray King, Mike Kinkade, Matt Kinney, Steve Kline, Brandon Knight, Gary Knotts, Masahide Kobayashi, Satoru Komiyama, Dae-Sung Koo, Joe Koshansky, Casey Kotchman, Mark Kotsay, Kevin Kouzmanoff, Rusty Kuntz, Hong-Chih Kuo, Hiroki Kuroda, Art Kusnyer, Masumi Kuwata, Tony La Russa, Rene Lachemann, Mike Lamb, Tom Lampkin, Rick Langford, Mark Langston, John Lannan, Barry Larkin, Adam LaRoche, Matt Lawton, Brandon League, Cliff Lee, Derek Lee, Travis Lee, Joe Lefebvre, Al Leiter, Mark Lemke, Patrick Lennon, Curtis Leskanic, Jesse Levis, Allen Levrault, Darren Lewis, Richie Lewis, Jim Leyritz, Brad Lidge, Cory Lidle, Jon Lieber, Brent Lillibridge, Derek Lilliquist, Ted Lilly, Jose Lima, Tim Lincecum, Adam Lind, Jose Lind, Doug Linton, Felipe Lira, Jesse Litsch, Brian Little, Graeme Lloyd, Paul Lo Duca, Esteban Loaiza, Kameron Loe, Nook Logan, Rich Loiselle, Kevin Long, Evan Longoria, Braden Looper, Davey Lopes, Aquilino Lopez, Felipe Lopez, Javier Lopez, Juan Lopez, Rodrigo Lopez, Mark Loretta, Mike Lowell, Noah Lowry, Julio Lugo, Fernando Lunar, Wayne Lydon, John Mabry, Bob MacDonald, Mike MacDougal, Ken Macha, Drew Macias, Greg Maddux, Mike Maddux, Warner Madrigal, Ryan Madson, Calvin Maduro, Ron Mahay, Pat Mahomes, John Maine, Gary Majewski, Omar Malave, Jack Maloof, Julio Manon,

Matt Mantei, Charlie Manuel, Jerry Manuel, Josias Manzanillo, Shaun Marcum, Nick Markakis, Carlos Marmol, Jason Marquis, Jay Marshall, Andy Marte, Damaso Marte, Tom Martin, Dave Martinez, Felix Martinez, Jose Martinez, Pedro Martinez, Tino Martinez, Roger Mason, Nick Masset, Mike Matheny, Rick Mathews, Luis Matos, Kaz Matsui, Gary Matthews Jr., Don Mattingly, Todd Maulding, Tim Mauser, Justin Maxwell, Derrick May, Brent Mayne, Leo Mazzone, Brian McCann, Lloyd McClendon, Mike McClendon, Quinton McCracken, Ben McDonald, Darnell McDonald, John McDonald, Roger McDowell, Chuck McElroy, Joe McEwing, Terry McGriff, Ryan McGuire, Mark McGwire, Jack McKeon, Jeff McKnight, Greg McMichael, Rusty Meacham, Brian Meadows, Brandon Medders, Jenrry Mejia, Orlando Mercado, Cla Meredith, Jose Mesa, Randy Messenger, Hensley Meulens, Dan Miceli, Doug Mientkiewicz, Kevin Millar, Lastings Milledge, Andrew Miller, Ray Miller, Trever Miller, Alan Mills, Blas Minor, Kevin Mitchell, Sergio Mitre, Garrett Mock, Chad Moeller, Bengie Molina, Raul Mondesi, Craig Monroe, Rich Monteleone, Jeff Montgomery, Melvin Mora, Jerry Morales, Mike Mordecai, Nyjer Morgan, Hal Morris, Brandon Morrow, Brandon Moss, Guillermo Mota, Jeff Motuzas, Edward Mujica, Terry Mulholland, Bobby Munoz, Scott Munter, Jeff Murphy, Matt Murton, Mike Mussina, Mike Myers, Charles Nagy, Mike Napoli, Johnny Narron, Bob Natal, Dioner Navarro, Jaime Navarro, Denny Neagle, Blaine Neal, Jeff Nelson, Robb Nen, Pat Neshek, Josh Newman, Kevin Nicholson, Randy Niemann, Jon Niese, Tom Nieto, Juan Nieves, Melvin Nieves, Wilbert Nieves, Dustin Nippert, C. J. Nitkowski, Jayson Nix, Matt Nokes, Ricky Nolasco, Vladimir Nunez, Jon Nunnally, Alex Ochoa, Ron Oester,

Jose Offerman, Will Ohman, Darren Oliver, Garrett Olson, Greg Olson, Paul O'Neill, Magglio Ordonez, Rey Ordonez, Ramon Ortiz, Daniel Ortmeier, Donovan Osborne, Keith Osik, Antonio Osuna, Ricky Otero, Akinori Otsuka, Lyle Overbay, Jerry Owens, Micah Owings, Juan Padilla, Angel Pagan, Matt Pagnozzi, Tom Pagnozzi, Dean Palmer, Mark Parent, Bobby Parnell, Chad Paronto, Gerardo Parra, Lance Parrish, Corey Patterson, Gil Patterson, John Patterson, Carl Pavano, Greg Pavlick, Jay Payton, Jake Peavy, Bill Pecota, Mike Pelfrey, Alejandro Pena, Carlos Pena, Jesus Pena, Terry Pendleton, Brad Penny, Jhonny Peralta, Troy Percival, Carlos Perez, Chris Perez, Eddie Perez, Melido Perez, Oliver Perez, Rafael Perez, Timo Perez, Yorkis Perez, Matt Perisho, Gerald Perry, Herbert Perry, Robert Person, Johnny Pesky, Rick Peterson, Gary Pettis, Marty Pevey, Tommy Phelps, Brandon Phillips, Jason Phillips, Mike Piazza, Renyel Pinto, Jim Pittsley, Dan Plesac, Scott Podsednik, Kevin Polcovich, Dick Pole, Luis Polonia, Bo Porter, Lou Pote, Jeremy Powell, Martin Prado, Todd Pratt, Bryan Price, Curtis Pride, Tom Prince, Bret Prinz, Tim Pugh, Albert Pujols, Luis Pujols, Bill Pulsipher, J. J. Putz, Chad Qualls, Paul Quantrill, Ruben Quevedo, Robb Quinlan, Omar Quintanilla, Ryan Raburn, Dave Racaniello, Brad Radke, Tim Raines, Edwar Ramirez, Hanley Ramirez, Bobby Ramos, Pat Rapp, Darrell Rasner, Jon Rauch, Claude Raymond, Britt Reames, Jeff Reardon, Mike Redmond, Jeff Reed, Chad Reineke, Desi Relaford, Mike Remlinger, Al Reyes, Dennys Reyes, Jo-Jo Reyes, Jose Reyes, Rene Reyes, Armando Reynoso, Arthur Rhodes, Jeff Ridgway, Dave Righetti, Jose Rijo, Juan Rincon, Ricardo Rincon, Royce Ring, Billy Ripken, David Riske, Bill Risley, Luis Rivas, Ben Rivera, Luis Rivera, Mariano Rivera, Saul Rivera, Joe

Roa, Bip Roberts, Brian Roberts, Grant Roberts, Ryan Roberts, Willis Roberts, David Robertson, Bill Robinson, Tom Robson, John Rocker, Fernando Rodney, Eddie Rodriguez, Felix Rodriguez, Francisco Rodriguez, Luis Rodriguez, Rich Rodriguez, Wandy Rodriguez, Cookie Rojas, Mel Rojas, Scott Rolen, Jimmy Rollins, Ron Romanick, J. C. Romero, Adam Rosales, Brian Rose, Cody Ross, Vern Ruhle, Glendon Rusch, B. J. Ryan, CC Sabathia, Bret Saberhagen, Chris Sabo, Juan Salas, Roger Salkeld, Jeff Samardzija, Anibal Sanchez, Duaner Sanchez, Freddy Sanchez, Gaby Sanchez, Reggie Sanders, Tommy Sandt, Johan Santana, Julio Santana, Jose Santiago, Ramon Santiago, Omir Santos, Victor Santos, Dennis Sarfate, Mackey Sasser, Joe Saunders, Michael Saunders, Bob Scanlan, Gene Schall, Nate Schierholtz, Brian Schneider, Scott Schoeneweis, Pete Schourek, Steve Schrenk, Tim Scott, Tony Scott, Marco Scutaro, Bobby Seay, Kevin Sefcik, Zack Segovia, Aaron Sele, Jae Weong Seo, Jeff Shaw, Danny Sheaffer, Ryan Shealy, Ben Sheets, Gary Sheffield, John Shelby, Glenn Sherlock, Darrell Sherman, George Sherrill, Razor Shines, Tsuyoshi Shinjo, Rick Short, Ruben Sierra, Carlos Silva, Jose Silva, Nelson Silverio, Bill Simas, Randall Simon, Grady Sizemore, Scott Sizemore, Joel Skinner, Doug Slaten, Terrmel Sledge, Heathcliff Slocumb, Aaron Small, John Smiley, Dwight Smith, Jason Smith, Joe Smith, Ozzie Smith, John Smoltz, Ian Snell, Sam Snider, J. T. Snow, Alay Soler, Steve Soliz, Joakim Soria, Rafael Soriano, Jorge Sosa, Jeff Sparks, Chris Speier, Ryan Speier, Paul Spoljaric, Tim Spooneybarger, Dennis Springer, Russ Springer, Chris Spurling, Mike Stanton, John Stearns, John Stephenson, Kelly Stinnett, Kevin Stocker, Brian Stokes, Todd Stottlemyre, Darryl Strawberry, Scott Strickland, Mark Strittmatter, Brent Strom, Tanyon Sturtze, Cory Sullivan, Ichiro Suzuki, Nick Swisher, Kazuhito Tadano, So Taguchi, Hisanori Takahashi, Ken Takahashi, Taylor Tankersley, Jack Taschner, Fernando Tatis, Eddie Taubensee, Julian Tavarez, Willy Taveras, Reggie Taylor, Miguel Tejada, Anthony Telford, Dave Telgheder, Bob Tewksbury, Josh Thole, Brad Thomas, Jim Thome, Justin Thompson, Milt Thompson, Ryan Thompson, John Thomson, Matt Thornton, Mike Timlin, Matt Tolbert, Brett Tomko, Jeff Torborg, Yorvit Torrealba, Carlos Tosca, Josh Towers, Steve Trachsel, Chad Tracy, Matt Treanor, Tom Trebelhorn, Ramon Troncoso, Troy Tulowitzki, Jason Tyner, Dan Uggla, Willie Upshaw, Tom Urbani, Juan Uribe, Merkin Valdez, Eric Valent, John Valentin, Jose Valentin, Bobby Valentine, Claudio Vargas, Jason Vargas, Gary Varsho, Esmerling Vasquez, Joe Vavra, Randy Velarde, Guillermo Velasquez, Will Venable, Michael Venafro, Robin Ventura, Jose Veras, Justin Verlander, Ron Villone, Fernando Vina, Joe Vitiello, Jose Vizcaino, Luis Vizcaino, Omar Vizquel, Ed Vosberg, Pete Vuckovich, Billy Wagner, Rick Waits, Matt Walbeck, Chico Walker, Jamie Walker, Kevin Walker, Pete Walker, Dave Wallace, Tim Wallach, Chien-Ming Wang, Duane Ward, Turner Ward, Jarrod Washburn, Ron Washington, Chris Waters, Alan Watson, David Weathers, Jered Weaver, John Wehner, Robbie Weinhardt, Kip Wells, Vernon Wells, Turk Wendell, Jayson Werth, John Wetteland, Dan Wheeler, Gabe White, Jerry White, Rick White, Rondell White, Sean White, Wally Whitehurst, Ernie Whitt, Ty Wigginton, Marc Wilkins, Rick Wilkins, Bernie Williams, Brian Williams, Eddie Williams, Gerald Williams, Mike Williams, Mark Williamson, Scott Williamson, Carl Willis, Reggie Willits, Bobby Wilson, C. J. Wilson, Jack Wilson, Josh Wilson, Mookie Wilson, Paul Wilson, Vance Wilson,

DeWayne Wise, Jay Witasick, Bobby Witt, Randy Wolf, Tony Womack, Kerry Wood, Tim Wood, Chris Woodward, David Wright, Michael Wuertz, Esteban Yan, Masato Yoshii, Chris Young, Carlos Zambrano, Victor Zambrano, Clay Zavada, Todd Zeile, Ryan Zimmerman, and Barry Zito.

PHOTO AND ILLUSTRATION CREDITS

Page 12:   Photo of Charles Weeghman—National Baseball Hall of Fame Library, Cooperstown, NY.

Page 20:   *Up for Grabs* poster—courtesy of Laemmle/Zeller Films, Inc.

Page 21:   Photo of Barry Bonds's 756th home run ball—National Baseball Hall of Fame Library, Cooperstown, NY.

Page 25:   Photo of Waveland Avenue—Zack Hample.

Page 32:   Photo of Luke Appling—National Baseball Hall of Fame Library, Cooperstown, NY.

Page 34:   Topps 1959 Norm Zauchin baseball card—courtesy of The Topps Company, Inc.

Page 41:   Photo of the Grasshopper airplane—courtesy of Mick Bajcar.

Page 43:   Photo of Herb Score—Bettmann/Corbis

Page 57:   Drawing of building and blimp heights—Zack Hample.

Page 80:   *B.C.* comic strip—reprinted by permission of John L. Hart FLP © 2010.

Page 86:   Photo of Justin Bieber—Kevin Aranibar, Kerosene Photography

Page 91:   Photo of the "lemon-peel" and "belt" balls—National Baseball Hall of Fame Library, Cooperstown, NY.

Page 96:   Photo of the painted ball—National Baseball Hall of Fame Library, Cooperstown, NY.

Page 100:   Patent diagram—courtesy of the U.S. Patent and Trademark Office.

Page 102:   Spalding baseball advertisement—National Baseball Hall of Fame Library, Cooperstown, NY.

Page 109:   Albert G. Spalding portrait—National Baseball Hall of Fame Library, Cooperstown, NY.

Page 124:   *Baseball* magazine cover—reproduced from the original held by the Department of Special Collections of the Hesburgh Libraries of the University of Notre Dame.

Page 131:   *Peanuts* comic strip—© 2010 PEANUTS Worldwide LLC.

Page 136:   Photo of the Astrodome—National Baseball Hall of Fame Library, Cooperstown, NY.

Page 146:   Photos of the baseballs from 1999 and 2000—Zack Hample.

Page 152:   Photo of a ball being dismantled—Zack Hample.

Page 154:   Photo of the pill components—Zack Hample.

Page 155:   Photo of the outside of the Rawlings factory—Zack Hample.

Page 158:   Photo of the cross section of a baseball—Zack Hample.

Page 161:   Photo of the hydraulic press—Zack Hample.

Page 161:   Photo of the figure-eight-shaped cutting tool—Zack Hample.

Page 163:   Photo of the stitching room—Zack Hample.

Page 167:   Photo of the inspection room—Zack Hample.

Page 172:   Photo of the 1978 World Series ball—courtesy of Zach Mazefsky.

Page 172: Photo of the 1979 All-Star Game ball—courtesy of Zach Mazefsky.

Page 172: Photo of the Comiskey Park ball—courtesy of Zach Mazefsky.

Page 173: Photo of the 1992 All-Star Game ball—courtesy of Zach Mazefsky.

Page 173: Photo of the Cal Ripken ball—courtesy of Zach Mazefsky.

Page 173: Photo of the "Primera Serie" ball—courtesy of Zach Mazefsky.

Page 174: Photo of the Jackie Robinson ball—courtesy of Zach Mazefsky.

Page 174: Photo of the Hank Aaron ball—courtesy of Zach Mazefsky.

Page 174: Photo of the American League 100th anniversary ball—courtesy of Zach Mazefsky.

Page 175: Photo of the 9/11 ball—courtesy of Zach Mazefsky.

Page 175: Photo of the Yankees' 100th anniversary ball—Zack Hample.

Page 175: Photo of the Don Larsen ball—courtesy of Zach Mazefsky.

Page 176: Photo of the Joe DiMaggio ball—courtesy of Zach Mazefsky.

Page 176: Photo of the Tiger Stadium ball—courtesy of Zach Mazefsky.

Page 176: Photo of the July 4th ball—courtesy of Zach Mazefsky.

Page 177: Photo of the 2004 Opening Day ball—courtesy of Zach Mazefsky.

Page 177: Photo of the Rogers Centre ball—courtesy of Zach Mazefsky.

Page 177: Photo of the Busch Stadium ball—courtesy of Zach Mazefsky.

Page 178: Photo of the 1986 World Series ball—courtesy of Zach Mazefsky.

Page 178: Photo of the 1989 World Series ball—courtesy of Zach Mazefsky.

Page 178: Photo of the 1996 National League Division Series ball—courtesy of Zach Mazefsky.

Page 179: Photo of the 1999 American League Championship Series ball—courtesy of Zach Mazefsky.

Page 179: Photo of the 2000 World Series ball—courtesy of Zach Mazefsky.

Page 179: Photo of the 2009 World Series ball—courtesy of Zach Mazefsky.

Page 180: Photo of the "Month of the Americas" ball—courtesy of Zach Mazefsky.

Page 180: Photo of the "Serie de los Expos de Montreal" ball—courtesy of Zach Mazefsky.

Page 180: Photo of the 2006 Japan All-Star Series ball—courtesy of Zach Mazefsky.

Page 181: Photo of the 2008 China Series ball—courtesy of Zach Mazefsky.

Page 181: Photo of the 2009 World Baseball Classic ball—courtesy of Zach Mazefsky.

Page 181: Photo of the 2010 Taiwan Games ball—courtesy of Zach Mazefsky.

Page 182: Photo of the Enron Field ball—Zack Hample.

Page 182: Photo of the 2000 All-Star Game ball—Zack Hample.

Page 182: Photo of the Grammy Awards ball—courtesy of Zach Mazefsky.

Page 183: Photo of the Ashburn Alley ball—Zack Hample.

Page 183: Photo of the 2007 Home Run Derby ball—courtesy of Zach Mazefsky.

Page 183: Photo of the 2K Sports ball—Zack Hample.

Page 187: Photo of the Rockies' humidor—Zack Hample.

Page 190: Photo of Lena Blackburne—National Baseball Hall of Fame Library, Cooperstown, NY.

Page 191: Photo of the mud container—Zack Hample.

Page 209: Photo of players wearing shirts over their jerseys—Zack Hample.

Page 213: Photo of a baseball in the empty stands—Zack Hample.

Page 218: Photo of Great American Ball Park—Zack Hample.

Page 221: Photo of Fenway Park—Zack Hample.

Page 224: Photos of the glove trick—Zack Hample.

Page 231: Photo of Heath Bell—© Andy Hayt; courtesy of the San Diego Padres.

Page 240: Photo of the Red Sox playing catch—Zack Hample.

Page 271: Photo of Moe Mullins—Zack Hample.

Page 273: Photo of Rich Buhrke—Zack Hample.

Page 277: Photo of Artie Laurain—Zack Hample.

Page 279: Photo of John Witt—courtesy of Cydney Hebert.

Page 281: Photo of Tracy Collins—Zack Hample.

Page 283: Photo of Alex Patino—Zack Hample.

Page 285: Photo of Lee Wilson—courtesy of Tommy O'Boyle.

Page 287: Photo of Emily and Dan Sauvageau—Julie Sauvageau.

Page 289: Photo of Greg Dryden—Zack Hample.

Page 297: Photo of Camden Yards—courtesy of Brandon Sloter.

Page 298: Photo of Kauffman Stadium—Zack Hample.

Page 299: Photo of AT&T Park—Zack Hample.

Page 300: Photo of Rangers Ballpark—Zack Hample.

Page 302: Photo of Progressive Field—Zack Hample.

Page 303: Photo of Turner Field—Zack Hample.

Page 304: Photo of Miller Park—Zack Hample.

Page 305: Photo of PETCO Park—Zack Hample.

Page 307: Photo of Chase Field—Zack Hample.

Page 308: Photo of PNC Park—Zack Hample.

Page 319: Photo of Bob Feller—© AP/Wide World Photos.

INDEX